# THE CONFESSIONS OF
# St Augustine

# THE CONFESSIONS OF

# St Augustine

In the translation of J. G. Pilkington
with an introduction by George N. Shuster
and illustrated with paintings by

EDY LEGRAND

*New York*

THE HERITAGE PRESS

B-0
Augustine

# INTRODUCTION

Mᴏʀᴇ than fifteen hundred years have passed since this book was written by a Roman, but it has lost none of its freshness and appeal. Here a Christian saint who has influenced the thought and feeling of the West as perhaps no other man has, tells the story of his life with the utmost candor and pertinence of phrase. He considers himself a brand saved from the burning through the goodness of God, to whom he pays tribute. The book is, indeed, above all an act of thanksgiving. But no doubt it was also written because Augustine hoped he could outline a goal for many young men and women of his time who were going nowhere in particular.

This is likewise a book about a student and professor of the fourth century, a book which in spite of its historical coloring seems to be describing the life of an intellectual in our own time. Augustine was born on November 13, 354, in Tagaste, a little town in the then flourishing Roman province of Numidia. This is now Algeria, by no means so tranquil or urbane. His parents were intelligent and moderately well-to-do; and so they planned an education for their son. The father, who until much later was what Augustine calls a pagan, wanted the boy to amount to something and so saved up money to meet the tuition costs, even as his counterparts do now. The mother, a pious Christian, thought her son would grow in sanctity and wisdom if his mind were properly trained. Accordingly during his early years he went to school, either in his home community or in a neighboring small city. He was taught the languages then in vogue, namely Latin and Greek, and a certain amount of mathematics and Christian doctrine. At the time the Roman Empire was officially Christian, having been so decreed by Constantine the Great. This Emperor appears not to have led an exemplary life, but he listened to his virtuous spouse and in addition was persuaded that the Christian Cross on his battleflags was an omen of victory. The heroic days of the persecutions were therefore over. No more would loyal Christians be carted off to arenas to be devoured by wild beasts for the pleasure of the mob. Nero was long since dead, and it seemed almost incredible that he had ever caused followers of the Nazarene to be coated with tallow and left to burn like torches in the palace gardens. But there lived in the minds of women like Augustine's mother, Monica, the memory of and a profound reverence for the martyrs. For them the Christian faith retained its immediacy and its poignant implications of sacrifice.

Her son, however, was a quite normal, active lad, strong, supple, and burned by the African sun, who found school a dreadful bore and did whatever he could to make life miserable for his teachers. The more they ranted the greater became his interest in games. They seem to have been a dreadful lot. They flogged whatever boy happened to be to the right or the left of them, and meanwhile judged the prowess of their brood by what each could commit to memory. Augustine wished a plague on all their houses. What he says about education reminds one of literature about English schools as they were in the days of yore, of Shakespeare's lad trudging like a snail unwillingly to school, or of Oliver Twist and David Copperfield. Then during his sixteenth year, while waiting for his father to save money enough to send him to a Carthage school for rhetoricians, Augustine had twelve months of idleness which must have been delightful, however heartily he disapproved of them in retrospect. Looking back on that time from the point of view of an ardent convert to the Christian faith, he virtually makes one suppose he had been a juvenile delinquent. But in all probability what he did was pretty much what many an American boy now does during a long vacation time, if he is not saddled with a job. He went to see plays that were perhaps no worse than our movies, though they doubtless were indecent enough, tossed dice on the hot pavement, and made eyes at the girls. There is also the famous episode of the pear orchard, at which Bertrand Russell has poked fun. But it should be noted that Augustine does not so much repent of having stolen a pear or two as of having stripped an orchard of fruit which was then wantonly thrown away. For this a man might well feel the same remorse.

Then he went to Carthage to study, and this being a big city was another matter. From our modern point of view the Christian rule of those days was strange in that a young person was seldom baptized until the fever had presumably died down in his blood. On the one hand the Sacrament of election was thought so august that misdeeds thereafter done could be atoned only with austere penitence, while on the other hand sins of the flesh were deemed practically unavoidable in a man's younger years. Augustine took a mistress of whom he was exceedingly fond. They had a child whom he piously called 'the gift of God.' The girl may well have been some beautiful waif, for marriage seems to have been out of the question. Meanwhile he had prepared for his profession, which today would be dubbed teaching rhetoric and public speaking. Subsequently he taught in Carthage, Rome, and Milan. What he says about his work seems to echo our own time. He was not very well paid, and therefore heartily enjoyed offers of hospitality. Teaching was a heavy chore, though the companionship of his best students was immensely stimulating. There were also congenial colleagues. Every modern professor must have some publications to his credit, and in Augustine's day fame likewise depended not a little on the written word. He wrote a number of essays which attracted attention. Like many a brilliant young scholar of our day, he was both fascinated and tormented by the clash of ideas taking place round about him.

The *Confessions* provide something more, which many readers throughout subsequent generations have found particularly satisfying. This is a book about friendships, some of them very beautiful while others were disappointing. Refreshingly enough, these intimate and often cordial relationships were not with those we like to refer to as important people. For example, Augustine would have dearly loved to make the acquaintance of Saint Anselm, a sturdy Roman official who was elected Bishop of Milan by its people and who in addition to having a great deal of common sense which he expounded in sermons wrote good religious verse in almost classical Latin. But Anselm was too busy. It seems rather odd, though quite comforting, that whenever Augustine, whom we now all recognize as the most illustrious man of his time, sought the companionship of somebody of genuine social importance, he was rebuffed and told to mind his business. But when he dealt with lesser folk he fastened them to his heart with nails and bolts. Never was this more amply demonstrated than at Cassiacum, to which he went with a few academic friends for a round of talks. Above all, there was his mother. She did not set the Christian world of her time on fire, as had Helena, the mother of Constantine, or Cecilia, the famed Roman musician. Yet she was no doubt a person of substance, of nimble wit, and of fortitude.

Augustine's friends in Rome and Milan were of course greatly affected by the official allegiance of the Empire to Christianity. But by and large the educated clung to the notion that the literature of Greece and Rome was vastly superior in quality to the Testaments in which the Judæo-Christian creed was set forth. In part this was due to the prevalence of poor and badly translated texts, for Saint Jerome's Latin translation was not yet available. Yet men could not let those texts be. The overripe civilization of the Empire did not permit alert young men to lie at ease in their intellectual beds, any more than does ours. Some took refuge in older Roman doctrines, notably those of the Stoics, as Augustine did for a time after coming upon the philosophy of Cicero. There were also skeptics for skepticism's sake, as well as those whose model was Lucretius, the Roman poet of Naturalism, whom Augustine also seems to have read. And how could he have failed to come upon the recent followers of Plato, doubtless read in translation because he had no adequate command of Greek? The ideas set forth in the *Enneads* of Plotinus were to remain deeply embedded in his mind. But the dominant concern of the time was with varying forms of what we should now term Theosophy. The countries bordering on rich Constantinople and learned Alexandria were hotbeds of mystical cults and symbolistic religions, several of which were then very influential. Augustine describes those which especially fascinated him, in particular the teaching of the Manichæans, who believed that the world is ruled by two Principles, one Good and the other Evil, and that the conflict between them cannot be resolved. A modern reader is also likely to be impressed by Augustine's concern with mathematics and science. His knowledge of the second was of course rudimentary, but he is shown to have been a keen observer who upon occasion also resorted to experimentation.

The *Confessions* were written to indicate how a young man who had carefully considered such doctrines and philosophies and who had been in bondage to sexual urges, without however having been in any sense libertine or degenerate (Augustine's reputation for wickedness has been exaggerated), elected to be baptized at the age of thirty-three and to set out for the quest of sanctity in the spirit of the Catholic Church. Augustine makes it plain that the decision was far from easy, but he does not pose as a hero or a man of exceptional ability. The narrative is fascinating by reason above all of its austere honesty. Augustine stresses first of all the enduring influence of his boyhood environment, which his faithful mother personifies. Sometimes no doubt he had thought her old-fashioned or even a nuisance. But having been united with her in the Church, he recognizes her goodness, self-denial, and gift of spiritual vision. The pages in which he describes his last conversations with her, her death, and the emotions that afterwards arose within his spirit have always been rightly thought incomparably beautiful. It would seem certain that her resolve never to cease keeping him in her heart was in a good measure responsible for his conversion.

But Augustine was also an artist of a rare kind, though he may have shown his gift only in his chosen field of Rhetoric, and who therefore proceeded from Platonism to Christianity by a kind of inner law. El Greco, who painted Augustine as he conceived of him, was in this respect his peer. To see that the soul is the ultimate, genuine reality and can be apprehended in outward things only by analogy—this gift, which was the great Spanish painter's and which also lights up Augustine's colloquies with his God which give the *Confessions* so much radiance, cannot but have spurred Augustine on. This is no doubt why so many poets have felt an inner kinship with him, among them Milton, Longfellow, and Francis Thompson, whose 'Hound of Heaven' is in part an ornate rhyming of Augustine's words:

> *Nature, poor step-dame, cannot slake my drouth;*
> *Let her, if she would owe me,*
> *Drop yon blue bosom-veil of sky, and show me*
> *The breasts o' her tenderness:*
> *Never did any milk of hers once bless*
> *My thirsting mouth,*
> *Nigh and nigh draws the chase*
> *With unperturbèd pace,*
> *Deliberate speed, majestic instancy*
> *And past those noisèd Feet*
> *A Voice comes yet more fleet —*
> *Lo! naught contents thee, who contents not Me.*

Yet there was doubtless something of deeper import still, closer to the innermost core of the spirit and of the religious life. It is, one thinks, correct to say that Augustine's book is a chronicle of how he elected to make himself over into a likeness of Paul of Tarsus. Quotations from the letters of this Apostle dot the prose of the *Confessions* as flowers do a lawn in spring. Was this merely the result of intellectual compatibility? Obviously not. For though the experience which was Augustine's on the threshold of his conversion was by no means as startling as that which had befallen Paul on the road to Damascus, there is a clear resemblance. A voice said, 'Take and read'; and the page to which the Scripture opened was one in which Paul enjoins the faithful, 'Put ye on the Lord Jesus Christ.' The import of such experiences may be questioned but they are not to be denied. One thinks of the sheet of paper on which Pascal recorded his 'Joy,' or of Paul Claudel leaning against a pillar in Notre Dame and believing, in the twinkling of an eye.

Even so, dialectic was as native to Augustine's mind as the vision of form was to Michelangelo's. He would go on to the priesthood and a bishopric in Hippo, Africa, but his mature strength would be expended on the great works of exposition and controversy through which he influenced the course of speculative thought, both theological and philosophical, of the Western world. The present edition therefore properly includes, in an admirable translation, the last four books of the *Confessions*, which are autobiographical in the sense only that Augustine outlines the reasoning about time and eternity which undergirded his religious decision. He busies himself in particular with the great riddle presented by the confrontation between Divine eternity and human time; and what he writes concerning it has been viewed by all subsequent generations even to our own day as having opened new perspectives to human thought. Perhaps it will be helpful to place the argument against the background of Augustine's total philosophical position, though this can be done here only in the briefest and most cursory way.

He would sometimes be led by the heat of debate, for which art he had been specially trained, to bend an argument to his purpose until it all but snapped in two. But this is an inevitable human failing and does not impair his basic intellectual position. Since every greatly endowed thinker begins with an intuition which he follows to its logical conclusions and which may often be best understood by means of an image, it may be observed that this was in Augustine's case a ladder by means of which one could ascend to a desired height. The ladder is first of all that which symbolizes the soul's awareness of Reality from the depths of entanglement in the 'material' to awareness of the Divine sovereignty. In a comparable way, Dante found symbolic expression for the stages of spiritual cleansing and emancipation which form the theme of the *Purgatorio* and the *Paradiso*.

Second, the ladder can be used to indicate the gradations of created being, which rises from a state of deprivation—that is, from the original 'chaos' upon which order was imprinted—to the greatest possible richness of the contingent spirit, whether human or angelic. Though Augustine did not lack interest in the intermediate rungs of the ladder, what actively concerned him were the bottom and the top. Down among the urges and the primitive needs, into the depths of which Freud and Jung later tried to probe, we all begin. But the desire to ascend, Augustine contends, is implanted in man. In the giant gnarled roots of a tree, life struggles towards expression in every branch and twig. So also there stir in the human soul the desires which can find their fulfillment only in God. 'Our hearts,' he says, 'are restless until they rest in Thee!'

Yet how shall we know God? Augustine takes it for granted that the world is, and must therefore have been caused. The world is likewise beautiful, as mathematical patterns are, and must therefore have been designed. But the place to seek Him out is none the less in our 'own inward things.' What are these? Knowledge and the love of knowledge are inextricably bound together in man's spirit. He does not see what *is* in isolation. What *ought to be* is always conjoined. Down these twin roads that are nevertheless one he enters into contact with a Reality implicit in which is perfection. The more we know of it, the more we shall necessarily know of God, for in a sense it is God. Man's closest, fullest awareness of this 'realm of truth' is dependent on his will to conform with the Divine plan in so far as he himself is concerned—that is, to live according to the 'verities of righteousness' which are the counterparts of the 'verities of being.' Very summarily stated, the position is this: knowing one part of 'truth,' we are able to see the whole in outline, even as Cuvier could visualize what an animal looked like after seeing a rib or a thigh-bone; we are, as a matter of plain fact, driven to acquire such knowledge of the whole by an urge innate in man's being; and, finally, this 'whole' includes the forms of righteousness which in turn, having been grasped, help us to a better understanding of the rest of 'truth.'

This conviction that knowledge of being and obligation are one, because knit together indissolubly in the human soul, cast a spell over Europe for many centuries—a spell which was not wholly broken even when Immanuel Kant sundered the speculative from the practical Reason. The Elizabethan time in England, for example, lived by the image of the 'ladder' or the 'chain' of Being. When Othello says that if Desdemona has sinned 'chaos is come again,' he alludes to the unity of the cosmic and moral order and so reflects Augustinian thinking. This has special appeal for our own time because while he was not a 'mystic' in the generally accepted sense, Augustine recognized in the human person a stature and range of creative endeavor that the newer Platonists he so genuinely admired had not accorded to it. The ultimate certitudes were knowable, in his view, not through a vision of the 'Ideas' which hover far above the world of sense, but through full awareness of the Self. 'I cannot doubt that I doubt' was for him the first immovable stone on the road to knowledge of Reality. And so inevitably a man of our own era who cannot follow Augustine to the faith in theological doctrine he so ardently espoused will nevertheless recognize with a kind of awe the brilliance of his insights into the nature of the psyche, as witness the analysis of memory which makes the Tenth Book of the *Confessions* so absorbing.

One cannot easily put the book aside without reaching two conclusions. How rich and varied, how lofty and challenging, Græco-Roman culture was when fused with the convictions derived from Jewish and Christian sources! And how truly regal man is when like Augustine he strips from himself all that is mortal in life for the sake of the radiance of immortality, keeping about him all the while a warmth which heartens and cleanses! It was, alas, true that he and those who were in some measure like him could not keep the walls and towers of Rome from tottering. Too much of the human substance of the Empire was gone. No new youth could be made to rise from its streets. The barbarian outsider, driving with his hordes against the ramparts like a mighty and incessant storm, would after his victory sit in darkness amidst the holy places. When Augustine,

Bishop of Hippo, died on August 28, 430, the Vandals were laying siege to the city. But after a while the children who were born to them would begin to think of what treasure might be gleaned not from the shrines and palaces of Rome but from the memorials of its mind and heart. Then random sentences Augustine had written became texts used in schools. More and more were added until his doctrine was once more available. In particular, texts of the *Confessions* were found—imperfect, sometimes garbled, but rich in meaning. Therewith the time in which we now live had properly begun. Upon this the memory of Augustine still rests.

GEORGE N. SHUSTER

# CONTENTS

Introduction   *page* v

*A Note on the Illustrations*   xxvii

I   Commencing with the invocation of God, Augustine relates in detail the beginning of his life, his infancy and boyhood up to his fifteenth year; at which age he acknowledges that he was more inclined to all youthful pleasures and vices than to the study of letters.   I

II   He advances to puberty, and indeed to the early part of the sixteenth year of his age, in which, having abandoned his studies, he indulged in lustful pleasures, and, with his companions, committed theft.   20

III   Of the seventeenth, eighteenth, and nineteenth years of his age, passed at Carthage, when, having completed his course of studies, he is caught in the snares of a licentious passion, and falls into the snares of the Manichæans.   30

IV   Then follows a period of nine years from the nineteenth year of his age, during which, having lost a friend, he followed the Manichæans —and wrote books 'on the fair and fit,' and published a work on the liberal arts, and the categories of Aristotle.   44

V   He describes the twenty-ninth year of his age, in which, having discovered the fallacies of the Manichæans, he professed rhetoric at Rome and Milan. Having heard Ambrose, he begins to come to himself.   62

VI   Attaining his thirtieth year, he, under the admonition of the discourses of Ambrose, discovered more and more the truth of the Catholic doctrine, and deliberates as to the better regulation of his life.   80

VII    *He recalls the beginning of his youth, i.e. the thirty-first year of his age, in which very grave errors as to the nature of God, and the origin of evil, being distinguished, and the sacred books more accurately known, he at length arrives at a clear knowledge of God, not yet rightly apprehending Jesus Christ.*    page 101

VIII    *He finally describes the thirty-second year of his age, the most memorable of his whole life, in which, being instructed by Simplicianus concerning the conversion of others, and the manner of acting, he is, after a severe struggle, renewed in his whole mind, and is converted unto God.*    122

IX    *He speaks of his design of forsaking the profession of rhetoric; of the death of his friends, Nebridius and Verecundus, of having received baptism in the thirty-third year of his age; and of the virtues and death of his mother, Monica.*    143

X    *Having manifested what he was and what he is, he shows the great fruit of his confession; and being about to examine by what method God and the happy life may be found, he enlarges on the nature and power of memory. Then he examines his own acts, thoughts, and affections, viewed under the threefold division of temptation; and commemorates the Lord, the one mediator of God and men.*    166

XI    *The design of his confessions being declared, he seeks from God the knowledge of the Holy Scriptures, and begins to expound the words of Genesis I. 1, concerning the creation of the world. The questions of rash disputers being refuted, 'What did God before He created the world?' That he might the better overcome his opponents, he adds a copious disquisition concerning time.*    206

XII    *He continues his explanation of the first chapter of Genesis according to the Septuagint, and by its assistance he argues, especially, concerning the double Heaven, and the formless matter out of which the whole world may have been created; afterwards of the interpretations of others not disallowed, and sets forth at great length the sense of the Holy Scripture.*    229

XIII    *Of the goodness of God explained in the creation of things, and of the Trinity as found in the first words of Genesis. The story concerning the origin of the world (Gen. I.) is allegorically explained, and he applies it to those things which God works for sanctified and blessed man. Finally, he makes an end of this work, having implored eternal rest from God.*    page 255

Notes    287

# LIST OF PLATES

## WITH THE ARTIST'S COMMENTS AND RELATED TEXTS

Plate Number                                                    Facing page

1   THE GIFTS OF GOD TO THE YOUNG CHILD                              8
    'Thus it was that the comforts of a woman's milk entertained me;
    for neither my mother nor my nurses filled their own breasts, but
    Thou by them didst give me the nourishment of infancy according to
    Thy ordinance and that bounty of Thine which underlieth all things.'
    (Book I.)

2   ST. AUGUSTINE AS AN OLD MAN, AT PRAYER                          16
    St. Augustine in the attitude of prayer, on his knees, hands
    extended. He is represented in his old age, having long since over-
    come the mistakes and errors of his youth. The 'Confessions' are the
    inner history of a soul, which he undertook to write when he was
    forty-five years old in order to demonstrate what grace can achieve
    when it is bestowed upon the most desperate. St. Augustine is
    therefore, in this drawing, far along in his thinking, rather than at
    a certain period of his life. (Book I.)

3   THE DEPTHS OF THE ABYSS                                          25
    'And to what end, these my writings? That I and all who read the
    same may reflect out of what depths we are to cry unto Thee.'
    (Book II.)

4   MONICA'S DREAM                                                   40
    'For in that dream she saw herself standing on a certain wooden
    rule, and a bright youth advancing towards her, joyous and smiling
    upon her, whilst she was grieving and bowed down with sorrow.

*Plate number*                                                                          *Facing page*

But he having inquired of her the cause of her sorrow . . . and she
answering that it was my perdition she was lamenting, he bade her
rest contented, and told her to behold and see "that where she was,
there was I also." And when she looked she saw me standing near her
on the same rule.' *(Book III.)*

The 'wooden rule' is the rule of the Church ('regula fidei,
regula disciplinæ,' the rule of faith, the rule of discipline).
Monica, a short distance away from St. Augustine, seems to be
touching him lightly with her hands in order to warn him. . . . By
an effect of perspective, the rule seems to sink down towards the
terrestrial horizon, while the influx of the Spirit draws the gazes of
the two characters upwards.

Augustine is much taller than the frail Monica, although she
seems to be of the same height: she thus reigns over her son by her
spirit. He will be converted by her—it is a premonitory dream. At
the bottom of the page, on the left, we have again represented
Monica, but sleeping—the 'earthly' Monica.

5   ST. AUGUSTINE AND HIS PUPILS IN CARTHAGE                    57
    Augustine's first Manichæan commentaries in Carthage. *(Book IV.)*

6   'LET THOSE GO WHO WILL!'                                    64
    'Let the restless and the unjust depart and flee from Thee!'
    *(Book V.)*

    In the background, the glittering light of God. A man is
    running away, his arms extended. Another seems to be asleep,
    half-lying along a slope, holding a stone in his hand.

7   ST. AMBROSE IN MILAN                                        80
    We have represented the Bishop of Milan meditating after reading,
    his face emaciated because of the hard discipline of which Augustine
    speaks in the book. Near St. Ambrose is seen a man praying,
    turned towards him, his eyes closed. *(Book VI.)*

8   CONVERSATIONS WITH MONICA                                   88
    'My mother, made strong by her piety, had come to me [in Rome].
    . . . She found me in grievous danger, through despair of ever finding
    truth.' *(Book VI.)*

*Plate number*                                                                    *Facing page*

9    THE GREAT MASS OF THE HEAVENS                                                    105

'*In like manner did I conceive of Thee, Life of my life, as vast through infinite spaces, on every side penetrating the whole mass of the world, and beyond it, all ways, through immeasurable and boundless spaces; so that the earth should have Thee, the heaven have Thee, all things have Thee . . .' (Book VII.)*

10   GOD'S CREATION, NATURE                                                          120

'*That Thou art to be praised is shown from the earth, dragons, and all deeps; fire, and hail; snow and vapours; stormy winds fulfilling Thy word; mountains, and all hills; fruitful trees, and all cedars; beasts, and all cattle; creeping things, and flying fowl; kings of the earth, and all people; princes, and all judges of the earth; both young men and maidens; old men and children, praise Thy name.' (Book VII.)*

*In the center of the drawing is a throne on which is seated a king wearing a crown. He holds a sword in his left hand, and in his right hand a vain emblem of his power. Two armed men keep watch over him. Birds are flying, horses frisking. In the foreground, young people clasping one another go off singing and manifest their 'joie de vivre.' The background represents virgin nature, as sprung forth from Creation, dominated by the great movements of Heaven, the domain of God.*

11   THE CONVERSION OF VICTORINUS                                                    128

'*How much less ought [Victorinus], when pronouncing Thy word, to dread Thy meek flock, who, in the delivery of his own words, had not feared the mad multitudes! . . . And having been admitted to the first sacraments of instruction, he not long after gave in his name, that he might be regenerated by baptism.' (Book VIII.)*

*We have therefore represented the baptism of Victorinus in the rather shallow octagonal basin (8 being the figure for Jesus, following the figure 7 of the Father). In the Apocalypse of St. John the triple 8 (888) is the Lord's gematrical figure: the Lord in the Trinity of 8.*

*Plate number*                                                                                                   *Facing page*

12   THE GARDEN IN MILAN                                                                    137
*Augustine, his friend Alypius, and another catechumen sit and
discourse in the little garden where 'the tempest within my breast'
had thrown Augustine. (Book VIII.)*

13   THE SONG OF DEGREES                                                                   144
*'Our intention then was known to Thee; but to men—excepting our
own friends—was it not known . . . although Thou hadst given to
us, ascending from the valley of tears, and singing the song of
degrees, sharp arrows and destroying coals against the deceitful
tongue. . . .' (Book IX.)*

*The song of degrees, or hymn of the Ascension, is here represented
by persons who are physically rising to a superior stage of prayer: they
mount to heaven in procession, singing, with hands clasped. Above
them the Saints, who are God's representatives, are seated motionless
upon the clouds. Their majestic calm (signifying that they are the
possessors of God's truth) contrasts with the agitation of the men
praying in the foreground. At the upper left, far off in the sky, can
be made out another procession mounting into space. . . .*

14   AUGUSTINE AND HIS MOTHER: ECSTASY IN OSTIA                    160
*The scene takes place on the banks of the Tiber, in Ostia. Augustine
is with Monica, who is nearing the day on which she is to depart this
life. He supports her. They are alone. After having raised themselves by degrees, in ecstasy, towards the 'Being Himself,' they
'gradually pass through all corporeal things, and even the heaven
itself, whence sun, and moon, and stars shine upon the earth. . . .'
They reach that region of souls where the inexhaustible abundance
of the food of truth prevails, where the place of Wisdom is located,
without past or future since it is eternal.*

*Above Monica, who is soon to die—and whose ecstasy is still
deeper than that of Augustine, only just converted by his mother—
the sky opens up and illuminates her as well as her son. (Book IX.)*

15   ST. AUGUSTINE BEFORE GOD                                                          177
*The Saint, his face showing the signs of mortification of the flesh,
is going to write the inner story of his soul, concealing none of his*

*Plate number*                                                                                    *Facing page*

*faults or weaknesses. We have represented him in the midst of his colloquy with God, his eyes turned toward Him, but his flesh ravaged by the mortal signs of his sufferings and his doubts. We have meant him to be thus, an aged man at the end of his terrestrial voyage. (Book X.)*

16    O LIGHT OF JACOB!                                                                    192
'*O Thou Light which Jacob saw when, blind through great age, with an enlightened heart, in the persons of his own sons, he threw light upon the races of the future people, pre-signified in them. . . .' (Book X.)*

17    THE HEAVENS AND THE EARTH                                              216
'*Behold, the heaven and earth . . . proclaim that they made not themselves; "therefore we are, because we have been made; we were not therefore before we were, so that we could have made ourselves." And the voice of those that speak is in itself an evidence. Thou, therefore, Lord, didst make these things; . . . Thou who art, for they are.' (Book XI.)*
    *A small being finds himself alone before the immensity of heaven and earth, the work of God. Day is breaking.*

18    'WISDOM, WHICH CLEARS MY CLOUDINESS'                          233
'*What is that which shines through me, and strikes my heart without injury, and I both shudder and burn? It is Wisdom itself that shines through me, clearing my cloudiness, which again overwhelms me, fainting from it, in the darkness and amount of my punishment.' (Book XI.)*

19    THEY DISCUSS THE THINGS OF THE LAW                            248
*I listen, I study all the interpretations, says St. Augustine, but* 'I *am unwilling to contend about words, for that is profitable to nothing "but to the subverting of the hearers." ' (Book XII.)*
    *Beside the sea, original element of life and fruit of the first day of Creation, men are discussing endlessly; their attitudes bear witness to their anxiety. Above them the sky, tracing a tremendous orb of light, is like God's eye, half-open and gazing down.*

*Plate number*                                                          *Facing page*

20    THE TRINITY, ABOVE THE PRIMARY WATERS, AT THE
       MOMENT OF CREATION                                                  280

'Thou, therefore, O Lord, . . . didst in the beginning, which is of
Thee, in Thy Wisdom, which was born of Thy Substance, create
something, and that out of nothing. . . . And aught else except
Thee there was not whence Thou mightest create these things, O
God, One Trinity, and Trine Unity; and, therefore, out of nothing
didst Thou create heaven and earth,—a great thing and a small . . .
' "Thou wast," and there was naught else from which Thou didst
create heaven and earth; two such things, one near unto Thee, the
other near to nothing—one to which Thou shouldest be superior, the
other to which nothing should be inferior.' (Book XII.)

We have represented the three elements of the Trinity: the Father
supporting before Him his consubstantial Son and the dove of the
Holy Ghost, which seems to take wing from the breast of the Son,
whose arms are extended. The Father's face, indescribable, is
merged with the sky of dawn rising up from the Creation.

This Trinitarian group is located above the waters of the earth
(between the waters from above and the waters from underneath,
separated since the first day of Genesis). The waters from beneath are
illuminated by the group which rises up at the same time as the
vapors of the waters from above, which become lost in space. Above
the central group, and on each side of it, are the Sun and the Moon,
symbols of the divine power, as used in all Christian iconography.

Jesus the Son, like the Father, being outside of time—beyond
past, present, and future—therefore in His eternity, holds His arms
like a cross, His hands open, offered for suffering and also for benediction. His body shows the stigmata of the sufferings which He is
to undergo when He dwells among men. His right hand (the hand of
the Last Judgment) bears the head of a nail driven into the flesh. His
glance is pregnant with all human pain, which He has taken upon
Himself since the original sin and which will culminate on the Cross.

This drawing attempts to translate the inexpressible; in it are
superimposed the ineffability and virtual unrepresentability of
Father and Son amid the vapors of the beginning of Creation, when
the Word (the Spirit) sounded with the noise of thunder. . . .

## DOUBLE PLATES

I  ST. AUGUSTINE SAILS FOR ITALY                    Front end leaves

*The ancient pagan world at the time of St. Augustine. The artist had in mind the harbor at Carthage, but having given pre-eminence to the departing galley on the right-hand side, he could not further extend the description of the town on the left side.*

*The idea of the drawing, half-descriptive, half-symbolic, is translated in these two sections: On the right, the galley leaving the shore—the men rowing and beginning to hoist the sails—is St. Augustine's ship leaving the soil of Africa on his way to Italy. The emblem on the stern of the ship, which might have been a Roman eagle, is in reality the watchful dove of the Holy Ghost. We have here 'the image of departure': It is in Italy that, when Monica has rejoined him, St. Augustine will become converted. It is therefore the meaning of this right-hand side which must be determinative for the whole drawing.*

*On the left half is a staircase on which people are seen 'descending' (by contrast with the right half, where the ship seems to be taking flight). In the background are ancient monuments of the Roman era.*

II  ST. AUGUSTINE IN HIPPO                          Back end leaves

*Our drawing represents not one fact, but the unfolding of an aggregate of facts: After his mother's death and his baptism by St. Ambrose, Augustine returns to his native Tagaste. Despite a reluctance due to his humility, Augustine is ordained a priest by the Bishop Valerius in Hippo, the harbor near Tagaste. Augustine had given away all his belongings to the poor. He then became the coadjutor of Bishop Valerius and, after the latter's death, his successor to the Bishopric of Hippo. There he died at the age of seventy-six, during the siege of that town by the barbarians.*

*The right-hand page represents Augustine, his only badge that of coadjutor, before the little church of Tagaste. In front of him are people kneeling; he is teaching them poverty and the doctrinal errors of the Manichæans, Donatists, and Arians, and the love of Christ.*

*In the distance, on the left side, is depicted the town of Hippo, where the Saint will continue his teaching. Between Hippo and*

Tagaste are ships which have just landed a crowd of pilgrims who are hastening towards the sound of Augustine's voice.

In order to render the scene intelligible, as it is composed of so many elements, the artist has shortened the distance separating the two cities, but Tagaste was located at a distance of about twenty-five miles from Hippo.

Here the color attempts to bring out the emotion of the whole and to give a concise description of the African terrain, which is outstripped as a mere location by the universality of its spiritual meaning.

# A NOTE ON THE ILLUSTRATIONS

It would have been easy for the artist who had been granted the privilege and task of illustrating the *Confessions* to depict the scenery of that Roman world of the decadent age in which the action takes place, from Tagaste to Hippo, from Carthage to Milan and to Rome. He could have taken that background as his canvas in translating the psychological and spiritual action of St. Augustine's colloquy with God. But it seemed to us that by representing the circus games (in the first part of the book) and the theatre, and by picturing the historical events of that time, with its material atmosphere, its luxury, we would be working in a manner opposed to the consistent spiritual atmosphere of the book. For the *Confessions* were written completely under the spell of repentance, conversion, and faith, and indeed rather late in the life of the Bishop of Hippo, since he composed and revised the work between the ages of forty-five and fifty.

We have therefore relinquished that convenient setting in order to concentrate our attention upon the positive data of the purely spiritual debate, the only one that the sublime grandeur of the *Confessions* seems to allow to any translator, even if his medium of translation is the picture.

The matter here is the inner story of a soul. This soul could not, in our opinion, be represented as imprisoned in the picturesqueness of a scene, or localized by some event that occurred in Augustine's life. For instance, our point of view impelled us to represent not the embarking of the Saint at Ostia on his return to Africa, but the ecstasy in Ostia; nor Augustine's baptism (*signaculum*) and the preparatory training that led to it—on which he does not insist—but rather to stress Monica's persistent and admirable influence, as well as Victorinus' conversion, which has the tremendous importance of example. This conversion was related by Simplicianus* to Augustine, with whom he discussed it at length when Augustine came to consult him regarding his errors, his anxiety, and the torments that beset him.

In Book II, we have chosen to illustrate the paragraph where Augustine justifies his *Confessions* by the possibility that any who may chance to light upon them 'may reflect out of what depths we [who live in error] are to cry unto Thee.' And so we have given the reader a glimpse of a small being struggling at the bottom of a dark abyss, dominated by a sky projected as a sheet of light 'gazing.' We have preferred these lines to those which refer to the author's stay in Madaura (near Tagaste), where he had settled down to study literature and oratory.

In Book III, the picture which thrust itself upon us was not that referring to the student's life in Carthage, but Monica's dream, which was premonitory of Augustine's future life and of his conversion. This is of prime importance and loaded with symbols.

Again, in Book V, it was not Augustine's life as a student in Carthage, nor his discussions with the Manichæan Bishop Faustus, who had arrived with great pomp, nor his departure for Rome, nor his illness, that we wished to stress. All our attention was focused upon that terrible cry to the Lord: 'Let the restless and the unjust depart and flee from Thee!'

These few examples may perhaps help the reader to understand better the meaning that we wanted to give to our illustration of the book and what we thought was the essential thing to be placed in relief throughout: The spiritual unity of the *Confessions* could not be interrupted by the external facts—even if utilized as they appear in evocations of nature, as in the double plate at the beginning of the book where a galley is being rowed towards Rome. For even then the external fact would place itself above daily life, with its symbolic and spiritual meaning—far above, on a level where the essentials of meditation are met. Then, color would help the

* Simplicianus succeeded Ambrose to the Bishopric of Milan in 397, i.e., ten years after the baptism of Augustine, who at about the same time was commencing to write his *Confessions*.

expression by confirming it. We beg the reader to refer, on this subject, to Plates 8, 9, 10, 12, 17, and 19.

As for Plate 20 (the last), it is a crowning-point of the book—an attempt to represent the great mystery of the Trinity. The Christ is placed in His eternal essence as Creator and Redeemer, His arms forming a cross. He represents the sufferings of men, in the midst of the primitive chaos which had issued from the *tehom*, the unformed, and which, through the power of His Word, is beginning to take shape around Him. God the Father supports Him above what is still disorder and nothingness, before the task of each of the six days, after which will come the seventh—in Genesis: 'And God saw that it was good. . . .'

There remains one point that requires explanation: We have insisted on a St. Augustine in his old age, even at the end of his life. But the *Confessions*— a kind of narrative monograph, written 'face to face' with God—were entirely composed at the end of the fourth century, and the development of the action stops at Monica's death in 387, therefore at the beginning of Augustine's vocation, when he was only thirty-three.

His biographer, Possidius, who knew him well since he never left his side, tells us: 'Augustine wanted to bear witness publicly lest, in the words of Paul the Apostle, someone appraise him above what he knew himself to be, or above what his words let people know of him: for he did not want to delude anyone, but was endeavouring to find in the blessing of his own deliverance and in the grace he had received, the Lord's glory and not his own.'

It is a question of the hard Christian discipline which invites the faithful to scan himself, to judge himself pitilessly, to retire within himself in order to unravel amidst his recollections and inclinations, his advance or his backslidings. Such hard discipline could not stop chronologically once the *Confessions* had been written. They were but the beginning of a long justification with regard to the writer and with regard to God, which extended itself right up to Augustine's death; he was the very expression of Wisdom definitely acquired after the disorders of youth and after repentance.

But this Wisdom is also a long patience, and the hardships caused by its attainment have left traces on Augustine's face like a stigma. Therefore the artist, choosing not to embroider the story of the life and errors of a young man in accordance with the succession of actual events, wished to represent an aged St. Augustine, conceived in the full compass of his thought, in the entirety of his Christian spirit.

Such has been our point of view.

EDY LEGRAND

# THE CONFESSIONS OF
# St Augustine

# BOOK I

*Commencing with the invocation of God, Augustine relates in detail the beginning of his life, his infancy and boyhood, up to his fifteenth year; at which age he acknowledges that he was more inclined to all youthful pleasures and vices than to the study of letters.*

GREAT art Thou, O Lord, and greatly to be praised; great is Thy power, and of Thy wisdom there is no end. And man, being a part of Thy creation, desires to praise Thee,—man, who bears about with him his mortality, the witness of his sin, even the witness that Thou 'resistest the proud,'—yet man, this part of Thy creation, desires to praise Thee. Thou movest us to delight in praising Thee; for Thou hast formed us for Thyself, and our hearts are restless till they find rest in Thee. Lord, teach me to know and understand which of these should be first, to call on Thee, or to praise Thee; and likewise to know Thee, or to call upon Thee. But who is there that calls upon Thee without knowing Thee? For he that knows Thee not may call upon Thee as other than Thou art. Or perhaps we call on Thee that we may know Thee. 'But how shall they call on Him in whom they have not believed? or how shall they believe without a preacher?' And those who seek the Lord shall praise Him. For those who seek shall find Him, and those who find Him shall praise Him. Let me seek Thee, Lord, in calling on Thee, and call on Thee in believing in Thee; for Thou hast been preached unto us. O Lord, my faith calls on Thee,—that faith which Thou hast imparted to me, which Thou hast breathed into me through the incarnation of Thy Son, through the ministry of Thy preacher.[1]

And how shall I call upon my God—my God and my Lord? For when

I

I call on Him I ask Him to come into me. And what place is there in me into which my God can come—into which God can come, even He who made heaven and earth? Is there anything in me, O Lord my God, that can contain Thee? Do indeed the very heaven and the earth, which Thou hast made, and in which Thou hast made me, contain Thee? Or, as nothing could exist without Thee, doth whatever exists contain Thee? Why, then, do I ask Thee to come into me, since I indeed exist, and could not exist if Thou wert not in me? Because I am not yet in hell, though Thou art even there; for 'if I go down into hell Thou art there.' I could not therefore exist, could not exist at all, O my God, unless Thou wert in me. Or should I not rather say, that I could not exist unless I were in Thee from whom are all things, by whom are all things, in whom are all things? Even so, Lord; even so. Where do I call Thee to, since Thou art in me, or whence canst Thou come into me? For where outside heaven and earth can I go that from thence my God may come into me who has said, 'I fill heaven and earth'?

Since, then, Thou fillest heaven and earth, do they contain Thee? Or, as they contain Thee not, dost Thou fill them, and yet there remains something over? And where dost Thou pour forth that which remaineth of Thee when the heaven and earth are filled? Or, indeed, is there no need that Thou who containest all things shouldest be contained of any, since those things which Thou fillest Thou fillest by containing them? For the vessels which Thou fillest do not sustain Thee, since should they even be broken Thou wilt not be poured forth. And when Thou art poured forth on us, Thou art not cast down, but we are uplifted; nor art Thou dissipated, but we are drawn together. But, as Thou fillest all things, dost Thou fill them with Thy whole self, or, as even all things cannot altogether contain Thee, do they contain a part, and do all at once contain the same part? Or has each its own proper part—the greater more, the smaller less? Is, then, one part of Thee greater, another less? Or is it that Thou art wholly everywhere whilst nothing altogether contains Thee?

What, then, art Thou, O my God—what, I ask, but the Lord God? For who is Lord but the Lord? or who is God save our God? Most high, most excellent, most potent, most omnipotent; most piteous and most just; most hidden and most near; most beauteous and most strong; stable, yet contained of none; unchangeable, yet changing all things; never new, never old; making all things new, yet bringing old age upon the proud and they know it not; always working, yet ever at rest; gathering, yet needing nothing; sustaining, pervading, and protecting; creating, nourishing, and developing; seeking, and yet possessing all things. Thou lovest, and burnest not; art jealous, yet free from care; repentest, and hast no sorrow; art angry, yet serene; changest Thy ways, leaving unchanged Thy plans; recoverest what Thou findest, having yet never lost; art never in want, whilst Thou rejoicest in gain; never covetous, though requiring usury. That Thou mayest owe, more than enough is given to Thee; yet who hath anything that is not Thine? Thou payest debts while owing nothing; and when Thou forgivest debts, losest nothing. Yet, O my God, my life, my holy joy, what is this that I have said? And what saith any man when he speaks of Thee? Yet woe to them that keep silence, seeing that even they who say most are as the dumb.

Oh! how shall I find rest in Thee? Who will send Thee into my heart to inebriate it, so that I may forget my woes, and embrace Thee, my only good? What art Thou to me? Have compassion on me, that I may speak. What am I to Thee that Thou demandest my love, and unless I give it Thee art angry, and threatenest me with great sorrows? Is it, then, a light sorrow not to love Thee? Alas! alas! tell me of Thy compassion, O Lord my God, what Thou art to me. 'Say unto my soul, I am thy salvation.' So speak that I may hear. Behold, Lord, the ears of my heart are before Thee; open Thou them, and 'say unto my soul, I am thy salvation.' When I hear, may I run and lay hold on Thee. Hide not Thy face from me. Let me die, lest I die, if only I may see Thy face.

Cramped is the dwelling of my soul; do Thou expand it, that Thou mayest enter in. It is in ruins, restore Thou it. There is that about it which must offend Thine eyes; I confess and know it, but who will cleanse it? or to whom shall I cry but to Thee? Cleanse me from my secret sins, O Lord, and keep Thy servant from those of other men. I believe, and therefore do I speak; Lord, Thou knowest. Have I not confessed my transgressions unto Thee, O my God; and Thou hast put away the iniquity of my heart? I do not contend in judgment with Thee, who art the Truth; and I would not deceive myself, lest my iniquity lie against itself. I do not, therefore, contend in judgment with Thee, for 'if Thou, Lord, shouldest mark iniquities, O Lord, who shall stand?'

Still suffer me to speak before Thy mercy—me, 'dust and ashes.' Suffer me to speak, for, behold, it is Thy mercy I address, and not derisive man. Yet perhaps even Thou deridest me; but when Thou art turned to me Thou wilt have compassion on me. For what do I wish to say, O Lord my God, but that I know not whence I came hither into this—shall I call it dying life or living death? Yet, as I have heard from my parents, from whose substance Thou didst form me,—for I myself cannot remember it,— Thy merciful comforts sustained me. Thus it was that the comforts of a woman's milk entertained me; for neither my mother nor my nurses filled their own breasts, but Thou by them didst give me the nourishment of infancy according to Thy ordinance and that bounty of Thine which underlieth all things. For Thou didst cause me not to want more than Thou gavest, and those who nourished me willingly to give me what Thou gavest them. For they, by an instinctive affection, were anxious to give me what Thou hadst abundantly supplied. It was, in truth, good for them that my good should come from them, though, indeed, it was not from them, but by them; for from Thee, O God, are all good things, and from my God is all my safety. This is what I have since discovered, as Thou hast declared Thyself to me by the blessings both within me and without me which Thou hast bestowed upon me. For at that time I knew how to suck, to be satisfied when comfortable, and to cry when in pain—nothing beyond.

Afterwards I began to laugh,—at first in sleep, then when waking. For this I have heard mentioned of myself, and I believe it (though I cannot remember it), for we see the same in other infants. And now little by little I realized where I was, and wished to tell my wishes to those who might satisfy them, but I could not! for my wants were within me, while they were without, and could not by any faculty of theirs enter into my soul. So I cast about limbs and voice, making the few and feeble signs I could, like, though indeed not much like, unto what I wished; and when I was not satisfied—either not being understood, or because it would have been injurious to me—I grew indignant that my elders were not subject unto me, and that those on whom I had no claim did not wait on me, and avenged myself on them by tears. That infants are such I have been able to learn by watching them; and they, though unknowing, have better shown me that I was such an one than my nurses who knew it.

And, behold, my infancy died long ago, and I live. But Thou, O Lord, who ever livest, and in whom nothing dies (since before the world was, and indeed before all that can be called 'before,' Thou existest, and art the God and Lord of all Thy creatures; and with Thee fixedly abide the causes of all unstable things, the unchanging sources of all things changeable, and the eternal reasons of all things unreasoning and temporal), tell me, Thy suppliant, O God; tell, O merciful One, Thy miserable servant—tell me whether my infancy succeeded another age of mine which had at that time perished. Was it that which I passed in my mother's womb? For of that something has been made known to me, and I have myself seen women with child. And what, O God, my joy, preceded that life? Was I, indeed, anywhere, or anybody? For no one can tell me these things, neither father nor mother, nor the experience of others, nor my own memory. Dost Thou laugh at me for asking such things, and command me to praise and confess Thee for what I know?

I give thanks to Thee, Lord of heaven and earth, giving praise to Thee for that my first being and infancy, of which I have no memory; for Thou hast granted to man that from others he should come to conclusions as to himself, and that he should believe many things concerning himself on the authority of feeble women. Even then I had life and being; and as my infancy closed I was already seeking for signs by which my feelings might be made known to others. Whence could such a creature come but from Thee, O Lord? Or shall any man be skilful enough to fashion himself? Or is there any other vein by which being and life runs into us save this, that 'Thou, O Lord, hast made us,' with whom being and life are one, because Thou Thyself art being and life in the highest? Thou art the highest, 'Thou changest not,' neither in Thee doth this present day come to an end, though it doth end in Thee, since in Thee all such things are; for they would have no way of passing away unless Thou sustainedst them. And since 'Thy years shall have no end,' Thy years are an ever present day. And how many of ours and our fathers' days have passed through this Thy day, and received from it their measure and fashion of being, and others yet to come shall so receive and pass away! 'But Thou art the same;' and all the things of to-morrow and the days yet to come, and all of yesterday and the days that are past, Thou wilt do to-day, Thou hast done to-day. What is it to me if any understand not? Let him still rejoice and say, 'What *is* this?'² Let him rejoice even so, and rather love to discover in failing to discover, than in discovering not to discover Thee.

Hearken, O God! Alas for the sins of men! Man saith this, and Thou dost compassionate him; for Thou didst create him, but didst not create the sin that is in him. Who bringeth to my remembrance the sin of my infancy? For before Thee none is free from sin, not even the infant which has lived but a day upon the earth. Who bringeth this to my remembrance? Doth not each little one, in whom I behold that which I do not remember of myself? In what, then, did I sin? Is it that I cried for the breast? If I should now so cry,—not indeed for the breast, but for the food suitable to my years,—I should be most justly laughed at and rebuked. What I then did deserved rebuke; but as I could not understand those who rebuked me, neither custom nor reason suffered me to be rebuked. For as we grow we root out and cast from us such habits. I have not seen any one who is wise, when 'purging' anything cast away the good. Or was it good, even for a time, to strive to get by crying that which, if given, would be hurtful—

to be bitterly indignant that those who were free and its elders, and those to whom it owed its being, besides many others wiser than it, who would not give way to the nod of its good pleasure, were not subject unto it—to endeavour to harm, by struggling as much as it could, because those commands were not obeyed which only could have been obeyed to its hurt? Then, in the weakness of the infant's limbs, and not in its will, lies its innocency. I myself have seen and known an infant to be jealous though it could not speak. It became pale, and cast bitter looks on its foster-brother. Who is ignorant of this? Mothers and nurses tell us that they appease these things by I know not what remedies; and may this be taken for innocence, that when the fountain of milk is flowing fresh and abundant, one who has need should not be allowed to share it, though needing that nourishment to sustain life? Yet we look leniently on these things, not because they are not faults, nor because the faults are small, but because they will vanish as age increases. For although you may allow these things now, you could not bear them with equanimity if found in an older person.

Thou, therefore, O Lord my God, who gavest life to the infant, and a frame which, as we see, Thou hast endowed with senses, compacted with limbs, beautified with form, and, for its general good and safety, hast introduced all vital energies—Thou commandest me to praise Thee for these things, 'to give thanks unto the Lord, and to sing praise unto Thy name, O Most High;' for Thou art a God omnipotent and good, though Thou hadst done nought but these things, which none other can do but Thou, who alone madest all things, O Thou most fair, who madest all things fair, and orderest all according to Thy law. This period, then, of my life, O Lord, of which I have no remembrance, which I believe on the word of others, and which I guess from other infants, it chagrins me—true though the guess be—to reckon in this life of mine which I lead in this world; inasmuch as, in the darkness of my forgetfulness, it is like to that which I passed in my mother's womb. But if 'I was shapen in iniquity, and in sin did my mother conceive me,' where, I pray Thee, O my God, where, Lord, or when was I, Thy servant, innocent? But behold, I pass by that time, for what have I to do with that, the memories of which I cannot recall?

Did I not, then, growing out of the state of infancy, come to boyhood, or rather did it not come to me, and succeed to infancy? Nor did my infancy depart (for whither went it?); and yet it did no longer abide, for I was no longer an infant that could not speak, but a chattering boy. I remember this, and I afterwards observed how I first learned to speak, for my elders did not teach me words in any set method, as they did letters afterwards; but I myself, when I was unable to say all I wished and to whomsoever I desired, by means of the whimperings and broken utterances and various motions of my limbs, which I used to enforce my wishes, repeated the sounds in my memory by the mind, O my God, which Thou gavest me. When they called anything by name, and moved the body towards it while they spoke, I saw and gathered that the thing they wished to point out was called by the name they then uttered; and that they did mean this was made plain by the motion of the body, even by the natural language of all nations expressed by the countenance, glance of the eye, movement of other members, and by the sound of the voice indicating the affections of the mind, as it seeks, possesses, rejects, or avoids. So it was that by frequently hearing words, in duly placed sentences, I gradually gathered what things they were the signs of; and having formed my mouth to the utterance of these signs, I thereby expressed my will. Thus I exchanged with those about me the signs by which we express our wishes, and advanced deeper into the stormy fellowship of human life, depending the while on the authority of parents, and the beck of elders.

O my God! what miseries and mockeries did I then experience, when obedience to my teachers was set before me as proper to my boyhood, that I might flourish in this world, and distinguish myself in the science of speech, which should get me honour amongst men, and deceitful riches! After that I was put to school to get learning of which I (worthless as I was) knew not what use there was; and yet, if slow to learn, I was flogged! For this was deemed praiseworthy by our forefathers; and many before us passing the same course, had appointed beforehand for us these troublesome

ways by which we were compelled to pass, multiplying labour and sorrow upon the sons of Adam. But we found, O Lord, men praying to Thee, and we learned from them to conceive of Thee, according to our ability, to be some Great One, who was able (though not visible to our senses) to hear and help us. For as a boy I began to pray to Thee, my 'help' and my 'refuge,' and in invoking Thee broke the bands of my tongue, and entreated Thee though little, with no little earnestness, that I might not be beaten at school. And when Thou heardest me not, giving me not over to folly thereby, my elders, yea, and my own parents too, who wished me no ill, laughed at my stripes, my then great and grievous ill.

Is there any one, Lord, with so high a spirit, cleaving to Thee with so strong an affection—for even a kind of obtuseness may do that much—but is there, I say, any one who, by cleaving devoutly to Thee, is endowed with so great a courage that he can esteem lightly those racks and hooks, and varied tortures of the same sort, against which, throughout the whole world, men supplicate Thee with great fear, deriding those who most bitterly fear them, just as our parents derided the torments with which our masters punished us when we were boys? For we were no less afraid of our pains, nor did we pray less to Thee to avoid them; and yet we sinned, in writing, or reading, or reflecting upon our lessons less than was required of us. For we wanted not, O Lord, memory or capacity,—of which, by Thy will, we possessed enough for our age,—but we delighted only in play; and we were punished for this by those who were doing the same things themselves. But the idleness of our elders they call business, whilst boys who do the like are punished by those same elders, and yet neither boys nor men find any pity. For will any one of good sense approve of my being whipped because, as a boy, I played ball, and so was hindered from learning quickly those lessons by means of which, as a man, I should play more unbecomingly? And did he by whom I was beaten do other than this, who, when he was overcome in any little controversy with a co-tutor, was more tormented by anger and envy than I when beaten by a playfellow in a match at ball?

And yet I erred, O Lord God, the Creator and Disposer of all things in Nature,—but of sin the Disposer only,—I erred, O Lord my God, in doing contrary to the wishes of my parents and of those masters; for this learning which they (no matter for what motive) wished me to acquire, I might have put to good account afterwards. For I disobeyed them not because I had chosen a better way, but from a fondness for play, loving the honour of victory in the matches and to have my ears tickled with lying fables, in order that they might itch the more furiously—the same curiosity beaming more and more in my eyes for the shows and sports of my elders. Yet those who give these entertainments are held in such high repute, that almost all desire the same for their children, whom they are still willing should be beaten, if so be these same games keep them from the studies by which they desire them to arrive at being the givers of them. Look down upon these things, O Lord, with compassion, and deliver us who now call upon Thee; deliver those also who do not call upon Thee, that they may call upon Thee, and that Thou mayest deliver them.

Even as a boy I had heard of eternal life promised to us through the humility of the Lord our God condescending to our pride, and I was signed with the sign of the cross, and was seasoned with His salt[3] even from the womb of my mother, who greatly trusted in Thee. Thou sawest, O Lord, how at one time, while yet a boy being suddenly seized with pains in the stomach, and being at the point of death—Thou sawest, O my God, for even then Thou wast my keeper, with what emotion of mind and with what faith I solicited from the piety of my mother, and of Thy Church, the mother of us all, the baptism of Thy Christ, my Lord and my God. On which, the mother of my flesh being much troubled,—since she, with a heart pure in Thy faith, travailed in birth more lovingly for my eternal salvation,—would, had I not quickly recovered, have without delay provided for my initiation and washing by Thy life-giving sacraments, confessing Thee, O Lord Jesus, for the remission of sins. So my cleansing was deferred, as if I must needs, should I live, be further polluted; because, indeed, the guilt contracted by sin would, after baptism, be greater and more perilous.[4] Thus I at that time believed with my mother and the whole house, except my father; yet he did not overcome the influence of my mother's piety in me so as to prevent my believing in Christ, as he had not yet believed in Him. For she was desirous that Thou, O my God, shouldst be my Father rather than he; and in this Thou didst aid her to overcome her husband, to whom, though the better of the two, she yielded obedience, because in this she yielded obedience to Thee, who dost so command.

I beseech Thee, my God, I would gladly know, if it be Thy will, to what end my baptism was then deferred? Was it for my good that the reins were slackened, as it were upon me for me to sin? Or were they not slackened? If not, whence comes it that it is still dinned into our ears on all sides, 'Let him alone, let him act as he likes, for he is not yet baptized'? But as regards bodily health, no one exclaims, 'Let him be more seriously wounded, for he is not yet cured!' How much better, then, had it been for me to have been cured at once; and then, by my own and my friends' diligence, my soul's restored health had been kept safe in Thy keeping, who gavest it! Better, in truth. But how numerous and great waves of temptation appeared to hang over me after my childhood! These were foreseen by my mother; and she preferred that the unformed clay should be exposed to them rather than the image itself.

But in this my childhood (which was far less dreaded for me than youth) I had no love of learning, and hated to be forced to it, yet was I forced to it notwithstanding; and this was well done towards me, but I did not well, for I would not have learned had I not been compelled. For no man doth well against his will, even if that which he doth be well. Neither did they who forced me do well, but the good that was done to me came from Thee, my God. For they considered not in what way I should employ what they forced me to learn, unless to satisfy the inordinate desires of a rich beggary and a shameful glory. But Thou, by whom the very hairs of our heads are numbered, didst use for my good the error of all who pressed me to learn; and my own error in willing not to learn, didst Thou make use of for my punishment—of which I, being so small a boy and so great a sinner, was not unworthy. Thus by the instrumentality of those who did not well didst Thou well for me; and by my own sin didst Thou justly punish me. For it is even as Thou hast appointed, that every inordinate affection should bring its own punishment.

But what was the cause of my dislike of Greek literature, which I studied from my boyhood, I cannot even now understand. For the Latin I loved exceedingly—not what our first masters, but what the grammarians teach; for those primary lessons of reading, writing, and ciphering, I considered no less of a burden and a punishment than Greek. Yet whence was this unless from the sin and vanity of this life? for I was 'but flesh, a wind that passeth away and cometh not again.' For those primary lessons were better, assuredly, because more certain; seeing that by their agency I acquired, and still retain, the power of reading what I find written, and writing myself what I will; whilst in the others I was compelled to learn about the wanderings of a certain Æneas, oblivious of my own, and to weep for Dido dead, because she slew herself for love; while at the same time I brooked with dry eyes my wretched self dying far from Thee, in the midst of those things, O God, my life.

For what can be more wretched than the wretch who pities not himself shedding tears over the death of Dido for love of Æneas, but shedding no tears over his own death in not loving Thee, O God, light of my heart, and bread of the inner mouth of my soul, and the power that weddest my mind with my innermost thoughts? I did not love Thee, and committed fornication against Thee; and those around me thus sinning cried, 'Well done! Well done!' For the friendship of this world is fornication against Thee; and 'Well done! Well done!' is cried until one feels ashamed not to be such a man. And for this I shed no tears, though I wept for Dido, who sought death at the sword's point, myself the while seeking the lowest of Thy creatures—having forsaken Thee—earth tending to the earth; and if forbidden to read these things, how grieved would I feel that I was not permitted to read what grieved me. This sort of madness is considered a more honourable and more fruitful learning than that by which I learned to read and write.

But now, O my God, cry unto my soul; and let Thy Truth say unto me, 'It is not so, it is not so; better much was that first teaching.' For behold, I would rather forget the wanderings of Æneas, and all such things, than how to write and read. But it is true that over the entrance of the grammar school there hangs a vail[5]; but this is not so much a sign of the majesty of the mystery, as of a covering for error. Let not them exclaim against me of whom I am no longer in fear, whilst I confess to Thee, my God, that which my soul desires, and acquiesce in reprehending my evil ways, that I may love Thy good ways. Neither let those cry out against me who buy or sell grammar-learnings. For if I ask them whether it be true, as the poet says, that Æneas once came to Carthage, the unlearned will reply that they do not know, the learned will deny it to be true. But if I ask with what letters the name Æneas is written, all who have learnt this will answer truly, in accordance with the conventional understanding men have arrived at as to these signs. Again, if I should ask which, if forgotten, would cause the greatest inconvenience in our life, reading and writing, or these poetical fictions, who does not see what every one would answer who had not entirely forgotten himself? I erred, then, when as a boy I preferred those vain studies to those more profitable ones, or rather loved the one and hated the other. 'One and one are two, two and two are four,' this was then in truth a hateful song to me; while the wooden horse full of armed men, and the burning of Troy, and the 'spectral image' of Creusa were a most pleasant spectacle of vanity.

But why, then, did I dislike Greek learning, which was full of like tales? For Homer also was skilled in inventing similar stories, and is most sweetly vain, yet was he disagreeable to me as a boy. I believe Virgil, indeed, would be the same to Grecian children, if compelled to learn him as I was Homer. The difficulty, in truth, the difficulty of learning a foreign language mingled as it were with gall all the sweetness of those fabulous Grecian stories. For not a single word of it did I understand, and to make me do so, they vehemently urged me with cruel threatenings and punishments. There was a time also when (as an infant) I knew no Latin; but this I acquired without any fear or tormenting, by merely taking notice, amid the blandishments of my nurses, the jests of those who smiled on me, and the sportiveness of those who toyed with me. I learnt all this, indeed, without being urged by any pressure of punishment, for my own heart urged me to bring forth its own conceptions, which I could not do unless by learning words, not of those who taught me, but of those who talked to me; into whose ears, also, I brought forth whatever I discerned. From this it is sufficiently clear that a free curiosity hath more influence in our learning these things than a necessity full of fear. But this last restrains the overflowings of that freedom, through Thy laws, O God,—Thy laws, from the ferrule of the schoolmaster to the trials of the martyr, being effective to mingle for us a salutary bitter, calling us back to Thyself from the pernicious delights which allure us from Thee.

Hear my prayer, O Lord; let not my soul faint under Thy discipline, nor let me faint in confessing unto Thee Thy mercies, whereby Thou hast saved me from all my most mischievous ways, that Thou mightest become sweet to me beyond all the seductions which I used to follow; and that I may love Thee entirely, and grasp Thy hand with my whole heart, and that Thou mayest deliver me from every temptation, even unto the end. For lo, O Lord, my King and my God, for Thy service be whatever useful thing I learnt as a boy—for Thy service what I speak, and write, and count. For when I learned vain things, Thou didst grant me Thy discipline; and my sin in taking delight in those vanities, Thou hast forgiven me. I learned, indeed, in them many useful words; but these may be learned in things not vain, and that is the safe way for youths to walk in.

But woe unto thee, thou stream of human custom! Who shall stay thy course? How long shall it be before thou art dried up? How long wilt thou carry down the sons of Eve into that huge and formidable ocean, which even they who are embarked on the cross (*lignum*) can scarce pass over? Do I not read in thee of Jove the thunderer and adulterer? And the

two verily he could not be; but it was that, while the fictitious thunder
served as a cloak, he might have warrant to imitate real adultery. Yet which
of our gowned masters can lend a temperate ear to a man of his school who
cries out and says: 'These were Homer's fictions; he transfers things human
to the gods. I could have wished him to transfer divine things to us.' But
it would have been more true had he said: 'These are, indeed, his fictions,
but he attributed divine attributes to sinful men, that crimes might not be
accounted crimes, and that whosoever committed any might appear to
imitate the celestial gods and not abandoned men.'

And yet, thou stream of hell, into thee are cast the sons of men, with
rewards for learning these things; and much is made of it when this is
going on in the forum in the sight of laws which grant a salary over and
above the rewards. And thou beatest against thy rocks and roarest, saying,
'Hence words are learnt; hence eloquence is to be attained, most necessary
to persuade people to your way of thinking, and to unfold your opinions.'
So in truth we should never have understood these words, 'golden shower,'
'bosom,' 'intrigue,' 'highest heavens,' and other words written in the same
place, unless Terence had introduced a good-for-nothing youth upon the
stage, setting up Jove as his example of lewdness:—

> '*Viewing a picture, where the tale was drawn,*
> *Of Jove's descending in a golden shower*
> *To Danaë's bosom . . . with a woman to intrigue.*'

And see how he excites himself to lust, as if by celestial authority, when
he says:—

> '*Great Jove,*
> *Who shakes the highest heavens with his thunder,*
> *And I, poor mortal man, not do the same!*
> *I did it, and with all my heart I did it.*'

Not one whit more easily are the words learnt for this vileness, but by their
means is the vileness perpetrated with more confidence. I do not blame the

words, they being, as it were, choice and precious vessels, but the wine of error which was drunk in them to us by inebriated teachers; and unless we drank, we were beaten, without liberty of appeal to any sober judge. And yet, O my God,—in whose presence I can now with security recall this,—did I, unhappy one, learn these things willingly, and with delight, and for this was I called a boy of good promise.

Bear with me, my God, while I speak a little of those talents Thou hast bestowed upon me, and on what follies I wasted them. For a lesson sufficiently disquieting to my soul was given me, in hope of praise, and fear of shame or stripes, to speak the words of Juno, as she raged and sorrowed that she could not

*'Latium bar*
*From all approaches of the Dardan king,'*

which I had heard Juno never uttered. Yet were we compelled to stray in the footsteps of these poetic fictions, and to turn that into prose which the poet had said in verse. And his speaking was most applauded in whom, according to the reputation of the persons delineated, the passions of anger and sorrow were most strikingly reproduced, and clothed in the most suitable language. But what is it to me, O my true Life, my God, that my declaiming was applauded above that of many who were my contemporaries and fellow-students? Behold is not all this smoke and wind? Was there nothing else, too, on which I could exercise my wit and tongue? Thy praise, Lord, Thy praises might have supported the tendrils of my heart by Thy Scriptures; so had it not been dragged away by these empty trifles, a shameful prey of the fowls of the air. For there is more than one way in which men sacrifice to the fallen angels.

But what matter of surprise is it that I was thus carried towards vanity, and went forth from Thee, O my God, when men were proposed to me to imitate, who, should they in relating any acts of theirs—not in themselves evil—be guilty of a barbarism or solecism, when censured for it became confounded: but when they made a full and ornate oration, in well-chosen

words, concerning their own licentiousness, and were applauded for it, they boasted? Thou seest this, O Lord, and keepest silence, 'long-suffering, and plenteous in mercy and truth,' as Thou art. Wilt Thou keep silence for ever? And even now Thou drawest out of this vast deep the soul that seeketh Thee and thirsteth after Thy delights, whose 'heart said unto Thee,' I have sought Thy face, 'Thy face, Lord, will I seek.' For I was far from Thy face, through my darkened affections. For it is not by our feet, nor by change of place, that we either turn from Thee or return to Thee. Or, indeed, did that younger son look out for horses, or chariots, or ships, or fly away with visible wings, or journey by the motion of his limbs, that he might, in a far country, prodigally waste all that Thou gavest him when he set out? A kind Father when Thou gavest, and kinder still when he returned destitute! So, then, in wanton, that is to say, in darkened affections, lies distance from Thy face.

Behold, O Lord God, and behold patiently, as Thou art wont to do, how diligently the sons of men observe the conventional rules of letters and syllables, received from those who spoke prior to them, and yet neglect the eternal rules of everlasting salvation received from Thee, insomuch that he who practises or teaches the hereditary rules of pronunciation, if, contrary to grammatical usage, he should say, without aspirating the first letter, a *uman* being, will offend men more than if, in opposition to Thy commandments, he, a human being, were to hate a human being. As if, indeed, any man should feel that an enemy could be more destructive to him than that hatred with which he is excited against him, or that he could destroy more utterly him whom he persecutes than he destroys his own soul by his enmity. And of a truth, there is no science of letters more innate than the writing of conscience—that he is doing unto another what he himself would not suffer. How mysterious art Thou, who in silence 'dwellest on high,' Thou God, the only great, who by an unwearied law dealest out the punishment of blindness to illicit desires! When a man seeking for the reputation of eloquence stands before a human judge while a thronging multitude surrounds him, inveighs against his enemy with the most fierce hatred, he takes most vigilant heed that his tongue slips not into grammatical error, but takes no heed lest through the fury of his spirit he cut off a man from his fellow-men.

These were the customs in the midst of which I, unhappy boy, was cast, and on that arena it was that I was more fearful of perpetrating a barbarism than, having done so, of envying those who had not. These things I declare and confess unto Thee, my God, for which I was applauded by them whom I then thought it my whole duty to please, for I did not perceive the gulf of infamy wherein I was cast away from Thine eyes. For in Thine eyes what was more infamous than I was already, displeasing even those like myself, deceiving with innumerable lies both tutor, and masters, and parents, from love of play, a desire to see frivolous spectacles, and a stage-struck restlessness, to imitate them? Pilferings I committed from my parents' cellar and table, either enslaved by gluttony, or that I might have something to give to boys who sold me their play, who, though they sold it, liked it as well as I. In this play, likewise, I often sought dishonest victories, I myself being conquered by the vain desire of pre-eminence. And what could I so little endure, or, if I detected it, censured I so violently, as the very things I did to others, and, when myself detected I was censured, preferred rather to quarrel than to yield? Is this the innocence of childhood? Nay, Lord, nay, Lord; I entreat Thy mercy, O my God. For these same sins, as we grow older, are transferred from governors and masters, from nuts, and balls, and sparrows, to magistrates and kings, to gold, and lands, and slaves, just as the rod is succeeded by more severe chastisements. It was, then, the stature of childhood that Thou, O our King, didst approve of as an emblem of humility when Thou saidst: 'Of such is the kingdom of heaven.'

But yet, O Lord, to Thee, most excellent and most good, Thou Architect and Governor of the universe, thanks had been due unto Thee, our God, even hadst Thou willed that I should not survive my boyhood. For I existed even then; I lived, and felt, and was solicitous about my own well-being,— a trace of that most mysterious unity from whence I had my being; I kept watch by my inner sense over the wholeness of my senses, and in these insignificant pursuits, and also in my thoughts on things insignificant, I learnt to take pleasure in truth. I was averse to being deceived, I had a vigorous memory, was provided with the power of speech, was softened by friendship, shunned sorrow, meanness, ignorance. In such a being what was not wonderful and praiseworthy? But all these are gifts of my God; I did not give them to myself; and they are good, and all these constitute myself. Good, then, is He that made me, and He is my God; and before Him will I rejoice exceedingly for every good gift which, as a boy, I had. For in this lay my sin, that not in Him, but in His creatures—myself and the rest—I sought for pleasures, honours, and truths, falling thereby into sorrows, troubles, and errors. Thanks be to Thee, my joy, my pride, my confidence, my God—thanks be to Thee for Thy gifts; but preserve Thou them to me. For thus wilt Thou preserve me; and those things which Thou hast given me shall be developed and perfected, and I myself shall be with Thee, for from Thee is my being.

# BOOK II

*He advances to puberty, and indeed to the early part of the sixteenth year of his age, in which, having abandoned his studies, he indulged in lustful pleasures, and, with his companions, committed theft.*

I WILL now call to mind my past foulness, and the carnal corruptions of my soul, not because I love them, but that I may love Thee, O my God. For love of Thy love do I it, recalling, in the very bitterness of my remembrance, my most vicious ways, that Thou mayest grow sweet to me,—Thou sweetness without deception! Thou sweetness happy and assured!—and re-collecting myself out of that my dissipation, in which I was torn to pieces, while, turned away from Thee the One, I lost myself among many vanities. For I even longed in my youth formerly to be satisfied with worldly things, and I dared to grow wild again with various and shadowy loves; my form consumed away, and I became corrupt in Thine eyes, pleasing myself, and eager to please in the eyes of men.

But what was it that I delighted in save to love and to be beloved? But I held it not in moderation, mind to mind, the bright path of friendship, but out of the dark concupiscence of the flesh and the effervescence of youth exhalations came forth which obscured and overcast my heart, so that I was unable to discern pure affection from unholy desire. Both boiled confusedly within me, and dragged away my unstable youth into the rough places of unchaste desires, and plunged me into a gulf of infamy. Thy anger had overshadowed me, and I knew it not. I was become deaf by the rattling of the chains of my mortality, the punishment for my soul's pride; and I wandered farther from Thee, and Thou didst 'suffer' me; and I was tossed to and fro, and wasted, and poured out, and boiled over in my fornications, and Thou didst hold Thy peace, O Thou my tardy joy! Thou then didst hold Thy peace, and I wandered still farther from Thee, into more and more barren seed-plots of sorrows, with proud dejection and restless lassitude.

Oh for one to have regulated my disorder, and turned to my profit the fleeting beauties of the things around me, and fixed a bound to their sweetness, so that the tides of my youth might have spent themselves upon the conjugal shore, if so be they could not be tranquillized and satisfied within the object of a family, as Thy law appoints, O Lord,—who thus formest the offspring of our death, being able also with a tender hand to blunt the thorns which were excluded from Thy paradise! For Thy omnipotency is not far from us even when we are far from Thee, else in truth ought I more vigilantly to have given heed to the voice from the clouds: 'Nevertheless, such shall have trouble in the flesh, but I spare you;' and, 'It is good for a man not to touch a woman;' and, 'He that is unmarried careth for the things that belong to the Lord, how he may please the Lord; but he that is married careth for the things that are of the world, how he may please his wife.' I should, therefore, have listened more attentively to these words, and, being severed 'for the kingdom of heaven's sake,' I would with greater happiness have expected Thy embraces.

But I, poor fool, seethed as does the sea, and, forsaking Thee, followed the violent course of my own stream, and exceeded all Thy limitations; nor did I escape Thy scourges. For what mortal can do so? But Thou wert always by me, mercifully angry, and dashing with the bitterest vexations all my illicit pleasures, in order that I might seek pleasures free from vexation. But where I could meet with such except in Thee, O Lord, I could not find,—except in Thee, who teachest by sorrow, and woundest us to heal us, and killest us that we may not die from Thee. Where was I, and how far was I exiled from the delights of Thy house, in that sixteenth year of the age of my flesh, when the madness of lust—to the which human shamelessness granteth full freedom, although forbidden by Thy laws—

held complete sway over me, and I resigned myself entirely to it? Those about me meanwhile took no care to save me from ruin by marriage, their sole care being that I should learn to make a powerful speech, and become a persuasive orator.

And for that year my studies were intermitted, while after my return from Madaura[6] (a neighbouring city, whither I had begun to go in order to learn grammar and rhetoric), the expenses for a further residence at Carthage were provided for me; and that was rather by the determination than the means of my father, who was but a poor freeman of Thagaste. To whom do I narrate this? Not unto Thee, my God; but before Thee unto my own kind, even to that small part of the human race who may chance to light upon these my writings. And to what end? That I and all who read the same may reflect out of what depths we are to cry unto Thee. For what cometh nearer to Thine ears than a confessing heart and a life of faith? For who did not extol and praise my father, in that he went even beyond his means to supply his son with all the necessaries for a far journey for the sake of his studies? For many far richer citizens did not the like for their children. But yet this same father did not trouble himself how I grew towards Thee, nor how chaste I was, so long as I was skilful in speaking—however barren I was to Thy tilling, O God, who art the sole true and good Lord of my heart, which is Thy field.

But while, in that sixteenth year of my age, I resided with my parents, having holiday from school for a time (this idleness being imposed upon me by my parents' necessitous circumstances), the thorns of lust grew rank over my head, and there was no hand to pluck them out. Moreover when my father, seeing me at the baths, perceived that I was becoming a man, and was stirred with a restless youthfulness, he, as if from this anticipating future descendants, joyfully told it to my mother; rejoicing in that intoxication wherein the world so often forgets Thee, its Creator, and falls in love with Thy creature instead of Thee, from the invisible wine of its own perversity turning and bowing down to the most infamous things. But in my mother's breast Thou hadst even now begun Thy temple, and the commencement of Thy holy habitation, whereas my father was only a catechumen as yet, and that but recently. She then started up with a pious fear and trembling; and, although I had not yet been baptized, she feared those crooked ways in which they walk who turn their back to Thee, and not their face.

Woe is me! and dare I affirm that Thou heldest Thy peace, O my God, while I strayed farther from Thee? Didst Thou then hold Thy peace to me? And whose words were they but Thine which by my mother, Thy faithful handmaid, Thou pouredst into my ears, none of which sank into my heart to make me do it? For she despised, and I remember privately warned me, with a great solicitude, 'not to commit fornication; but above all things never to defile another man's wife.' These appeared to me but womanish counsels, which I should blush to obey. But they were Thine, and I knew it not, and I thought that Thou heldest Thy peace, and that it was she who spoke, through whom Thou heldest not Thy peace to me, and in her person wast despised by me, her son, 'the son of Thy handmaid, Thy servant.' But this I knew not, and rushed on headlong with such blindness, that amongst my equals I was ashamed to be less shameless, when I heard them pluming themselves upon their disgraceful acts, yea, and glorying all the more in proportion to the greatness of their baseness; and I took pleasure in doing it, not for the pleasure's sake only, but for the praise. What is worthy of dispraise but vice? But I made myself out worse than I was, in order that I might not be dispraised; and when in anything I had not sinned as the abandoned ones, I would affirm that I had done what I had not, that I might not appear abject for being more innocent, or of less esteem for being more chaste.

Behold with what companions I walked the streets of Babylon, in whose filth I was rolled, as if in cinnamon and precious ointments. And that I might cleave the more tenaciously to its very centre, my invisible enemy trod me down, and seduced me, I being easily seduced. Nor did the mother of my flesh, although she herself had ere this fled 'out of the midst of Babylon,'—progressing, however, but slowly in the skirts of it,—in counselling me to chastity, so bear in mind what she had been told about me by her husband as to restrain in the limits of conjugal affection (if it could not be cut away to the quick) what she knew to be destructive in the present and dangerous in the future. But she took no heed of this, for she was afraid lest a wife should prove a hindrance and a clog to my hopes. Not those hopes of the future world, which my mother had in Thee; but the hope of learning, which both my parents were too anxious that I should acquire,—he, because he had little or no thought of Thee, and but vain thoughts for me—she, because she calculated that those usual courses of learning would not only be no drawback, but rather a furtherance towards my attaining Thee. For thus I conjecture, recalling as well as I can the dispositions of my parents. The reins, meantime, were slackened towards me beyond the restraint of due severity, that I might play, yea, even to dissoluteness, in whatsoever I fancied. And in all there was a mist, shutting out from my sight the brightness of Thy truth, O my God; and my iniquity displayed itself as from very 'fatness.'

Theft is punished by Thy law, O Lord, and by the law written in men's hearts, which iniquity itself cannot blot out. For what thief will suffer a thief? Even a rich thief will not suffer him who is driven to it by want. Yet had I a desire to commit robbery, and did so, compelled neither by hunger, nor poverty, but through a distaste for well-doing, and a lustiness of iniquity. For I pilfered that of which I had already sufficient, and much better. Nor did I desire to enjoy what I pilfered, but the theft and sin itself. There was a pear-tree close to our vineyard, heavily laden with fruit, which was tempting neither for its colour nor its flavour. To shake and rob this some of us wanton young fellows went, late one night (having, according to our disgraceful habit, prolonged our games in the streets until then), and carried away great loads, not to eat ourselves, but to fling to the very swine, having only eaten some of them; and to do this pleased us all the more because it was not permitted. Behold my heart, O my God; behold my heart, which Thou hadst pity upon when in the bottomless pit. Behold, now, let my heart tell Thee what it was seeking there, that I should be

gratuitously wanton, having no inducement to evil but the evil itself. It was foul, and I loved it. I loved to perish. I loved my own error—not that for which I erred, but the error itself. Base souls, falling from Thy firmament to utter destruction—not seeking aught through the shame but the shame itself!

There is a desirableness in all beautiful bodies, and in gold, and silver, and all things; and in bodily contact sympathy is powerful, and each other sense hath his proper adaptation of body. Worldly honour hath also its glory, and the power of command, and of overcoming; whence proceeds also the desire for revenge. And yet to acquire all these, we must not depart from Thee, O Lord, nor deviate from Thy law. The life which we live here hath also its peculiar attractiveness, through a certain measure of comeliness of its own, and harmony with all things here below. The friendships of men also are endeared by a sweet bond, in the oneness of many souls. On account of all these, and such as these, is sin committed; while through an inordinate preference for these goods of a lower kind, the better and higher are neglected,—even Thou, our Lord God, Thy truth, and Thy law. For these meaner things have their delights, but not like unto my God, who hath created all things; for in Him doth the righteous delight, and He is the sweetness of the upright in heart.

When, therefore, we inquire why a crime was committed, we do not believe it, unless it appear that there might have been the wish to obtain some of those which we designated meaner things, or else a fear of losing them. For truly they are beautiful and comely, although in comparison with those higher and celestial goods they be abject and contemptible. A man hath murdered another; what was his motive? He desired his wife or his estate; or would steal to support himself; or he was afraid of losing something of the kind by him; or, being injured, he was burning to be revenged. Would he commit murder without a motive, taking delight simply in the act of murder? Who would credit it? For as for that savage and brutal man, of whom it is declared that he was gratuitously wicked and cruel, there is yet a motive assigned. 'Lest through idleness,' he says, 'hand or heart should grow inactive.' And to what purpose? Why, even that, having once got possession of the city through that practice of wickedness, he might attain unto honours, empire, and wealth, and be exempt from the fear of the laws, and his difficult circumstances from the needs of his family, and the consciousness of his own wickedness. So it seems that even Catiline himself loved not his own villainies, but something else, which gave him the motive for committing them.

What was it, then, that I, miserable one, so doted on in thee, thou theft of mine, thou deed of darkness, in that sixteenth year of my age? Beautiful thou wert not, since thou wert theft. But art thou anything, that so I may argue the case with thee? Those pears that we stole were fair to the sight, because they were Thy creation, Thou fairest of all, Creator of all, Thou good God—God, the highest good, and my true good. Those pears truly were pleasant to the sight; but it was not for them that my miserable soul lusted, for I had abundance of better, but those I plucked simply that I might steal. For, having plucked them, I threw them away, my sole gratification in them being my own sin, which I was pleased to enjoy. For if any of these pears entered my mouth, the sweetener of it was my sin in eating it. And now, O Lord my God, I ask what it was in that theft of mine that caused me such delight; and behold it hath no beauty in it—not such, I mean, as exists in justice and wisdom; nor such as is in the mind, memory, senses, and animal life of man; nor yet such as is the glory and beauty of the stars in their courses; or the earth, or the sea, teeming with incipient life, to replace, as it is born, that which decayeth; nor, indeed, that false and shadowy beauty which pertaineth to deceptive vices.

For thus doth pride imitate high estate, whereas Thou alone art God, high above all. And what does ambition seek but honours, and renown, whereas Thou alone art to be honoured above all, and renowned for evermore? The cruelty of the powerful wishes to be feared; but who is to be feared but God only, out of whose power what can be forced away or withdrawn—when, or where, or whither, or by whom? The entice-ments of the wanton would fain be deemed love; and yet is naught more enticing than Thy charity, nor is aught loved more healthfully than that, Thy truth, bright and beautiful above all. Curiosity affects a desire for knowledge, whereas it is Thou who supremely knowest all things. Yea, ignorance and foolishness themselves are concealed under the names of ingenuousness and harmlessness, because nothing can be found more ingenuous than Thou; and what is more harmless, since it is a sinner's own works by which he is harmed? And sloth seems to long for rest; but what sure rest is there besides the Lord? Luxury would fain be called plenty and abundance; but Thou art the fulness and unfailing plenteousness of unfading joys. Prodigality presents a shadow of liberality; but Thou art the most lavish giver of all good. Covetousness desires to possess much; and Thou art the Possessor of all things. Envy contends for excellence; but what so excellent as Thou? Anger seeks revenge; who avenges more justly than Thou? Fear starts at unwonted and sudden chances which threaten things beloved, and is wary for their security; but what can happen that is unwonted or sudden to Thee? or who can deprive Thee of what Thou lovest? or where is there unshaken security save with Thee? Grief languishes for things lost in which desire had delighted itself, even because it would have nothing taken from it, as nothing can be from Thee.

Thus doth the soul commit fornication when she turns away from Thee, and seeks without Thee what she cannot find pure and untainted until she returns to Thee. Thus all pervertedly imitate Thee who separate themselves far from Thee, and raise themselves up against Thee. But even by thus imitating Thee they acknowledge Thee to be the Creator of all nature, and so that there is no place whither they can altogether retire from Thee. What, then, was it that I loved in that theft? And wherein did I, even corruptedly and pervertedly, imitate my Lord? Did I wish, if only by artifice, to act contrary to Thy law, because by power I could not, so that, being a captive, I might imitate an imperfect liberty by doing with impunity things which I was not allowed to do, in obscured likeness of Thy omnipotency?[7] Behold this servant of Thine, fleeing from his Lord, and following a shadow! O rottenness! O monstrosity of life and profundity of death! Could I like that which was unlawful only because it was un-lawful?

'What shall I render unto the Lord,' that whilst my memory recalls these things my soul is not appalled at them? I will love Thee, O Lord, and thank Thee, and confess unto Thy name, because Thou hast put away from me these so wicked and nefarious acts of mine. To Thy grace I attribute it, and to Thy mercy, that Thou hast melted away my sin as it were ice. To Thy grace also I attribute whatsoever of evil I have not committed; for what might I not have committed, loving as I did the sin for the sin's sake? Yea, all I confess to have been pardoned me, both those which I committed by my own perverseness, and those which, by Thy guidance, I committed not. Where is he who, reflecting upon his own infirmity, dares to ascribe his chastity and innocency to his own strength, so that he should love Thee the less, as if he had been in less need of Thy mercy, whereby Thou dost forgive the transgressions of those that turn to Thee? For whosoever, called by Thee, obeyed Thy voice, and shunned those things which he reads me recalling and confessing of myself, let him not despise me, who, being sick, was healed by that same Physician by whose aid it was that he was not sick, or rather was less sick. And for this let him love Thee as much, yea, all the more, since by whom he sees me to have been restored from so great a feebleness of sin, by Him he sees himself from a like feebleness to have been preserved.

'What fruit had I then,' wretched one, in those things which, when I remember them, cause me shame—above all in that theft, which I loved only for the theft's sake? And as the theft itself was nothing, all the more wretched was I who loved it. Yet by myself alone I would not have done it—I recall what my heart was—alone I could not have done it. I loved, then, in it the companionship of my accomplices with whom I did it. I did not, therefore, love the theft alone—yea, rather, it was that alone that I loved, for the companionship was nothing. What is the fact? Who is it that can teach me, but He who illuminateth mine heart and searcheth out the dark corners thereof? What is it that hath come into my mind to inquire about, to discuss, and to reflect upon? For had I at that time loved the pears I stole, and wished to enjoy them, I might have done so alone, if I could have been satisfied with the mere commission of the theft by which my pleasure was secured; nor needed I have provoked that itching of my own passions, by the encouragement of accomplices. But as my enjoyment was not in those pears it was in the crime itself, which the company of my fellow-sinners produced.

By what feelings, then, was I animated? For it was in truth too shameful; and woe was me who had it. But still what was it? 'Who can understand his errors?' We laughed, because our hearts were tickled at the thought of deceiving those who little imagined what we were doing, and would have vehemently disapproved of it. Yet, again, why did I so rejoice in this, that I did not alone? Is it that no one readily laughs alone? No one does so readily; but yet sometimes, when men are alone by themselves, nobody being by, a fit of laughter overcomes them when anything very droll presents itself to their senses or mind. Yet alone I would not have done it—alone I could not at all have done it. Behold, my God, the lively recollection of my soul is laid bare before Thee—alone I had not committed that theft, wherein what I stole pleased me not, but rather the act of stealing; nor to have done it alone would I have liked so well, neither would I have done it. O Friendship too unfriendly! thou mysterious seducer of the soul, thou greediness to do mischief out of mirth and wantonness, thou craving for others' loss, without desire for my own profit or revenge; but when they say, 'Let us go, let us do it,' we are ashamed not to be shameless.

Who can unravel that twisted and tangled knottiness? It is foul. I hate to reflect on it. I hate to look on it. But thee do I long for, O righteousness and innocency, fair and comely to all virtuous eyes, and of a satisfaction that never palls! With thee is perfect rest, and life unchanging. He who enters into thee enters into the joy of his Lord, and shall have no fear, and shall do excellently in the most Excellent. I sank away from Thee, O my God, and I wandered too far from Thee, my stay, in my youth, and became to myself an unfruitful land.

# BOOK III

*Of the seventeenth, eighteenth, and nineteenth years of his age, passed at Carthage, when, having completed his course of studies, he is caught in the snares of a licentious passion, and falls into the snares of the Manichæans.*

To Carthage I came, where a cauldron of unholy loves bubbled up all around me. I loved not as yet, yet I loved to love; and, with a hidden want, I abhorred myself that I wanted not. I searched about for something to love, in love with loving, and hating security, and a way not beset with snares. For within me I had a dearth of that inward food, Thyself, my God, though that dearth caused me no hunger; but I remained without all desire for incorruptible food, not because I was already filled thereby, but the more empty I was the more I loathed it. For this reason my soul was far from well, and, full of ulcers, it miserably cast itself forth, craving to be excited by contact with objects of sense. Yet, had these no soul, they would not surely inspire love. To love and to be loved was sweet to me, and all the more when I succeeded in enjoying the person I loved. I befouled, therefore, the spring of friendship with the filth of concupiscence, and I dimmed its lustre with the hell of lustfulness; and yet, foul and dishonourable as I was, I craved, through an excess of vanity, to be thought elegant and urbane. I fell precipitately, then, into the love in which I longed to be ensnared. My God, my mercy, with how much bitterness didst Thou, out of Thy infinite goodness, besprinkle for me that sweetness! For I was both beloved, and secretly arrived at the bond of enjoying; and was joyfully bound with troublesome ties, that I might be scourged with the burning iron rods of jealousy, suspicion, fear, anger, and strife.

30

Stage-plays also drew me away, full of representations of my miseries and of fuel to my fire. Why does man like to be made sad when viewing doleful and tragical scenes, which yet he himself would by no means suffer? And yet he wishes, as a spectator, to experience from them a sense of grief, and in this very grief his pleasure consists. What is this but wretched insanity? For a man is more affected with these actions, the less free he is from such affections. Howsoever, when he suffers in his own person, it is the custom to style it 'misery;' but when he compassionates others, then it is styled 'mercy.' But what kind of mercy is it that arises from fictitious and scenic passions? The hearer is not expected to relieve, but merely invited to grieve; and the more he grieves, the more he applauds the actor of these fictions. And if the misfortunes of the characters (whether of olden times or merely imaginary) be so represented as not to touch the feelings of the spectator, he goes away disgusted and censorious; but if his feelings be touched, he sits it out attentively, and sheds tears of joy.

Are sorrows, then, also loved? Surely all men desire to rejoice? Or, as man wishes to be miserable, is he, nevertheless, glad to be merciful, which, because it cannot exist without passion, for this cause alone are passions loved? This also is from that vein of friendship. But whither does it go? Whither does it flow? Wherefore runs it into that torrent of pitch,[8] seething forth those huge tides of loathsome lusts into which it is changed and trans-formed, being of its own will cast away and corrupted from its celestial clearness? Shall, then, mercy be repudiated? By no means. Let us, therefore, love sorrows sometimes. But beware of uncleanness, O my soul, under the protection of my God, the God of our fathers, who is to be praised and exalted above all for ever, beware of uncleanness. For I have not now ceased to have compassion; but then in the theatres I sympathized with lovers when they sinfully enjoyed one another, although this was done fictitiously in the play. And when they lost one another, I grieved with them, as if pitying them, and yet had delight in both. But now-a-days I feel much more pity for him that delighteth in his wickedness, than for him who is counted as enduring hardships by failing to obtain some pernicious pleasure, and the loss of some miserable felicity. This, surely, is the truer mercy, but grief hath no delight in it. For though he that condoles with the unhappy be approved for his office of charity, yet would he who had real compassion rather there were nothing for him to grieve about. For if good-will be ill-willed (which it cannot), then can he who is truly and sincerely commiserating wish that there should be some unhappy ones, that he might commiserate them. Some grief may then be justified, none loved. For thus dost Thou, O Lord God, who lovest souls far more purely than do we, and art more incorruptibly compassionate, although Thou art wounded by no sorrow. 'And who is sufficient for these things?'

But I, wretched one, then loved to grieve, and sought out what to grieve at, as when, in another man's misery, though feigned and counterfeited, that delivery of the actor best pleased me, and attracted me the most powerfully, which moved me to tears. What marvel was it that, an unhappy sheep, straying from Thy flock, and impatient of Thy care, I became infected with a foul disease? And hence came my love of griefs—not such as should probe me too deeply, for I loved not to suffer such things as I loved to look upon, but such as, when hearing their fictions, should lightly affect the surface; upon which, like as with empoisoned nails, followed burning, swelling, putrefaction, and horrible corruption. Such was my life! But was it life, O my God?

And Thy faithful mercy hovered over me afar. Upon what unseemly iniquities did I wear myself out, following a sacrilegious curiosity, that, having deserted Thee, it might drag me into the treacherous abyss, and to the beguiling obedience of devils unto whom I immolated my wicked deeds and in all which Thou didst scourge me! I dared, even while Thy solemn rites were being celebrated within the walls of Thy Church, to desire, and to plan a business sufficient to procure me the fruits of death; for which Thou chastisedst me with grievous punishments, but nothing in comparison with my fault, O Thou my greatest mercy, my God, my refuge from those terrible hurts, among which I wandered with presumptuous neck, receding farther from Thee, loving my own ways, and not Thine—loving a vagrant liberty.

Those studies, also, which were accounted honourable, were directed towards the courts of law; to excel in which, the more crafty I was, the more I should be praised. Such is the blindness of men that they even glory in their blindness. And now I was head in the School of Rhetoric, whereat I rejoiced proudly, and became inflated with arrogance, though more sedate, O Lord, as Thou knowest, and altogether removed from the sub-vertings of those 'subverters'[9] (for this stupid and diabolical name was held to be the very brand of gallantry) amongst whom I lived, with an impudent shamefacedness that I was not even as they were. And with them I was, and at times I was delighted with their friendship whose acts I ever abhorred, that is, their 'subverting,' wherewith they insolently attacked the modesty of strangers, which they disturbed by uncalled-for jeers, gratifying thereby their mischievous mirth. Nothing can more nearly resemble the actions of devils than these. By what name, therefore, could they be more truly called than 'subverters'?—being themselves subverted first, and altogether perverted—being secretly mocked at and seduced by the deceiving spirits, in what they themselves delight to jeer at and deceive others.

Among such as these, at that unstable period of my life, I studied books of eloquence, wherein I was eager to be eminent from a damnable and inflated purpose, even a delight in human vanity. In the ordinary course of study, I lighted upon a certain book of Cicero, whose language, though not his heart, almost all admire. This book of his contains an exhortation to philosophy, and is called *Hortensius*. This book, in truth, changed my affections, and turned my prayers to Thyself, O Lord, and made me have other hopes and desires. Worthless suddenly became every vain hope to me; and, with an incredible warmth of heart, I yearned for an immortality of wisdom, and began now to arise that I might return to Thee. Not, then, to improve my language—which I appeared to be purchasing with my mother's means, in that my nineteenth year, my father having died two years before—not to improve my language did I have recourse to that book; nor did it persuade me by its style, but its matter.

How ardent was I then, my God, how ardent to fly from earthly things to Thee! Nor did I know how Thou wouldst deal with me. For with Thee is wisdom. In Greek the love of wisdom is called 'philosophy,' with which that book inflamed me. There be some who seduce through philosophy, under a great, and alluring, and honourable name colouring and adorning their own errors. And almost all who in that and former times were such, are in that book censured and pointed out. There is also disclosed that most salutary admonition of Thy Spirit, by Thy good and pious servant: 'Beware lest any man spoil you through philosophy and vain deceit, after the tradition of men, after the rudiments of the world, and not after Christ: for in Him dwelleth all the fulness of the Godhead bodily.' And since at that time (as Thou, O Light of my heart, knowest) the words of the apostle were unknown to me, I was delighted with that exhortation, in so far only as I was thereby stimulated, and enkindled, and inflamed to love, seek, obtain, hold, and embrace, not this or that sect, but wisdom itself, whatever it were; and this alone checked me thus ardent, that the name of Christ was not in it. For this name, according to Thy mercy, O Lord, this name of my Saviour Thy Son, had my tender heart piously drunk in, deeply treasured even with my mother's milk; and whatsoever was without that name, though never so erudite, polished, and truthful, took not complete hold of me.

I resolved, therefore, to direct my mind to the Holy Scriptures, that I might see what they were. And behold, I perceive something not comprehended by the proud, not disclosed to children, but lowly as you approach, sublime as you advance, and veiled in mysteries; and I was not of the number of those who could enter into it, or bend my neck to follow its steps. For not as when now I speak did I feel when I turned towards those Scriptures, but they appeared to me to be unworthy to be compared with the dignity of Tully; for my inflated pride shunned their style, nor could the sharpness of my wit pierce their inner meaning. Yet, truly, were they such as would develope in little ones; but I scorned to be a little one, and, swollen with pride, I looked upon myself as a great one.

Therefore I fell among men proudly raving, very carnal, and voluble, in whose mouths were the snares of the devil—the bird-lime being composed of a mixture of the syllables of Thy name, and of our Lord Jesus Christ, and of the Paraclete, the Holy Ghost, the Comforter. These names departed not out of their mouths, but so far forth as the sound only and the clatter of the tongue, for the heart was empty of truth. Still they cried, 'Truth, Truth,' and spoke much about it to me, 'yet was it not in them;' but they spake falsely not of Thee only—who, verily, art the Truth—but also of these elements of this world, Thy creatures. And I, in truth, should have passed by philosophers, even when speaking truth concerning them, for love of Thee, my Father, supremely good, beauty of all things beautiful! O Truth, Truth! how inwardly even then did the marrow of my soul pant after Thee, when they frequently, and in a multiplicity of ways, and in numerous and huge books, sounded out Thy name to me, though it was but a voice![10] And these were the dishes in which to me, hungering for Thee, they, instead of Thee, served up the sun and moon, Thy beauteous works—but yet Thy works, not Thyself, nay, nor Thy first works. For before these corporeal works are Thy spiritual ones, celestial and shining though they be. But I hungered and thirsted not even after those first works of Thine, but after Thee Thyself, the Truth, 'with whom is no variableness, neither shadow of turning;' yet they still served up to me in those dishes glowing phantasies, than which better were it to love this very sun (which, at least, is true to our sight), than those illusions which deceive the mind through the eye. And yet, because I supposed them to be Thee, I fed upon them; not with avidity, for Thou didst not taste to my mouth as Thou art, for Thou wast not these empty fictions; neither was I nourished by them, but the rather exhausted. Food in our sleep appears like our food awake; yet the sleepers are not nourished by it, for they are asleep. But those things were not in any way like unto Thee as Thou hast now spoken unto me, in that those were corporeal phantasies, false bodies, than which these true bodies, whether celestial or terrestrial, which we perceive with our fleshly sight, are much more certain. These things the very beasts and birds perceive as well as we, and they are more certain than when we imagine them. And again, we do with more certainty imagine them, than by them conceive of other greater and infinite bodies which have no existence. With such empty husks was I then fed, and was not fed. But Thou, my Love, in looking for whom I fail that I may be strong, art neither those bodies that we see, although in heaven, nor art Thou those which we see not there; for Thou hast created them, nor dost Thou reckon them amongst Thy greatest works. How far, then, art Thou from those phantasies of mine, phantasies of bodies which are not at all, than which the images of those bodies which are, are more certain, and still more certain the bodies themselves, which yet Thou art not; nay, nor yet the soul, which is the life of the bodies. Better, then, and more certain is the life of bodies than the bodies themselves. But Thou art the life of souls, the life of lives, having life in Thyself; and Thou changest not, O Life of my soul.

Where, then, wert Thou then to me, and how far from me? Far, indeed, was I wandering away from Thee, being even shut out from the very husks of the swine, whom with husks I fed. For how much better, then, are the fables of the grammarians and poets than these snares! For verses, and poems, and Medea flying, are more profitable truly than these men's five elements, variously painted, to answer to the five caves of darkness, none of which exist, and which slay the believer. For verses and poems I can turn into true food, but the 'Medea flying,' though I sang, I maintained it not; though I heard it sung, I believed it not; but those things I did believe. Woe, woe, by what steps was I dragged down to 'the depths of hell'!—toiling and turmoiling through want of Truth, when I sought after Thee, my God, —to Thee I confess it, who hadst mercy on me when I had not yet confessed,—sought after Thee not according to the understanding of the mind, in which Thou desiredst that I should excel the beasts, but according to the sense of the flesh! Thou wert more inward to me than my most inward part; and higher than my highest. I came upon that bold woman, who 'is simple, and knoweth nothing,' the enigma of Solomon, sitting 'at the door of the house on a seat,' and saying, 'Stolen waters are sweet, and bread eaten in secret is pleasant.' This woman seduced me, because she found my soul beyond its portals, dwelling in the eye of my flesh, and thinking on such food as through it I had devoured.

For I was ignorant as to that which really is, and was, as it were, violently moved to give my support to foolish deceivers, when they asked me, 'Whence is evil?'[11]—and, 'Is God limited by a bodily shape, and has He hairs and nails?'—and, 'Are they to be esteemed righteous who had many wives at once, and did kill men, and sacrificed living creatures?' At which things I, in my ignorance, was much disturbed, and, retreating from the truth, I appeared to myself to be going towards it; because as yet I knew not that evil was naught but a privation of good, until in the end it ceases altogether to be; which how should I see, the sight of whose eyes saw no further than bodies, and of my mind no further than a phantasm? And I knew not God to be a Spirit, not one who hath parts extended in length and breadth, nor whose being was bulk; for every bulk is less in a part than in the whole, and, if it be infinite, it must be less in such part as is limited by a certain space than in its infinity; and cannot be wholly everywhere, as Spirit, as God is. And what that should be in us, by which we were like unto God, and might rightly in Scripture be said to be after 'the image of God,' I was entirely ignorant.

Nor had I knowledge of that true inner righteousness, which doth not judge according to custom, but out of the most perfect law of God Almighty, by which the manners of places and times were adapted to those places and times—being itself the while the same always and everywhere, not one thing in one place, and another in another; according to which Abraham, and Isaac, and Jacob, and Moses, and David, and all those commended by the mouth of God were righteous, but were judged unrighteous by foolish men, judging out of man's judgment, and gauging by the petty standard of their own manners the manners of the whole human race. Like as if in an armoury, one knowing not what were adapted to the several members should put greaves on his head, or boot himself with a helmet, and then complain because they would not fit. Or as if, on some day when in the afternoon business was forbidden, one were to fume at not being allowed to sell as it was lawful to him in the forenoon. Or when in some house he sees a servant take something in his hand which the butler is not permitted to touch, or something done behind a stable which would be prohibited in the dining-room, and should be indignant that in one house, and one family, the same thing is not distributed everywhere to all. Such are they who cannot endure to hear something to have been lawful for righteous men in former times which is not so now; or that God, for certain temporal reasons, commanded them one thing, and these another, but both obeying the same righteousness; though they see, in one man, one day, and one house, different things to be fit for different members, and a thing which was formerly lawful after a time unlawful—that permitted or commanded in one corner, which done in another is justly prohibited and punished. Is justice, then, various and changeable? Nay, but the times over which she presides are not all alike, because they are times. But men, whose days upon the earth are few, because by their own perception they cannot harmonize the causes of former ages and other nations, of which they had no experience, with these of which they have experience, though in one and the same body, day, or family, they can readily see what is suitable for each member, season, part, and person—to the one they take exception, to the other they submit.

These things I then knew not, nor observed. They met my eyes on every side, and I saw them not. I composed poems, in which it was not permitted me to place every foot everywhere, but in one metre one way, and in another another, nor even in any one verse the same foot in all places. Yet the art itself by which I composed had not different principles for these different cases, but comprised all in one. Still I saw not how that righteousness, which good and holy men submitted to, far more excellently and sublimely comprehended in one all those things which God commanded, and in no part varied, though in varying times it did not prescribe all things at once, but distributed and enjoined what was proper for each. And I, being blind, blamed those pious fathers, not only for making use of present things as God commanded and inspired them to do, but also for foreshowing things to come as God was revealing them.[12]

Can it at any time or place be an unrighteous thing for a man to love God with all his heart, with all his soul, and with all his mind, and his neighbour as himself? Therefore those offences which be contrary to nature are everywhere and at all times to be held in detestation and punished; such were those of the Sodomites, which should all nations commit, they should all be held guilty of the same crime by the divine law, which hath not so made men that they should in that way abuse one another. For even that fellowship which should be between God and us is violated, when that same nature of which He is author is polluted by the perversity of lust. But those offences which are contrary to the customs of men are to be avoided according to the customs severally prevailing; so that an agreement made, and confirmed by custom or law of any city or nation, may not be violated at the lawless pleasure of any, whether citizen or stranger. For any part which is not consistent with its whole is unseemly. But when God commands anything contrary to the customs or compacts of any nation to be done, though it were never done by them before, it is to be done; and if intermitted it is to be restored, and, if never established, to be established. For if it be lawful for a king, in the state over which he reigns, to command that which neither he himself nor any one before him had commanded, and to obey him cannot be held to be inimical to the public interest,—nay, it were so if he were not obeyed (for obedience to princes is a general compact of human society),—how much more, then, ought we unhesitatingly to obey God, the Governor of all His creatures! For as among the authorities of human society the greater authority is obeyed before the lesser, so must God above all.

So also in deeds of violence, where there is a desire to harm, whether by contumely or injury; and both of these either by reason of revenge, as one enemy against another; or to obtain some advantage over another, as the highwayman to the traveller; or for the avoiding of some evil, as with him who is in fear of another; or through envy, as the unfortunate man to one who is happy; or as he that is prosperous in anything to him who he fears will become equal to himself, or whose equality he grieves at; or for the mere pleasure in another's pains, as the spectators of gladiators, or the deriders and mockers of others. These be the chief iniquities which spring forth from the lust of the flesh, of the eye, and of power, whether singly, or two together, or all at once. And so do men live in opposition to the three and seven, that psaltery 'of ten strings,' Thy ten commandments, O God most high and most sweet. But what foul offences can there be against Thee who canst not be defiled? Or what deeds of violence against Thee who canst not be harmed? But Thou avengest that which men perpetrate against themselves, seeing also that when they sin against Thee, they do wickedly against their own souls; and iniquity gives itself the lie, either by corrupting or perverting their nature, which Thou hast made and ordained, or by an immoderate use of things permitted, or in 'burning' in things forbidden to that use which is against nature; or when convicted, raging with heart and voice against Thee, kicking against the pricks; or when, breaking through the pale of human society, they audaciously rejoice in private combinations or divisions, according as they have been pleased or offended. And these things are done whenever Thou art forsaken, O Fountain of Life, who art the only and true Creator and Ruler of the universe, and by a self-willed pride any one false thing is selected therefrom and loved. So, then, by a humble piety we return to Thee; and Thou purgest us from our evil customs, and art merciful unto the sins of those who confess unto Thee, and dost 'hear the groaning of the prisoner,' and dost loosen us from those fetters which we have forged for ourselves, if we lift not up against Thee the horns of a false liberty—losing all through craving more, by loving more our own private good than Thee, the good of all.

But amidst these offences of infamy and violence, and so many iniquities, are the sins of men who are, on the whole, making progress; which, by those who judge rightly, and after the rule of perfection, are censured, yet commended withal, upon the hope of bearing fruit, like as in the green blade of the growing corn. And there are some which resemble offences

of infamy or violence, and yet are not sins, because they neither offend Thee, our Lord God, nor social custom: when, for example, things suitable for the times are provided for the use of life, and we are uncertain whether it be out of a lust of having; or when acts are punished by constituted authority for the sake of correction, and we are uncertain whether it be out of a lust of hurting. Many a deed, then, which in the sight of men is disapproved, is approved by Thy testimony; and many a one who is praised by men is, Thou being witness, condemned; because frequently the view of the deed, and the mind of the doer, and the hidden exigency of the period, severally vary. But when Thou unexpectedly commandest an unusual and unthought-of thing—yea, even if Thou hast formerly forbidden it, and still for the time keepest secret the reason of Thy command, and it even be contrary to the ordinance of some society of men, who doubts but it is to be done, inasmuch as that society is righteous which serves Thee? But blessed are they who know Thy commands! For all things were done by them who served Thee[13] either to exhibit something necessary at the time, or to foreshow things to come.

These things being ignorant of, I derided those holy servants and prophets of Thine. And what did I gain by deriding them but to be derided by Thee, being insensibly, and little by little, led on to those follies, as to credit that a fig-tree wept when it was plucked, and that the mother-tree shed milky tears? Which fig notwithstanding, plucked not by his own but another's wickedness, had some 'saint' eaten and mingled with his entrails, he should breathe out of it angels; yea, in his prayers he shall assuredly groan and sigh forth particles of God, which particles of the most high and true God should have remained bound in that fig unless they had been set free by the teeth and belly of some 'elect saint'![14] And I, miserable one, believed that more mercy was to be shown to the fruits of the earth than unto men, for whom they were created; for if a hungry man—who was not a Manichæan—should beg for any, that morsel which should be given him would appear, as it were, condemned to capital punishment.

And Thou sendedst Thine hand from above, and drewest my soul out of that profound darkness, when my mother, Thy faithful one, wept to Thee on my behalf more than mothers are wont to weep the bodily deaths of their children. For she saw that I was dead by that faith and spirit which she had from Thee, and Thou heardest her, O Lord. Thou heardest her, and despisedst not her tears, when, pouring down, they watered the earth under her eyes in every place where she prayed[15]; yea, Thou heardest her. For whence was that dream with which Thou consoledst her, so that she permitted me to live with her, and to have my meals at the same table in the house, which she had begun to avoid, hating and detesting the blasphemies of my error? For she saw herself standing on a certain wooden rule, and a bright youth advancing towards her, joyous and smiling upon her, whilst she was grieving and bowed down with sorrow. But he having inquired of her the cause of her sorrow and daily weeping (he wishing to teach, as is their wont, and not to be taught), and she answering that it was my perdition she was lamenting, he bade her rest contented, and told her to behold and see 'that where she was, there was I also.' And when she looked she saw me standing near her on the same rule. Whence was this, unless that Thine ears were inclined towards her heart? O Thou Good Omnipotent, who so carest for every one of us as if Thou caredst for him only, and so for all as if they were but one!

Whence was this, also, that when she had narrated this vision to me, and I tried to put this construction on it, 'That she rather should not despair of being some day what I was,' she immediately, without hesitation, replied, 'No; for it was not told me that "where he is, there shalt thou be," but, "where thou art, there shall he be" '? I confess to Thee, O Lord, that, to the best of my remembrance (and I have oft spoken of this), Thy answer through my watchful mother—that she was not disquieted by the speciousness of my false interpretation, and saw in a moment what was to be seen, and which I myself had not in truth perceived before she spake—even then moved me more than the dream itself, by which the happiness to that pious woman, to be realized so long after, was, for the alleviation of her present anxiety, so long before predicted. For nearly nine years passed in which I wallowed in the slime of that deep pit and the darkness of falsehood, striving often to rise, but being all the more heavily dashed down. But yet that chaste, pious, and sober widow (such as Thou lovest), now more buoyed up with hope, though no whit less zealous in her weeping and mourning, desisted not, at all the hours of her supplications, to bewail my case unto Thee. And her prayers entered into Thy presence, and yet Thou didst still suffer me to be involved and re-involved in that darkness.

And meanwhile Thou grantedst her another answer, which I recall; for much I pass over, hastening on to those things which the more strongly impel me to confess unto Thee, and much I do not remember. Thou didst grant her then another answer, by a priest of Thine, a certain bishop, reared in Thy Church and well versed in Thy books. He, when this woman had entreated that he would vouchsafe to have some talk with me, refute my errors, unteach me evil things, and teach me good (for this he was in the habit of doing when he found people fitted to receive it), refused, very prudently, as I afterwards came to see. For he answered that I was still unteachable, being inflated with the novelty of that heresy, and that I had already perplexed divers inexperienced persons with vexatious questions, as she had informed him. 'But leave him alone for a time,' saith he, 'only pray God for him; he will of himself, by reading, discover what that error is, and how great its impiety.' He disclosed to her at the same time how he himself, when a little one, had, by his misguided mother, been given over to the Manichæans, and had not only read, but even written out almost all their books, and had come to see (without argument or proof from any one) how much that sect was to be shunned, and had shunned it. Which when he had said, and she would not be satisfied, but repeated more earnestly her entreaties, shedding copious tears, that he would see and discourse with me, he, a little vexed at her importunity, exclaimed, 'Go thy way, and God bless thee, for it is not possible that the son of these tears should perish.' Which answer (as she often mentioned in her conversations with me) she accepted as though it were a voice from heaven.

# BOOK IV

*Then follows a period of nine years from the nineteenth year of his age, during which, having lost a friend, he followed the Manichæans—and wrote books 'on the fair and fit,' and published a work on the liberal arts, and the categories of Aristotle.*

DURING this space of nine years, then, from my nineteenth to my eight and twentieth year, we went on seduced and seducing, deceived and deceiving, in divers lusts; publicly, by sciences which they style 'liberal'—secretly, with a falsity called religion. Here proud, there superstitious, everywhere vain! Here, striving after the emptiness of popular fame, even to theatrical applauses, and poetic contests, and strifes for grassy garlands, and the follies of shows and the intemperance of desire. There, seeking to be purged from these our corruptions by carrying food to those who were called 'elect' and 'holy,' out of which, in the laboratory of their stomachs, they should make for us angels and gods, by whom we might be delivered. These things did I follow eagerly, and practise with my friends—by me and with me deceived. Let the arrogant, and such as have not been yet savingly cast down and stricken by Thee, O my God, laugh at me; but notwithstanding I would confess to Thee mine own shame in Thy praise. Bear with me, I beseech Thee, and give me grace to retrace in my present remembrance the circlings of my past errors, and to 'offer to Thee the sacrifice of thanksgiving.' For what am I to myself without Thee, but a guide to mine own downfall? Or what am I even at the best, but one sucking Thy milk, and feeding upon Thee, the meat that perisheth not? But what kind of man is any man, seeing that he is but a man? Let, then, the strong and the mighty laugh at us, but let us who are 'poor and needy' confess unto Thee.

In those years I taught the art of rhetoric, and, overcome by cupidity, put to sale a loquacity by which to overcome. Yet I preferred—Lord, Thou knowest—to have honest scholars (as they are esteemed); and these I, without artifice, taught artifices, not to be put in practice against the life of the guiltless, though sometimes for the life of the guilty. And Thou, O God, from afar sawest me stumbling in that slippery path, and amid much smoke sending out some flashes of fidelity, which I exhibited in that my guidance of such as loved vanity and sought after leasing, I being their companion. In those years I had one (whom I knew not in what is called lawful wedlock, but whom my wayward passion, void of understanding, had discovered), yet one only, remaining faithful even to her; in whom I found out truly by my own experience what difference there is between the restraints of the marriage bonds, contracted for the sake of issue, and the compact of a lustful love, where children are born against the parents' will, although, being born, they compel love.

I remember, too, that when I decided to compete for a theatrical prize, a soothsayer demanded of me what I would give him to win; but I, detesting and abominating such foul mysteries, answered, 'That if the garland were of imperishable gold, I would not suffer a fly to be destroyed to secure it for me.' For he was to slay certain living creatures in his sacrifices, and by those honours to invite the devils to give me their support. But this ill thing I also refused, not out of a pure love for Thee, O God of my heart; for I knew not how to love Thee, knowing not how to conceive aught beyond corporeal brightness. And doth not a soul, sighing after such-like fictions, commit fornication against Thee, trust in false things, and nourish the wind? But I would not, forsooth, have sacrifices offered to devils on my behalf, though I myself was offering sacrifices to them by that superstition. For what else is nourishing the wind but nourishing them, that is, by our wanderings to become their enjoyment and derision?

Those impostors, then, whom they designate Mathematicians, I consulted without hesitation, because they used no sacrifices, and invoked the aid of no spirit for their divinations, which art Christian and true piety fitly rejects and condemns. For good it is to confess unto Thee, and to say, 'Be merciful unto me, heal my soul, for I have sinned against Thee;' and not to abuse Thy goodness for a license to sin, but to remember the words of the Lord, 'Behold, thou art made whole; sin no more, lest a worse thing come unto thee.' All of which salutary advice they endeavour to destroy when they say, 'The cause of thy sin is inevitably determined in heaven;' and, 'This did Venus, or Saturn, or Mars;' in order that man, forsooth, flesh and blood, and proud corruption, may be blameless, while the Creator and Ordainer of heaven and stars is to bear the blame. And who is this but Thee, our God, the sweetness and well-spring of righteousness, who renderest 'to every man according to his deeds,' and despisest not 'a broken and a contrite heart!'

There was in those days a wise man,[16] very skilful in medicine, and much renowned therein, who had with his own proconsular hand put the Agonistic garland upon my distempered head, not, though, as a physician; for this disease Thou alone healest, who resistest the proud, and givest grace to the humble. But didst Thou fail me even by that old man, or forbear from healing my soul? For when I had become more familiar with him, and hung assiduously and fixedly on his conversation (for though couched in simple language, it was replete with vivacity, life, and earnestness), when he had perceived from my discourse that I was given to books of the horoscope-casters, he, in a kind and fatherly manner, advised me to throw them away, and not vainly bestow the care and labour necessary for useful things upon these vanities; saying that he himself in his earlier years had studied that art with a view to gaining his living by following it as a profession, and that, as he had understood Hippocrates, he would soon have understood this, and yet he had given it up, and followed medicine, for no other reason than that he discovered it to be utterly false, and he, being a man of character, would not gain his living by beguiling people. 'But thou,' saith he, 'who hast rhetoric to support thyself by, so that thou followest this of free will, not of necessity—all the more, then, oughtest thou to give me credit herein, who laboured to attain it so perfectly, as I wished to gain my living by it alone.' When I asked him to account for so many true things being foretold by it, he answered me (as he could) 'that the force of chance, diffused throughout the whole order of nature, brought this about. For if when a man by accident opens the leaves of some poet, who sang and intended something far different, a verse oftentimes fell out wondrously apposite to the present business, it were not to be wondered at,' he continued, 'if out of the soul of man, by some higher instinct, not knowing what goes on within itself, an answer should be given by chance, not art, which should coincide with the business and actions of the question.'

And thus truly, either by or through him, Thou didst look after me. And Thou didst delineate in my memory what I might afterwards search out for myself. But at that time neither he, nor my most dear Nebridius, a youth most good and most circumspect, who scoffed at that whole stock of divination, could persuade me to forsake it, the authority of the authors influencing me still more; and as yet I had lighted upon no certain proof— such as I sought—whereby it might without doubt appear that what had been truly foretold by those consulted was by accident or chance, not by the art of the star-gazers.

In those years, when I first began to teach rhetoric in my native town, I had acquired a very dear friend, from association in our studies, of mine own age, and, like myself, just rising up into the flower of youth. He had grown up with me from childhood, and we had been both school-fellows and play-fellows. But he was not then my friend, nor, indeed, afterwards, as true friendship is; for true it is not but in such as Thou bindest together, cleaving unto Thee by that love which is shed abroad in our hearts by the Holy Ghost, which is given unto us. But yet it was too sweet, being ripened by the fervour of similar studies. For, from the true faith (which he, as a youth, had not soundly and thoroughly become master of), I had turned him aside towards those superstitious and pernicious fables which my mother mourned in me. With me this man's mind now erred, nor could my soul exist without him. But behold, Thou wert close behind Thy fugitives—at once God of vengeance and Fountain of mercies, who turnest us to Thyself by wondrous means. Thou removedst that man from this life when he had scarce completed one whole year of my friendship, sweet to me above all the sweetness of that my life.

'Who can show forth all Thy praise' which he hath experienced in himself alone? What was it that Thou didst then, O my God, and how unsearchable are the depths of Thy judgments! For when, sore sick of a fever, he long lay unconscious in a death-sweat, and all despaired of his recovery, he was baptized without his knowledge; myself meanwhile little caring, presuming that his soul would retain rather what it had imbibed from me, than what was done to his unconscious body. Far different, however, was it, for he was revived and restored. Straightaway, as soon as I could talk to him (which I could as soon as he was able, for I never left him, and we hung too much upon each other), I attempted to jest with him,[17] as if he also would jest with me at that baptism which he had received when mind and senses were in abeyance, but had now learnt that he had received. But he shuddered at me, as if I were his enemy; and, with a remarkable and unexpected freedom, admonished me, if I desired to continue his friend, to desist from speaking to him in such a way. I, confounded and confused, concealed all my emotions, till he should get well, and his health be strong enough to allow me to deal with him as I wished. But he was withdrawn from my frenzy, that with Thee he might be preserved for my comfort. A few days after, during my absence, he had a return of the fever, and died.

At this sorrow my heart was utterly darkened, and whatever I looked upon was death. My native country was a torture to me, and my father's house a wondrous unhappiness; and whatsoever I had participated in with him, wanting him, turned into a frightful torture. Mine eyes sought him everywhere, but he was not granted them; and I hated all places because he was not in them; nor could they now say to me, 'Behold, he is coming,' as they did when he was alive and absent. I became a great puzzle to myself, and asked my soul why she was so sad, and why she so exceedingly disquieted me; but she knew not what to answer me. And if I said, 'Hope thou in God,' she very properly obeyed me not; because that most dear friend whom she had lost was, being man, both truer and better than that phantasm she was bid to hope in. Naught but tears were sweet to me, and they succeeded my friend in the dearest of my affections.

And now, O Lord, these things are passed away, and time hath healed my wound. May I learn from Thee, who art Truth, and apply the ear of my heart unto Thy mouth, that Thou mayest tell me why weeping should be so sweet to the unhappy. Hast Thou—although present everywhere—cast away far from Thee our misery? And Thou abidest in Thyself, but we are disquieted with divers trials; and yet, unless we wept in Thine ears, there would be no hope for us remaining. Whence, then, is it that such sweet fruit is plucked from the bitterness of life, from groans, tears, sighs, and lamentations? Is it the hope that Thou hearest us that sweetens it? This is true of prayer, for therein is a desire to approach unto Thee. But is it also in grief for a thing lost, and the sorrow with which I was then over-whelmed? For I had neither hope of his coming to life again, nor did I seek this with my tears; but I grieved and wept only, for I was miserable, and had lost my joy. Or is weeping a bitter thing, and for distaste of the things which aforetime we enjoyed before, and even then, when we are loathing them, does it cause us pleasure?

But why do I speak of these things? For this is not the time to question, but rather to confess unto Thee. Miserable I was, and miserable is every soul fettered by the friendship of perishable things—he is torn to pieces when he loses them, and then is sensible of the misery which he had before ever he lost them. Thus was it at that time with me; I wept most bitterly, and found rest in bitterness. Thus was I miserable, and that life of misery I accounted dearer than my friend. For though I would willingly have changed it, yet I was even more unwilling to lose it than him; yea, I knew not whether I was willing to lose it even for him, as is handed down to us (if not an invention) of Pylades and Orestes, that they would gladly have died one for another, or both together, it being worse than death to them not to live together. But there had sprung up in me some kind of feeling, too, contrary to this, for both exceedingly wearisome was it to me to live, and dreadful to die. I suppose, the more I loved him, so much the more did I hate and fear, as a most cruel enemy, that death which had robbed me of him; and I imagined it would suddenly annihilate all men, as it had power over him. Thus, I remember, it was with me. Behold my heart, O my God! Behold and look into me, for I remember it well, O my Hope! who cleansest me from the uncleanness of such affections, directing mine eyes towards Thee, and plucking my feet out of the net. For I was astonished that other mortals lived, since he whom I loved, as if he would never die, was dead; and I wondered still more that I, who was to him a second self, could live when he was dead. Well did one say of his friend, 'Thou half of my soul,' for I felt that my soul and his soul were but one soul in two bodies; and, consequently, my life was a horror to me, because I would not live in half. And therefore, perchance, was I afraid to die, lest he should die wholly whom I had so greatly loved.

O madness, which knowest not how to love men as men should be loved! O foolish man that I then was, enduring with so much impatience the lot of man! So I fretted, sighed, wept, tormented myself, and took neither rest nor advice. For I bore about with me a rent and polluted soul, impatient of being borne by me, and where to repose it I found not. Not in pleasant groves, not in sport or song, not in fragrant spots, nor in magnificent banquetings, nor in the pleasures of the bed and the couch, nor, finally, in books and songs did it find repose. All things looked terrible, even the very light itself; and whatsoever was not what he was, was repulsive and hateful, except groans and tears, for in those alone found I a little repose. But when my soul was withdrawn from them, a heavy burden of misery weighed me down. To Thee, O Lord, should it have been raised, for Thee to lighten and avert it. This I knew, but was neither willing nor able; all the more since, in my thoughts of Thee, Thou wert not any solid or substantial thing to me. For Thou wert not Thyself, but an empty phantasm, and my error was my god. If I attempted to discharge my burden thereon, that it might find rest, it sank into emptiness, and came rushing down again upon me, and I remained to myself an unhappy spot, where I could neither stay nor depart from. For whither could my heart fly from my heart? Whither could I fly from mine own self? Whither not follow myself? And yet fled I from my country; for so should my eyes look less for him where they were not accustomed to see him. And thus I left the town of Thagaste, and came to Carthage.

Times lose no time, nor do they idly roll through our senses. They work strange operations on the mind. Behold, they came and went from day to day, and by coming and going they disseminated in my mind other ideas and other remembrances, and by little and little patched me up again with the former kind of delights, unto which that sorrow of mine yielded. But yet there succeeded, not certainly other sorrows, yet the causes of other sorrows. For whence had that former sorrow so easily penetrated to the quick, but that I had poured out my soul upon the dust, in loving one who must die as if he were never to die? But what revived and refreshed me especially was the consolations of other friends, with whom I did love what instead of Thee I loved. And this was a monstrous fable and pro-tracted lie, by whose adulterous contact our soul, which lay itching in our ears, was being polluted. But that fable would not die to me so oft as any of my friends died. There were other things in them which did more lay hold of my mind,—to discourse and jest with them; to indulge in an inter-change of kindness; to read together pleasant books; together to trifle, and together to be earnest; to differ at times without ill-humour, as a man would do with his own self; and even by the infrequency of these differences to give zest to our more frequent consentings; sometimes teaching, some-times being taught; longing for the absent with impatience, and welcoming the coming with joy. These and similar expressions, emanating from the hearts of those who loved and were beloved in return, by the countenance, the tongue, the eyes, and a thousand pleasing movements, were so much fuel to melt our souls together, and out of many to make but one.

This is it that is loved in friends; and so loved that a man's conscience accuses itself if he love not him by whom he is beloved, or love not again him that loves him, expecting nothing from him but indications of his love. Hence that mourning if one die, and gloom of sorrow, that steeping of the heart in tears, all sweetness turned into bitterness, and upon the loss of the life of the dying, the death of the living. Blessed be he who loveth Thee, and his friend in Thee, and his enemy for Thy sake. For he alone loses none dear to him to whom all are dear in Him who cannot be lost. And who is this but our God, the God that created heaven and earth, and filleth them because by filling them He created them? None loseth Thee but he who leaveth Thee. And he who leaveth Thee, whither goeth he, or whither fleeth he, but from Thee well pleased to Thee angry? For where doth not he find Thy law in his own punishment? 'And Thy law is the truth,' and truth Thou.

'Turn us again, O Lord God of Hosts, cause Thy face to shine; and we shall be saved.' For whithersoever the soul of man turns itself, unless towards Thee, it is affixed to sorrows, yea, though it is affixed to beauteous things without Thee and without itself. And yet they were not unless they were from Thee. They rise and set; and by rising, they begin as it were to be; and they grow, that they may become perfect; and when perfect, they wax old and perish; and all wax not old, but all perish. Therefore when they rise and tend to be, the more rapidly they grow that they may be, so much the more they hasten not to be. This is the way of them. Thus much hast Thou given them, because they are parts of things, which exist not all at the same time, but by departing and succeeding they together make up the universe, of which they are parts. And even thus is our speech accomplished by signs emitting a sound; but this, again, is not perfected unless one word pass away when it has sounded its part, in order that another may succeed it. Let my soul praise Thee out of all these things, O God, the Creator of all; but let not my soul be affixed to these things by the glue of love, through the senses of the body. For they go whither they were to go, that they might no longer be; and they rend her with pestilent desires, because she longs to be, and yet loves to rest in what she loves. But in these things no place is to be found; they stay not—they flee; and who is he that is able to follow them with the senses of the flesh? Or who can grasp them, even when they are near? For tardy is the sense of the flesh, because it is the sense of the flesh, and its boundary is itself. It sufficeth for that for which it was made, but it is not sufficient to stay things running their course from their appointed starting-place to the end appointed. For in Thy word, by which they were created, they hear the fiat, 'Hence and hitherto.'

Be not foolish, O my soul, and deaden not the ear of thine heart with the tumult of thy folly. Hearken thou also. The word itself invokes thee to return; and there is the place of rest imperturbable, where love is not abandoned if itself abandoneth not. Behold, these things pass away, that others may succeed them, and so this lower universe be made complete in all its parts. But do I depart anywhere, saith the word of God? There fix thy habitation. There commit whatsoever thou hast thence, O my soul; at all events now thou art tired out with deceits. Commit to truth whatso-ever thou hast from the truth, and nothing shalt thou lose; and thy decay shall flourish again, and all thy diseases be healed, and thy perishable parts shall be re-formed and renovated, and drawn together to thee; nor shall they put thee down where themselves descend, but they shall abide with thee, and continue for ever before God, who abideth and continueth for ever.

Why, then, be perverse and follow thy flesh? Rather let it be converted and follow thee. Whatever by her thou feelest, is but in part; and the whole, of which these are portions, thou art ignorant of, and yet they delight thee. But had the sense of thy flesh been capable of comprehending the whole, and not itself also, for thy punishment, been justly limited to a portion of the whole, thou wouldest that whatsoever existeth at the present time should pass away, that so the whole might please thee more. For what we speak, also by the same sense of the flesh thou hearest; and yet wouldest not thou that the syllables should stay, but fly away, that others may come, and the whole be heard. Thus it is always, when any single thing is com-posed of many, all of which exist not together, all together would delight more than they do singly could all be perceived at once. But far better than these is He who made all; and He is our God, and He passeth not away, for there is nothing to succeed Him. If bodies please thee, praise God for them, and turn back thy love upon their Creator, lest in those things which please thee thou displease.

If souls please thee, let them be loved in God; for they also are mutable, but in Him are they firmly stablished, else would they pass, and pass away. In Him, then, let them be beloved; and draw unto Him along with thee as many souls as thou canst, and say to them, 'Him let us love, Him let us love; He created these, nor is He far off. For He did not create them, and then depart; but they are of Him, and in Him. Behold, there is He wherever truth is known. He is within the very heart, but yet hath the heart wandered from Him. Return to your heart, O ye transgressors, and cleave fast unto Him that made you. Stand with Him and you shall stand fast. Rest in Him, and you shall be at rest. Whither go ye in rugged paths? Whither go ye? The good that you love is from Him; and as it has respect unto Him it is both good and pleasant, and justly shall it be embittered, because whatsoever cometh from Him is unjustly loved if He be forsaken for it. Why, then, will ye wander farther and farther in these difficult and toilsome ways? There is no rest where ye seek it. Seek what ye seek; but it is not there where ye seek. Ye seek a blessed life in the land of death; it is not there. For could a blessed life be where life itself is not?'

But our very Life descended hither and bore our death, and slew it, out of the abundance of His own life; and thundering He called loudly to us to return hence to Him into that secret place whence He came forth to us—first into the Virgin's womb, where the human creature was married to Him,—our mortal flesh, that it might not be for ever mortal,—and thence 'as a bridegroom coming out of his chamber, rejoicing as a strong man to run a race.' For He tarried not, but ran crying out by words, deeds, death, life, descent, ascension, crying aloud to us to return to Him. And He departed from our sight, that we might return to our heart, and there find Him. For He departed, and behold, He is here. He would not be long with us, yet left us not; for He departed thither, whence He never departed, because 'the world was made by Him.' And in this world He was, and into this world He came to save sinners, unto whom my soul doth confess, that He may heal it, for it hath sinned against Him. O ye sons of men, how long so slow of heart? Even now, after the Life is descended to you, will ye not ascend and live? But whither ascend ye, when ye are on high, and set your mouth against the heavens? Descend that ye may ascend, and ascend to God. For ye have fallen by 'ascending against Him.' Tell them this, that they may weep in the valley of tears, and so draw them with thee to God, because it is by His Spirit that thou speakest thus unto them, if thou speakest burning with the fire of love.

These things I knew not at that time, and I loved these lower beauties, and I was sinking to the very depths; and I said to my friends, 'Do we love anything but the beautiful? What, then, is the beautiful? And what is beauty? What is it that allures and unites us to the things we love; for unless there were a grace and beauty in them, they could by no means attract us to them?' And I marked and perceived that in bodies themselves there was a beauty from their forming a kind of whole, and another from mutual fitness, as one part of the body with its whole, or a shoe with a foot, and so on. And this consideration sprang up in my mind out of the recesses of my heart, and I wrote books (two or three, I think) 'on the fair and fit.' Thou knowest, O Lord, for it has escaped me; for I have them not, but they have strayed from me, I know not how.

But what was it that prompted me, O Lord my God, to dedicate these books to Hierius, an orator of Rome, whom I knew not by sight, but loved the man for the fame of his learning, for which he was renowned, and some words of his which I had heard, and which had pleased me? But the more did he please me in that he pleased others, who highly extolled him, astonished that a native of Syria, instructed first in Greek eloquence, should afterwards become a wonderful Latin orator, and one so well versed in studies pertaining unto wisdom. Thus a man is commended and loved when absent. Doth this love enter into the heart of the hearer from the mouth of the commender? Not so. But through one who loveth is another inflamed.

For hence he is loved who is commended when the commender is believed to praise him with an unfeigned heart; that is, when he that loves him praises him.

Thus, then, loved I men upon the judgment of men, not upon Thine, O my God, in which no man is deceived. But yet why not as the renowned charioteer, as the huntsman, known far and wide by a vulgar popularity— but far otherwise, and seriously, and so as I would desire to be myself commended? For I would not that they should commend and love me as actors are,—although I myself did commend and love them,—but I would prefer being unknown than so known, and even being hated than so loved. Where now are these influences of such various and divers kinds of loves distributed in one soul? What is it that I am in love with in another, which, if I did not hate, I should not detest and repel from myself, seeing we are equally men? For it does not follow that because a good horse is loved by him who would not, though he might, be that horse, the same should therefore be affirmed by an actor, who partakes of our nature. Do I then love in a man that which I, who am a man, hate to be? Man himself is a great deep, whose very hairs Thou numberest, O Lord, and they fall not to the ground without Thee. And yet are the hairs of his head more readily numbered than are his affections and the movements of his heart.

But that orator was of the kind that I so loved as I wished myself to be such a one; and I erred through an inflated pride, and was 'carried about with every wind,' but yet was piloted by Thee, though very secretly. And whence know I, and whence confidently confess I unto Thee that I loved him more because of the love of those who praised him, than for the very things for which they praised him? Because had he been unpraised, and these self-same men had dispraised him, and with dispraise and scorn told the same things of him, I should never have been so inflamed and provoked to love him. And yet the things had not been different, nor he himself different, but only the affections of the narrators. See where lieth the impotent soul that is not yet sustained by the solidity of truth! Just as the blasts of tongues blow from the breasts of conjecturers, so is it tossed this way and that,

driven forward and backward, and the light is obscured to it and the truth not perceived. And behold it is before us. And to me it was a great matter that my style and studies should be known to that man; the which if he approved, I were the more stimulated, but if he disapproved, this vain heart of mine, void of Thy solidity, had been offended. And yet that 'fair and fit,' about which I wrote to him, I reflected on with pleasure, and contemplated it, and admired it, though none joined me in doing so.

But not yet did I perceive the hinge on which this impotent matter turned in Thy wisdom, O Thou Omnipotent, 'who alone doest great wonders;' and my mind ranged through corporeal forms, and I defined and distinguished as 'fair,' that which is so in itself, and 'fit,' that which is beautiful as it corresponds to some other thing; and this I supported by corporeal examples. And I turned my attention to the nature of the mind, but the false opinions which I entertained of spiritual things prevented me from seeing the truth. Yet the very power of truth forced itself on my gaze, and I turned away my throbbing soul from incorporeal substance, to lineaments, and colours, and bulky magnitudes. And not being able to perceive these in the mind, I thought I could not perceive my mind. And whereas in virtue I loved peace, and in viciousness I hated discord, in the former I distinguished unity, but in the latter a kind of division. And in that unity I conceived the rational soul and the nature of truth and of the chief good[18] to consist. But in this division I, unfortunate one, imagined there was I know not what substance of irrational life, and the nature of the chief evil, which should not be a substance only, but real life also, and yet not emanating from Thee, O my God, from whom are all things. And yet the first I called a Monad, as if it had been a soul without sex, but the other a Duad,—anger in deeds of violence, in deeds of passion, lust,—not knowing of what I talked. For I had not known or learned that neither was evil a substance, nor our soul that chief and unchangeable good.

For even as it is in the case of deeds of violence, if that emotion of the soul from whence the stimulus comes be depraved, and carry itself insolently and mutinously; and in acts of passion, if that affection of the soul whereby carnal pleasures are imbibed is unrestrained,—so do errors and false opinions contaminate the life, if the reasonable soul itself be depraved, as it was at that time in me, who was ignorant that it must be enlightened by another light that it may be partaker of truth, seeing that itself is not that nature of truth. 'For Thou wilt light my candle; the Lord my God will enlighten my darkness;' and 'of His fulness have all we received,' for 'that was the true Light which lighted every man that cometh into the world;' for in Thee there is 'no variableness, neither shadow of turning.'

But I pressed towards Thee, and was repelled by Thee that I might taste of death, for Thou 'resistest the proud.' But what prouder than for me, with a marvellous madness, to assert myself to be that by nature which Thou art? For whereas I was mutable,—so much being clear to me, for my very longing to become wise arose from the wish from worse to become better, —yet chose I rather to think Thee mutable, than myself not to be that which Thou art. Therefore was I repelled by Thee, and Thou resistedst my changeable stiffneckedness; and I imagined corporeal forms, and, being flesh, I accused flesh, and, being 'a wind that passeth away,' I returned not to Thee, but went wandering and wandering on towards those things that have no being, neither in Thee, nor in me, nor in the body. Neither were they created for me by Thy truth, but conceived by my vain conceit out of corporeal things. And I used to ask Thy faithful little ones, my fellow-citizens,—from whom I unconsciously stood exiled,—I used flippantly and foolishly to ask, 'Why, then, doth the soul which God created err?' But I would not permit any one to ask me, 'Why, then, doth God err?' And I contended that Thy immutable substance erred of constraint, rather than admit that my mutable substance had gone astray of free will, and erred as a punishment.[19]

I was about six or seven and twenty years of age when I wrote those volumes—meditating upon corporeal fictions, which clamoured in the ears of my heart. These I directed, O sweet Truth, to Thy inward melody, pondering on the 'fair and fit,' and longing to stay and listen to Thee, and to rejoice greatly at the Bridegroom's voice, and I could not; for by the voices of my own errors was I driven forth, and by the weight of my own pride was I sinking into the lowest pit. For Thou didst not 'make me to hear joy and gladness;' nor did the bones which were not yet humbled rejoice.

And what did it profit me that, when scarce twenty years old, a book of Aristotle's, entitled *The Ten Predicaments*, fell into my hands,—on whose very name I hung as on something great and divine, when my rhetoric master of Carthage, and others who were esteemed learned, referred to it with cheeks swelling with pride,—I read it alone and understood it? And on my conferring with others, who said that with the assistance of very able masters—who not only explained it orally, but drew many things in the dust—they scarcely understood it, and could tell me no more about it than I had acquired in reading it by myself alone? And the book appeared to me to speak plainly enough of substances, such as man is, and of their qualities,—such as the figure of a man, of what kind it is; and his stature, how many feet high; and his relationship, whose brother he is; or where placed, or when born, or whether he stands or sits, or is shod or armed, or does or suffers anything; and whatever innumerable things might be classed under these nine categories,[20]—of which I have given some examples,—or under that chief category of substance.

What did all this profit me, seeing it even hindered me, when, imagining that whatsoever existed was comprehended in those ten categories, I tried so to understand, O my God, Thy wonderful and unchangeable unity as if Thou also hadst been subjected to Thine own greatness or beauty, so that they should exist in Thee as their subject, like as in bodies, whereas Thou Thyself art Thy greatness and beauty? But a body is not great or fair because it is a body, seeing that, though it were less great or fair, it should nevertheless be a body. But that which I had conceived of Thee was falsehood, not truth,—fictions of my misery, not the supports of Thy blessedness. For Thou hadst commanded, and it was done in me, that the earth should bring forth briars and thorns to me, and that with labour I should get my bread.

And what did it profit me that I, the base slave of vile affections, read unaided, and understood, all the books that I could get of the so-called liberal arts? And I took delight in them, but knew not whence came whatever in them was true and certain. For my back then was to the light, and my face towards the things enlightened; whence my face, with which I discerned the things enlightened, was not itself enlightened. Whatever was written either on rhetoric or logic, geometry, music, or arithmetic, did I, without any great difficulty, and without the teaching of any man, understand, as Thou knowest, O Lord my God, because both quickness of comprehension and acuteness of perception are Thy gifts. Yet did I not thereupon sacrifice to Thee. So, then, it served not to my use, but rather to my destruction, since I went about to get so good a portion of my substance into my own power; and I kept not my strength for Thee, but went away from Thee into a far country, to waste it upon harlotries. For what did good abilities profit me, if I did not employ them to good uses? For I did not perceive that those arts were acquired with great difficulty, even by the studious and those gifted with genius, until I endeavoured to explain them to such; and he was the most proficient in them who followed my explanations not too slowly.

But what did this profit me, supposing that Thou, O Lord God, the Truth, wert a bright and vast body, and I a piece of that body? Perverseness too great! But such was I. Nor do I blush, O my God, to confess to Thee Thy mercies towards me, and to call upon Thee—I, who blushed not then to avow before men my blasphemies, and to bark against Thee. What profited me then my nimble wit in those sciences and all those knotty volumes, disentangled by me without help from a human master, seeing that I erred so odiously, and with such sacrilegious baseness, in the doctrine of piety? Or what impediment was it to Thy little ones to have a far slower wit, seeing that they departed not far from Thee, that in the nest of Thy Church they might safely become fledged, and nourish the wings of charity by the food of a sound faith? O Lord our God, under the shadow of Thy wings let us hope, defend us, and carry us. Thou wilt carry us both when little, and even to grey hairs wilt Thou carry us; for our firmness, when it is Thou, then is it firmness; but when it is our own, then it is infirmity. Our good lives always with Thee, from which when we are averted we are perverted. Let us now, O Lord, return, that we be not overturned, because with Thee our good lives without any eclipse,—which good Thou Thyself art. And we need not fear lest we should find no place unto which to return because we fell away from it; for when we were absent, our home— Thy Eternity—fell not.

# BOOK V

*He describes the twenty-ninth year of his age, in which, having discovered the fallacies of the Manichæans, he professed rhetoric at Rome and Milan. Having heard Ambrose, he begins to come to himself.*

ACCEPT the sacrifice of my confessions by the agency of my tongue, which Thou hast formed and quickened, that it may confess to Thy name; and heal Thou all my bones, and let them say, 'Lord, who is like unto Thee?' For neither does he who confesses to Thee teach Thee what may be passing within him, because a closed heart doth not exclude Thine eye, nor does man's hardness of heart repulse Thine hand, but Thou dissolvest it when Thou willest, either in pity or in vengeance, 'and there is no one who can hide himself from Thy heat.' But let my soul praise Thee, that it may love Thee; and let it confess Thine own mercies to Thee, that it may praise Thee. Thy whole creation ceaseth not, nor is it silent in Thy praises—neither the spirit of man, by the voice directed unto Thee, nor animal nor corporeal things, by the voice of those meditating thereon, so that our souls may from their weariness arise towards Thee, leaning on those things which Thou hast made, and passing on to Thee, who hast made them wonderfully; and there is there refreshment and true strength.

Let the restless and the unjust depart and flee from Thee. Thou both seest them and distinguishest the shadows. And lo! all things with them are fair, yet are they themselves foul.[21] And how have they injured Thee? Or in what have they disgraced Thy government, which is just and perfect from heaven even to the lowest parts of the earth? For whither fled they when they fled from Thy presence? Or where dost Thou not find them? But they fled that they might not see Thee seeing them, and blinded might stumble against Thee; since Thou forsakest nothing that Thou hast made— that the unjust might stumble against Thee, and justly be hurt, withdrawing themselves from Thy gentleness, and stumbling against Thine uprightness, and falling upon their own roughness. Forsooth, they know not that Thou art everywhere whom no place encompasseth, and that Thou alone art near even to those that remove far from Thee. Let them, then, be converted and seek Thee; because not as they have forsaken their Creator hast Thou forsaken Thy creature. Let them be converted and seek Thee; and behold, Thou art there in their hearts, in the hearts of those who confess to Thee, and cast themselves upon Thee, and weep on Thy bosom after their obdurate ways, even Thou gently wiping away their tears. And they weep the more, and rejoice in weeping, since Thou, O Lord, not man, flesh and blood, but Thou, Lord, who didst make, remakest and comfortest them. And where was I when I was seeking Thee? And Thou wert before me, but I had gone away even from myself; nor did I find myself, much less Thee!

Let me lay bare before my God that twenty-ninth year of my age. There had at this time come to Carthage a certain bishop of the Manichæans, by name Faustus, a great snare of the devil, and many were entangled by him through the allurement of his smooth speech; the which, although I did commend, yet could I separate from the truth of those things which I was eager to learn. Nor did I esteem the small dish of oratory so much as the science, which this their so praised Faustus placed before me to feed upon. Fame, indeed, had before spoken of him to me, as most skilled in all becoming learning, and pre-eminently skilled in the liberal sciences. And as I had read and retained in memory many injunctions of the philosophers, I used to compare some teachings of theirs with those long fables of the Manichæans; and the former things which they declared, who could only prevail so far as to estimate this lower world, while its lord they could by no means find out, seemed to me the more probable. For Thou art great,

O Lord, and hast 'respect unto the lowly, but the proud Thou knowest afar off.' Nor dost Thou draw near but to the contrite heart, nor art Thou found by the proud,—not even could they number by cunning skill the stars and the sand, and measure the starry regions, and trace the courses of the planets.

For with their understanding and the capacity which Thou hast bestowed upon them they search out these things; and much have they found out, and foretold many years before,—the eclipses of those luminaries, the sun and moon, on what day, at what hour, and from how many particular points they were likely to come. Nor did their calculation fail them; and it came to pass even as they foretold. And they wrote down the rules found out, which are read at this day; and from these others foretell in what year, and in what month of the year, and on what day of the month, and at what hour of the day, and at what quarter of its light, either moon or sun is to be eclipsed, and thus it shall be even as it is foretold. And men who are ignorant of these things marvel and are amazed, and they that know them exult and are exalted; and by an impious pride, departing from Thee, and forsaking Thy light, they foretell a failure of the sun's light which is likely to occur so long before, but see not their own, which is now present. For they seek not religiously whence they have the ability wherewith they seek out these things. And finding that Thou hast made them, they give not themselves up to Thee, that Thou mayest preserve what Thou hast made, nor sacrifice themselves to Thee, even such as they have made themselves to be; nor do they slay their own pride, as fowls of the air, nor their own curiosities, by which (like the fishes of the sea) they wander over the unknown paths of the abyss, nor their own extravagance, as the 'beasts of the field,' that Thou, Lord, 'a consuming fire,' mayest burn up their lifeless cares and renew them immortally.

But the way—Thy Word, by whom Thou didst make these things which they number, and themselves who number, and the sense by which they perceive what they number, and the judgment out of which they number— they knew not, and that of Thy wisdom there is no number. But the

Only-begotten has been 'made unto us wisdom, and righteousness, and sanctification,' and has been numbered amongst us, and paid tribute to Cæsar. This way, by which they might descend to Him from themselves, they knew not; nor that through Him they might ascend unto Him. This way they knew not, and they think themselves exalted with the stars and shining, and lo! they fell upon the earth, and 'their foolish heart was darkened.' They say many true things concerning the creature; but Truth, the Artificer of the creature, they seek not with devotion, and hence they find Him not. Or if they find Him, knowing that He is God, they glorify Him not as God, neither are they thankful, but become vain in their imaginations, and say that they themselves are wise, attributing to themselves what is Thine; and by this, with most perverse blindness, they desire to impute to Thee what is their own, forging lies against Thee who art the Truth, and changing the glory of the incorruptible God into an image made like corruptible man, and to birds, and four-footed beasts, and creeping things,—changing Thy truth into a lie, and worshipping and serving the creature more than the Creator.

Many truths, however, concerning the creature did I retain from these men, and the cause appeared to me from calculations, the succession of seasons, and the visible manifestations of the stars; and I compared them with the sayings of Manichæus, who in his frenzy has written most extensively on these subjects, but discovered not any account either of the solstices, or the equinoxes, the eclipses of the luminaries, or anything of the kind I had learned in the books of secular philosophy. But therein I was ordered to believe, and yet it corresponded not with those rules acknowledged by calculation and my own sight, but was far different.

Doth, then, O Lord God of truth, whosoever knoweth those things therefore please Thee? For unhappy is the man who knoweth all those things, but knoweth Thee not; but happy is he who knoweth Thee, though these he may not know. But he who knoweth both Thee and them is not the happier on account of them, but is happy on account of Thee only, if knowing Thee he glorify Thee as God, and gives thanks, and becomes not vain in his thoughts. But as he is happier who knows how to possess a tree, and for the use thereof renders thanks to Thee, although he may not know how many cubits high it is, or how wide it spreads, than he that measures it and counts all its branches, and neither owns it nor knows or loves its Creator; so a just man, whose is the entire world of wealth, and who, as having nothing, yet possesseth all things by cleaving unto Thee, to whom all things are subservient, though he know not even the circles of the Great Bear, yet it is foolish to doubt but that he may verily be better than he who can measure the heavens, and number the stars, and weigh the elements, but is forgetful of Thee, 'who hast set in order all things in number, weight, and measure.'

But yet who was it that ordered Manichæus to write on these things likewise, skill in which was not necessary to piety? For Thou hast told man to behold piety and wisdom, of which he might be in ignorance although having a complete knowledge of these other things; but since, knowing not these things, he yet most impudently dared to teach them, it is clear that he had no acquaintance with piety. For even when we have a knowledge of these worldly matters, it is folly to make a profession of them; but confession to Thee is piety. It was therefore with this view that this straying one spake much of these matters, that, standing convicted by those who had in truth learned them, the understanding that he really had in those more difficult things might be made plain. For he wished not to be lightly esteemed, but went about trying to persuade men 'that the Holy Ghost, the Comforter and Enricher of Thy faithful ones, was with full authority personally resident in him.' When, therefore, it was discovered that his teaching concerning the heavens and stars, and the motions of sun and moon, was false, though these things do not relate to the doctrine of religion, yet his sacrilegious arrogance would become sufficiently evident, seeing that not only did he affirm things of which he knew nothing, but also perverted them, and with such egregious vanity of pride as to seek to attribute them to himself as to a divine being.

For when I hear a Christian brother ignorant of these things, or in error concerning them, I can bear with patience to see that man hold to his opinions; nor can I apprehend that any want of knowledge as to the situation or nature of this material creation can be injurious to him, so long as he does not entertain belief in anything unworthy of Thee, O Lord, the Creator of all. But if he conceives it to pertain to the form of the doctrine of piety, and presumes to affirm with great obstinacy that whereof he is ignorant, therein lies the injury. And yet even a weakness such as this in the dawn of faith is borne by our Mother Charity, till the new man may grow up 'unto a perfect man,' and not be 'carried about with every wind of doctrine.' But in him who thus presumed to be at once the teacher, author, head, and leader of all whom he could induce to believe this, so that all who followed him believed that they were following not a simple man only, but Thy Holy Spirit, who would not judge that such great insanity, when once it stood convicted of false teaching, should be abhorred and utterly cast off? But I had not yet clearly ascertained whether the changes of longer and shorter days and nights, and day and night itself, with the eclipses of the greater lights, and whatever of the like kind I had read in other books, could be expounded consistently with his words. Should I have found myself able to do so, there would still have remained a doubt in my mind whether it were so or no, although I might, on the strength of his reputed godliness, rest my faith on his authority.

And for nearly the whole of those nine years during which, with unstable mind, I had been their follower, I had been looking forward with but too great eagerness for the arrival of this same Faustus. For the other members of the sect whom I had chanced to light upon, when unable to answer the questions I raised, always bade me look forward to his coming, when, by discoursing with him, these, and greater difficulties if I had them, would be most easily and amply cleared away. When at last he did come, I found him to be a man of pleasant speech, who spoke of the very same things as they themselves did, although more fluently, and in better language. But of what profit to me was the elegance of my cup-bearer, since he offered me not the more precious draught for which I thirsted? My ears were already satiated with similar things; neither did they appear to me more conclusive, because better expressed; nor true, because oratorical; nor the spirit necessarily wise, because the face was comely and the language eloquent. But they who extolled him to me were not competent judges; and therefore, as he was possessed of suavity of speech, he appeared to them to be prudent and wise. Another sort of persons, however, was, I was aware, suspicious even of truth itself, if enunciated in smooth and flowing language. But me, O my God, Thou hadst already instructed by wonderful and mysterious ways, and therefore I believe that Thou instructedst me because it is truth; nor of truth is there any other teacher—where or whencesoever it may shine upon us—but Thee. From Thee, therefore, I had now learned, that because a thing is eloquently expressed, it should not of necessity seem to be true; nor, because uttered with stammering lips, should it be false; nor, again, perforce true, because unskilfully delivered; nor consequently untrue, because the language is fine; but that wisdom and folly are as food both wholesome and unwholesome, and courtly or simple words as town-made or rustic vessels,—and both kinds of food may be served in either kind of dish.

That eagerness, therefore, with which I had so long waited for this man was in truth delighted with his action and feeling when disputing, and the fluent and apt words with which he clothed his ideas. I was therefore filled with joy, and joined with others (and even exceeded them) in exalting and praising him. It was, however, a source of annoyance to me that I was not allowed at those meetings of his auditors to introduce and impart any of those questions that troubled me in familiar exchange of arguments with him. When I might speak, and began, in conjunction with my friends, to engage his attention at such times as it was not unseeming for him to enter into a discussion with me, and had mooted such questions as perplexed me, I discovered him first to know nothing of the liberal sciences save grammar, and that only in an ordinary way. Having, however, read some of Tully's Orations, a very few books of Seneca, and some of the poets, and such few volumes of his own sect as were written coherently in Latin,

and being day by day practised in speaking, he so acquired a sort of eloquence, which proved the more delightful and enticing in that it was
under the control of ready tact, and a sort of native grace. Is it not even as
I recall, O Lord my God, Thou judge of my conscience? My heart and my
memory are laid before Thee, who didst at that time direct me by the
inscrutable mystery of Thy Providence, and didst set before my face those
vile errors of mine, in order that I might see and loathe them.

For when it became plain to me that he was ignorant of those arts in
which I had believed him to excel, I began to despair of his clearing up and
explaining all the perplexities which harassed me: though ignorant of these,
however, he might still have held the truth of piety, had he not been a
Manichæan. For their books are full of lengthy fables concerning the
heaven and stars, the sun and moon, and I had ceased to think him able to
decide in a satisfactory manner what I ardently desired,—whether, on
comparing these things with the calculations I had read elsewhere, the
explanations contained in the works of Manichæus were preferable, or at
any rate equally sound. But when I proposed that these subjects should be
deliberated upon and reasoned out, he very modestly did not dare to endure
the burden. For he was aware that he had no knowledge of these things,
and was not ashamed to confess it. For he was not one of those loquacious
persons, many of whom I had been troubled with, who covenanted to
teach me these things, and said nothing; but this man possessed a heart,
which, though not right towards Thee, yet was not altogether false towards
himself. For he was not altogether ignorant of his own ignorance, nor
would he without due consideration be inveigled in a controversy, from
which he could neither draw back nor extricate himself fairly. And for
that I was even more pleased with him, for more beautiful is the modesty
of an ingenuous mind than the acquisition of the knowledge I desired,—
and such I found him to be in all the more abstruse and subtle questions.

My eagerness after the writings of Manichæus having thus received a
check, and despairing even more of their other teachers,—seeing that in
sundry things which puzzled me, he, so famous amongst them, had thus

turned out,—I began to occupy myself with him in the study of that literature which he also much affected, and which I, as Professor of Rhetoric,
was then engaged in teaching the young Carthaginian students, and in
reading with him either what he expressed a wish to hear, or I deemed
suited to his bent of mind. But all my endeavours by which I had concluded
to improve in that sect, by acquaintance with that man, came completely
to an end: not that I separated myself altogether from them, but, as one
who could find nothing better, I determined in the meantime upon contenting myself with what I had in any way lighted upon, unless, by chance,
something more desirable should present itself. Thus that Faustus, who had
entrapped so many to their death,—neither willing nor witting it,—now
began to loosen the snare in which I had been taken. For Thy hands, O my
God, in the hidden design of Thy Providence, did not desert my soul; and
out of the blood of my mother's heart, through the tears that she poured
out by day and by night, was a sacrifice offered unto Thee for me; and by
marvellous ways didst Thou deal with me. It was Thou, O my God, who
didst it, for the steps of a man are ordered by the Lord, and He shall dispose
his way. Or how can we procure salvation but from Thy hand, remaking
what it hath made?

Thou dealedst with me, therefore, that I should be persuaded to go to
Rome, and teach there rather what I was then teaching at Carthage. And
how I was persuaded to do this, I will not fail to confess unto Thee; for in
this also the profoundest workings of Thy wisdom, and Thy ever present
mercy to usward, must be pondered and avowed. It was not my desire to
go to Rome because greater advantages and dignities were guaranteed me
by the friends who persuaded me into this,—although even at this period I
was influenced by these considerations,—but my principal and almost sole
motive was, that I had been informed that the youths studied more quietly
there, and were kept under by the control of more rigid discipline, so that
they did not capriciously and impudently rush into the school of a master
not their own, into whose presence they were forbidden to enter unless
with his consent. At Carthage, on the contrary, there was amongst the

scholars a shameful and intemperate license. They burst in rudely, and, with almost furious gesticulations, interrupt the system which any one may have instituted for the good of his pupils. Many outrages they perpetrate with astounding phlegm, which would be punishable by law were they not sustained by custom; that custom showing them to be the more worthless, in that they now do, as according to law, what by Thy unchangeable law will never be lawful. And they fancy they do it with impunity, whereas the very blindness whereby they do it is their punishment, and they suffer far greater things than they do. The manners, then, which as a student I would not adopt, I was compelled as a teacher to submit to from others; and so I was too glad to go where all who knew anything about it assured me that similar things were not done. But Thou, 'my refuge and my portion in the land of the living,' didst while at Carthage goad me, so that I might thereby be withdrawn from it, and exchange my worldly habitation for the preservation of my soul; whilst at Rome Thou didst offer me enticements by which to attract me there, by men enchanted with this dying life,—the one doing insane actions, and the other making assurances of vain things and, in order to correct my footsteps, didst secretly employ their and my perversity. For both they who disturbed my tranquillity were blinded by a shameful madness, and they who allured me elsewhere smacked of the earth. And I, who hated real misery here, sought fictitious happiness there.

But the cause of my going thence and going thither, Thou, O God, knewest, yet revealedst it not, either to me or to my mother, who grievously lamented my journey, and went with me as far as the sea. But I deceived her, when she violently restrained me either that she might retain me or accompany me, and I pretended that I had a friend whom I could not quit until he had a favourable wind to set sail. And I lied to my mother—and such a mother!—and got away. For this also Thou hast in mercy pardoned me, saving me, thus replete with abominable pollutions, from the waters of the sea, for the water of Thy grace,[22] whereby, when I was purified, the fountains of my mother's eyes should be dried, from which for me she day by day watered the ground under her face. And yet, refusing to go back without me, it was with difficulty I persuaded her to remain that night in a place quite close to our ship, where there was an oratory in memory of the blessed Cyprian. That night I secretly left, but she was not backward in prayers and weeping. And what was it, O Lord, that she, with such an abundance of tears, was asking of Thee, but that Thou wouldest not permit me to sail? But Thou, mysteriously counselling and hearing the real purpose of her desire, granted not what she then asked, in order to make me what she was ever asking. The wind blew and filled our sails, and withdrew the shore from our sight; and she, wild with grief, was there on the morrow, and filled Thine ears with complaints and groans, which Thou didst disregard; whilst, by the means of my longings, Thou wert hastening me on to the cessation of all longing, and the gross part of her love to me was whipped out by the just lash of sorrow. But, like all mothers,—though even more than others,—she loved to have me with her, and knew not what joy Thou wert preparing for her by my absence. Being ignorant of this, she did weep and mourn, and in her agony was seen the inheritance of Eve,—seeking in sorrow what in sorrow she had brought forth. And yet, after accusing my perfidy and cruelty, she again continued her intercessions for me with Thee, returned to her accustomed place, and I to Rome.

And behold, there was I received by the scourge of bodily sickness, and I was descending into hell burdened with all the sins that I had committed, both against Thee, myself, and others, many and grievous, over and above that bond of original sin whereby we all die in Adam. For none of these things hadst Thou forgiven me in Christ, neither had He 'abolished' by His cross 'the enmity' which, by my sins, I had incurred with Thee. For how could He, by the crucifixion of a phantasm, which I supposed Him to be? As true, then, was the death of my soul, as that of His flesh appeared to me to be untrue; and as true the death of His flesh as the life of my soul, which believed it not, was false. The fever increasing, I was now passing away and perishing. For had I then gone hence, whither should I have gone but into the fiery torments meet for my misdeeds, in the truth of Thy ordinance?

She was ignorant of this, yet, while absent, prayed for me. But Thou, everywhere present, hearkened to her where she was, and hadst pity upon me where I was, that I should regain my bodily health, although still frenzied in my sacrilegious heart. For all that peril did not make me wish to be baptized, and I was better when, as a lad, I entreated it of my mother's piety, as I have already related and confessed. But I had grown up to my own dishonour, and all the purposes of Thy medicine I madly derided, who wouldst not suffer me, though such a one, to die a double death. Had my mother's heart been smitten with this wound, it never could have been cured. For I cannot sufficiently express the love she had for me, nor how she now travailed for me in the spirit with a far keener anguish than when she bore me in the flesh.

I cannot conceive, therefore, how she could have been healed if such a death of mine had transfixed the bowels of her love. Where then would have been her so earnest, frequent, and unintermitted prayers to Thee alone? But couldst Thou, most merciful God, despise the 'contrite and humble heart' of that pure and prudent widow, so constant in alms-deeds, so gracious and attentive to Thy saints, not permitting one day to pass without oblation at Thy altar, twice a day, at morning and even-tide, coming to Thy Church without intermission—not for vain gossiping, nor old wives' 'fables,' but in order that she might listen to Thee in Thy sermons, and Thou to her in her prayers? Couldst Thou—Thou by whose gift she was such—despise and disregard without succouring the tears of such a one, wherewith she entreated Thee not for gold or silver, nor for any changing or fleeting good, but for the salvation of the soul of her son? By no means, Lord. Assuredly Thou wert near, and wert hearing and doing in that method in which Thou hadst predetermined that it should be done. Far be it from Thee that Thou shouldst delude her in those visions and the answers she had from Thee,—some of which I have spoken of, and others not,—which she kept in her faithful breast, and, always petitioning, pressed upon Thee as Thine autograph. For Thou, 'because Thy mercy endureth for ever,' condescendest to those whose debts

Thou hast pardoned, to become likewise a debtor by Thy promises.

Thou restoredst me then from that illness, and made sound the son of Thy handmaid meanwhile in body, that he might live for Thee, to endow him with a higher and more enduring health. And even then at Rome I joined those deluding and deluded 'saints;' not their 'hearers' only,—of the number of whom was he in whose house I had fallen ill, and had recovered, —but those also whom they designate 'The Elect.' For it still seemed to me 'that it was not we that sin, but that I know not what other nature sinned in us.' And it gratified my pride to be free from blame, and, after I had committed any fault, not to acknowledge that I had done any,—'that Thou mightest heal my soul because it had sinned against Thee;' but I loved to excuse it, and to accuse something else (I wot not what) which was with me, but was not I. But assuredly it was wholly I, and my impiety had divided me against myself; and that sin was all the more incurable in that I did not deem myself a sinner. And execrable iniquity it was, O God omnipotent, that I would rather have Thee to be overcome in me to my destruction, than myself of Thee to salvation! Not yet, therefore, hadst Thou set a watch before my mouth, and kept the door of my lips, that my heart might not incline to wicked speeches, to make excuses of sins, with men that work iniquity—and, therefore, was I still united with their 'Elect.'

But now, hopeless of making proficiency in that false doctrine, even those things with which I had decided upon contenting myself, providing that I could find nothing better, I now held more loosely and negligently. For I was half inclined to believe that those philosophers whom they call 'Academics' were more sagacious than the rest, in that they held that we ought to doubt everything, and ruled that man had not the power of comprehending any truth; for so, not yet realizing their meaning, I also was fully persuaded that they thought just as they are commonly held to do.[23] And I did not fail frankly to restrain in my host that assurance which I observed him to have in those fictions of which the works of Manichæus are full. Notwithstanding, I was on terms of more intimate friendship with them than with others who were not of this heresy. Nor did I defend it with my former ardour; still my familiarity with that sect (many of them being concealed in Rome) made me slower to seek any other way,—particularly since I was hopeless of finding the truth, from which in Thy Church, O Lord of heaven and earth, Creator of all things visible and invisible, they had turned me aside,—and it seemed to me most unbecoming to believe Thee to have the form of human flesh, and to be bounded by the bodily lineaments of our members. And because, when I desired to meditate on my God, I knew not what to think of but a mass of bodies (for what was not such did not seem to me to be), this was the greatest and almost sole cause of my inevitable error.

For hence I also believed evil to be a similar sort of substance, and to be possessed of its own foul and misshapen mass—whether dense, which they denominated earth, or thin and subtle, as is the body of the air, which they fancy some malignant spirit crawling through that earth. And because a piety—such as it was—compelled me to believe that the good God never created any evil nature, I conceived two masses, the one opposed to the other, both infinite, but the evil the more contracted, the good the more expansive. And from this mischievous commencement the other profanities followed on me. For when my mind tried to revert to the Catholic faith, I was cast back, since what I had held to be the Catholic faith was not so. And it appeared to me more devout to look upon Thee, my God,—to whom I make confession of Thy mercies,—as infinite, at least, on other sides, although on that side where the mass of evil was in opposition to Thee I was compelled to confess Thee finite, than if on every side I should conceive Thee to be confined by the form of a human body. And better did it seem to me to believe that no evil had been created by Thee—which to me in my ignorance appeared not only some substance, but a bodily one, because I had no conception of the mind excepting as a subtle body, and that diffused in local spaces—than to believe that anything could emanate from Thee of such a kind as I considered the nature of evil to be. And our very Saviour Himself, also, Thine only-begotten, I believed to have been reached forth, as it were, for our salvation out of the lump of

Thy most effulgent mass, so as to believe nothing of Him but what I was able to imagine in my vanity. Such a nature, then, I thought could not be born of the Virgin Mary without being mingled with the flesh; and how that which I had thus figured to myself could be mingled without being contaminated, I saw not. I was afraid, therefore, to believe Him to be born in the flesh, lest I should be compelled to believe Him contaminated by the flesh. Now will Thy spiritual ones blandly and lovingly smile at me if they shall read these my confessions; yet such was I.

Furthermore, whatever they had censured in Thy Scriptures I thought impossible to be defended; and yet sometimes, indeed, I desired to confer on these several points with some one well learned in those books, and to try what he thought of them. For at this time the words of one Helpidius, speaking and disputing face to face against the said Manichæans, had begun to move me even at Carthage, in that he brought forth things from the Scriptures not easily withstood, to which their answer appeared to me feeble. And this answer they did not give forth publicly, but only to us in private,—when they said that the writings of the New Testament had been tampered with by I know not whom, who were desirous of ingrafting the Jewish law upon the Christian faith; but they themselves did not bring forward any uncorrupted copies. But I, thinking of corporeal things, very much ensnared and in a measure stifled, was oppressed by those masses; panting under which for the breath of Thy Truth, I was not able to breathe it pure and undefiled.

Then began I assiduously to practise that for which I came to Rome— the teaching of rhetoric; and first to bring together at my home some to whom, and through whom, I had begun to be known; when, behold, I learnt that other offences were committed in Rome which I had not to bear in Africa. For those subvertings by abandoned young men were not practised here, as I had been informed; yet, suddenly, said they, to evade paying their master's fees, many of the youths conspire together, and remove themselves to another,—breakers of faith, who, for the love of money, set a small value on justice. These also my heart 'hated,' though not with a 'perfect hatred;' for, perhaps, I hated them more in that I was to suffer by them, than for the illicit acts they committed. Such of a truth are base persons, and they are unfaithful to Thee, loving these transitory mockeries of temporal things, and vile gain, which begrimes the hand that lays hold on it; and embracing the fleeting world, and scorning Thee, who abidest, and invitest to return, and pardonest the prostituted human soul when it returneth to Thee. And now I hate such crooked and perverse men, although I love them if they are to be corrected so as to prefer the learning they obtain to money, and to learning Thee, O God, the truth and fulness of certain good and most chaste peace. But then was the wish stronger in me for my own sake not to suffer them evil, than was the wish that they should become good for Thine.

When, therefore, they of Milan had sent to Rome to the prefect of the city, to provide them with a teacher of rhetoric for their city, and to despatch him at the public expense, I made interest through those identical persons, drunk with Manichæan vanities, to be freed from whom I was going away,—neither of us, however, being aware of it,—that Symmachus, the then prefect, having proved me by proposing a subject, would send me. And to Milan I came, unto Ambrose the bishop, known to the whole world as among the best of men, Thy devout servant; whose eloquent discourse did at that time strenuously dispense unto Thy people the flour of Thy wheat, the 'gladness' of Thy 'oil,' and the sober intoxication of Thy 'wine.' To him was I unknowingly led by Thee, that by him I might knowingly be led to Thee. That man of God received me like a father, and looked with a benevolent and episcopal kindliness on my change of abode. And I began to love him, not at first, indeed, as a teacher of the truth,—which I entirely despaired of in Thy Church,—but as a man friendly to myself. And I studiously hearkened to him preaching to the people, not with the motive I should, but, as it were, trying to discover whether his eloquence came up to the fame thereof, or flowed fuller or lower than was asserted; and I hung on his words intently, but of the matter I was but as a careless and contemptuous spectator; and I was delighted with the pleasantness of his speech, more erudite, yet less cheerful and soothing in manner, than that of Faustus. Of the matter, however, there could be no comparison; for the latter was straying amid Manichæan deceptions, whilst the former was teaching salvation most soundly. But 'salvation is far from the wicked,' such as I then stood before him; and yet I was drawing nearer gradually and unconsciously.

For although I took no trouble to learn what he spake, but only to hear how he spake (for that empty care alone remained to me, despairing of a way accessible for man to Thee), yet, together with the words which I prized, there came into my mind also the things about which I was careless; for I could not separate them. And whilst I opened my heart to admit 'how skilfully he spake,' there also entered with it, but gradually, 'and how truly he spake!' For first, these things also had begun to appear to me to be defensible; and the Catholic faith, for which I had fancied nothing could be said against the attacks of the Manichæans, I now conceived might be maintained without presumption; especially after I had heard one or two parts of the Old Testament explained, and often allegorically—which when I accepted literally, I was 'killed' spiritually. Many places, then, of those books having been expounded to me, I now blamed my despair in having believed that no reply could be made to those who hated and derided[24] the Law and the Prophets. Yet I did not then see that for that reason the Catholic way was to be held because it had its learned advocates, who could at length, and not irrationally, answer objections; nor that what I held ought therefore to be condemned because both sides were equally defensible. For that way did not appear to me to be vanquished; nor yet did it seem to me to be victorious.

Hereupon did I earnestly bend my mind to see if in any way I could possibly prove the Manichæans guilty of falsehood. Could I have realized a spiritual substance, all their strongholds would have been beaten down, and cast utterly out of my mind; but I could not. But yet, concerning the body of this world, and the whole of nature, which the senses of the flesh can attain unto, I, now more and more considering and comparing things, judged that the greater part of the philosophers held much the more probable opinions. So, then, after the manner of the Academics (as they are supposed), doubting of everything and fluctuating between all, I decided that the Manichæans were to be abandoned; judging that, even while in that period of doubt, I could not remain in a sect to which I preferred some of the philosophers; to which philosophers, however, because they were without the saving name of Christ, I utterly refused to commit the cure of my fainting soul. I resolved, therefore, to be a catechumen in the Catholic Church, which my parents had commended to me, until something settled should manifest itself to me whither I might steer my course.

# BOOK VI

*Attaining his thirtieth year, he, under the admonition of the discourses of Ambrose, discovered more and more the truth of the Catholic doctrine, and deliberates as to the better regulation of his life.*

O THOU, my hope from my youth, where wert Thou to me, and whither hadst Thou gone? For in truth, hadst Thou not created me, and made a difference between me and the beasts of the field and fowls of the air? Thou hadst made me wiser than they, yet did I wander about in dark and slippery places, and sought Thee abroad out of myself, and found not the God of my heart; and had entered the depths of the sea, and distrusted and despaired finding out the truth. By this time my mother, made strong by her piety, had come to me, following me over sea and land, in all perils feeling secure in Thee. For in the dangers of the sea she comforted the very sailors (to whom the inexperienced passengers, when alarmed, were wont rather to go for comfort), assuring them of a safe arrival, because she had been so assured by Thee in a vision. She found me in grievous danger, through despair of ever finding truth. But when I had disclosed to her that I was now no longer a Manichæan, though not yet a Catholic Christian, she did not leap for joy as at what was unexpected; although she was now reassured as to that part of my misery for which she had mourned me as one dead, but who would be raised to Thee, carrying me forth upon the bier of her thoughts, that Thou mightest say unto the widow's son, 'Young man, I say unto Thee, arise,' and he should revive, and begin to speak, and Thou shouldest deliver him to his mother. Her heart, then, was not agitated with any violent

S<sup>T</sup> AMBROSIUS

exultation, when she had heard that to be already in so great a part accomplished which she daily, with tears, entreated of Thee might be done,—that though I had not yet grasped the truth, I was rescued from falsehood. Yea, rather, for that she was fully confident that Thou, who hadst promised the whole, wouldst give the rest, most calmly, and with a breast full of confidence, she replied to me, 'She believed in Christ, that before she departed this life, she would see me a Catholic believer.' And thus much said she to me; but to Thee, O Fountain of mercies, poured she out more frequent prayers and tears, that Thou wouldest hasten Thy aid, and enlighten my darkness; and she hurried all the more assiduously to the church, and hung upon the words of Ambrose, praying for the fountain of water[25] that springeth up into everlasting life. For she loved that man as an angel of God, because she knew that it was by him that I had been brought, for the present, to that perplexing state of agitation I was now in, through which she was fully persuaded that I should pass from sickness unto health, after an access, as it were, of a sharper fit, which doctors term the 'crisis.'

When, therefore, my mother had at one time—as was her custom in Africa—brought to the oratories built in the memory of the saints certain cakes, and bread, and wine, and was forbidden by the door-keeper, so soon as she learnt that it was the bishop who had forbidden it, she so piously and obediently acceded to it, that I myself marvelled how readily she could bring herself to accuse her own customs, rather than question his prohibition. For wine-bibbing did not take possession of her spirit, nor did the love of wine stimulate her to hatred of the truth, as it doth too many, both male and female, who nauseate at a song of sobriety, as men well drunk at a draught of water. But she, when she had brought her basket with the festive meats, of which she would taste herself first and give the rest away, would never allow herself more than one little cup of wine diluted according to her own temperate palate, which, out of courtesy, she would taste. And if there were many oratories of departed saints that ought to be honoured in the same way, she still carried round with her the selfsame cup, to be used everywhere; and this, which was not only very much watered, but was also very tepid with carrying about, she would distribute by small sips to those around; for she sought their devotion, not pleasure. As soon, therefore, as she found this custom to be forbidden by that famous preacher and most pious prelate, even to those who would use it with moderation, lest thereby an occasion of excess might be given to such as were drunken, and because these, so to say, festivals in honour of the dead were very like unto the superstition of the Gentiles, she most willingly abstained from it. And in lieu of a basket filled with fruits of the earth, she had learned to bring to the oratories of the martyrs a heart full of more purified petitions, and to give all that she could to the poor; that so the communion of the Lord's body might be rightly celebrated there, where, after the example of His passion, the martyrs had been sacrificed and crowned. But yet it seems to me, O Lord my God, and thus my heart thinks of it in thy sight, that my mother perhaps would not so easily have given way to the relinquishment of this custom had it been forbidden by another whom she loved not as Ambrose, whom, out of regard for my salvation, she loved most dearly; and he loved her truly, on account of her most religious conversation, whereby, in good works so 'fervent in spirit,' she frequented the church; so that he would often, when he saw me, burst forth into her praises, congratulating me that I had such a mother—little knowing what a son she had in me, who was in doubt as to all these things, and did not imagine the way of life could be found out.

Nor did I now groan in my prayers that Thou wouldest help me; but my mind was wholly intent on knowledge, and eager to dispute. And Ambrose himself I esteemed a happy man, as the world counted happiness, in that such great personages held him in honour; only his celibacy appeared to me a painful thing. But what hope he cherished, what struggles he had against the temptations that beset his very excellences, what solace in adversities, and what savoury joys Thy bread possessed for the hidden mouth of his heart when ruminating on it,[26] I could neither conjecture, nor had I experienced. Nor did he know my embarrassments, nor the pit of my danger. For I could not request of him what I wished as I wished, in that I was debarred from hearing and speaking to him by crowds of busy people, whose infirmities he devoted himself to. With whom when he was not engaged (which was but a little time), he either was refreshing his body with necessary sustenance, or his mind with reading. But while reading, his eyes glanced over the pages, and his heart searched out the sense, but his voice and tongue were silent. Ofttimes, when we had come (for no one was forbidden to enter, nor was it his custom that the arrival of those who came should be announced to him), we saw him thus reading to himself, and never otherwise; and, having long sat in silence (for who durst interrupt one so intent?), we were fain to depart, inferring that in the little time he secured for the recruiting of his mind, free from the clamour of other men's business, he was unwilling to be taken off. And perchance he was fearful lest, if the author he studied should express aught vaguely, some doubtful and attentive hearer should ask him to expound it, or to discuss some of the more abstruse questions, as that, his time being thus occupied, he could not turn over as many volumes as he wished; although the preservation of his voice, which was very easily weakened, might be the truer reason for his reading to himself. But whatever was his motive in so doing, doubtless in such a man was a good one.

But verily no opportunity could I find of ascertaining what I desired from that Thy so holy oracle, his breast, unless the thing might be entered into briefly. But those surgings in me required to find him at full leisure, that I might pour them out to him, but never were they able to find him so; and I heard him, indeed, every Lord's day, 'rightly dividing the word of truth' among the people; and I was all the more convinced that all those knots of crafty calumnies, which those deceivers of ours had knit against the divine books, could be unravelled. But so soon as I understood, withal, that man made 'after the image of Him that created him' was not so understood by Thy spiritual sons (whom of the Catholic mother Thou hadst begotten again through grace), as though they believed and imagined Thee to be bounded by human form,—although what was the nature of a spiritual substance I had not the faintest or dimmest suspicion,—yet rejoicing,

I blushed that for so many years I had barked, not against the Catholic faith, but against the fables of carnal imaginations. For I had been both impious and rash in this, that what I ought inquiring to have learnt, I had pronounced on condemning. For Thou, O most high and most near, most secret, yet most present, who hast not limbs some larger some smaller, but art wholly everywhere, and nowhere in space, nor art Thou of such corporeal form, yet hast Thou created man after Thine own image, and, behold, from head to foot is he confined by space.

As, then, I knew not how this image of Thine should subsist, I should have knocked and propounded the doubt how it was to be believed, and not have insultingly opposed it, as if it were believed. Anxiety, therefore, as to what to retain as certain, did all the more sharply gnaw into my soul, the more shame I felt that, having been so long deluded and deceived by the promise of certainties, I had, with puerile error and petulance, prated of so many uncertainties as if they were certainties. For that they were falsehoods became apparent to me afterwards. However, I was certain that they were uncertain, and that I had formerly held them as certain when with a blind contentiousness I accused Thy Catholic Church, which though I had not yet discovered to teach truly, yet not to teach that of which I had so vehemently accused her. In this manner was I confounded and converted, and I rejoiced, O my God, that the one Church, the body of Thine only Son (wherein the name of Christ had been set upon me when an infant), did not appreciate these infantile trifles, nor maintained, in her sound doctrine, any tenet that would confine Thee, the Creator of all, in space—though ever so great and wide, yet bounded on all sides by the restraints of a human form.

I rejoiced also that the old Scriptures of the Law and the Prophets were laid before me, to be perused, not now with that eye to which they seemed most absurd before, when I censured Thy holy ones for so thinking, whereas in truth they thought not so; and with delight I heard Ambrose, in his sermons to the people, oftentimes most diligently recommend this text as a rule,—'The letter killeth, but the Spirit giveth life;'[27] whilst, drawing aside the mystic veil, he spiritually laid open that which, accepted according to the 'letter,' seemed to teach perverse doctrines—teaching herein nothing that offended me, though he taught such things as I knew not as yet whether they were true. For all this time I restrained my heart from assenting to anything, fearing to fall headlong; but by hanging in suspense I was the worse killed. For my desire was to be as well assured of those things that I saw not, as I was that seven and three are ten. For I was not so insane as to believe that this could not be comprehended; but I desired to have other things as clear as this, whether corporeal things, which were not present to my senses, or spiritual, whereof I knew not how to conceive except corporeally. And by believing I might have been cured, that so the sight of my soul being cleared, it might in some way be directed towards Thy truth, which abideth always, and faileth in naught. But as it happens that he who has tried a bad physician fears to trust himself with a good one, so was it with the health of my soul, which could not be healed but by believing, and, lest it should believe falsehoods, refused to be cured—resisting Thy hands, who hast prepared for us the medicaments of faith, and hast applied them to the maladies of the whole world, and hast bestowed upon them so great authority.

From this, however, being led to prefer the Catholic doctrine, I felt that it was with more moderation and honesty that it commanded things to be believed that were not demonstrated (whether it was that they could be demonstrated, but not to any one, or could not be demonstrated at all), than was the method of the Manichæans, where our credulity was mocked by audacious promise of knowledge, and then so many most fabulous and absurd things were forced upon belief because they were not capable of demonstration. After that, O Lord, Thou, by little and little, with most gentle and most merciful hand, drawing and calming my heart, didst persuade me,—taking into consideration what a multiplicity of things which I had never seen, nor was present when they were enacted, like so many of the things in secular history, and so many accounts of places and cities which I had not seen; so many of friends, so many of physicians, so many now of these men, now of those, which unless we should believe, we should do nothing at all in this life; lastly, with how unalterable an assurance I believed of what parents I was born, which it would have been impossible for me to know otherwise than by hearsay,—taking into consideration all this, Thou persuadedst me that not they who believed Thy books (which, with so great authority, Thou hast established among nearly all nations), but those who believed them not were to be blamed; and that those men were not to be listened unto who should say to me, 'How dost thou know that those Scriptures were imparted unto mankind by the Spirit of the one true and most true God?' For it was this same thing that was most of all to be believed, since no wranglings of blasphemous questions, whereof I had read so many amongst the self-contradicting philosophers, could once wring the belief from me that Thou art,—whatsoever Thou wert, though what I knew not,—or that the government of human affairs belongs to Thee.

Thus much I believed, at one time more strongly than another, yet did I ever believe both that Thou wert, and hadst a care of us, although I was ignorant both what was to be thought of Thy substance, and what way led, or led back to Thee. Seeing, then, that we were too weak by unaided reason to find out the truth, and for this cause needed the authority of the holy writings, I had now begun to believe that Thou wouldest by no means have given such excellency of authority to those Scriptures throughout all lands, had it not been Thy will thereby to be believed in, and thereby sought. For now those things which heretofore appeared incongruous to me in the Scripture, and used to offend me, having heard divers of them expounded reasonably I referred to the depth of the mysteries, and its authority seemed to me all the more venerable and worthy of religious belief, in that, while it was visible for all to read it, it reserved the majesty of its secret within its profound significance, stooping to all in the great plainness of its language and lowliness of its style, yet exercising the application of such as are not light of heart; that it might receive all into its common bosom, and through narrow passages waft over some few towards Thee, yet many more than if it did not stand upon such a height of authority, nor allured multitudes within its bosom by its holy humility. These things I meditated upon, and Thou wert with me; I sighed, and Thou heardest me; I vacillated, and Thou didst guide me; I roamed through the broad way of the world, and Thou didst not desert me.

I longed for honours, gains, wedlock; and Thou mockedst me. In these desires I underwent most bitter hardships, Thou being the more gracious the less Thou didst suffer anything which was not Thou to grow sweet to me. Behold my heart, O Lord, who wouldest that I should recall all this, and confess unto Thee. Now let my soul cleave to Thee, which Thou hast freed from that fast-holding birdlime of death. How wretched was it! And Thou didst irritate the feeling of its wound, that, forsaking all else, it might be converted unto Thee,—who art above all, and without whom all things would be naught,—be converted and be healed. How wretched was I at that time, and how didst Thou deal with me, to make me sensible of my wretchedness on that day wherein I was preparing to recite a panegyric on the Emperor,[28] wherein I was to deliver many a lie, and lying was to be applauded by those who knew I lied; and my heart panted with these cares, and boiled over with the feverishness of consuming thoughts. For, while walking along one of the streets of Milan, I observed a poor mendicant,—then, I imagine, with a full belly,—joking and joyous; and I sighed, and spake to the friends around me of the many sorrows resulting from our madness, for that by all such exertions of ours,—as those wherein I then laboured, dragging along, under the spur of desires, the burden of my own unhappiness, and by dragging increasing it,—we yet aimed only to attain that very joyousness which that mendicant had reached before us, who, perchance, never would attain it! For what he had obtained through a few begged pence, the same was I scheming for by many a wretched and tortuous turning,—the joy of a temporary felicity. For he verily possessed not true joy, but yet I, with these my ambitions, was seeking one much more untrue. And in truth he was joyous, I anxious; he free from care, I full of alarms. But should any one inquire of me whether I would rather be merry or fearful, I would reply, Merry. Again, were I asked whether I would rather be such as he was, or as I myself then was, I should elect to be myself, though beset with cares and alarms, but out of perversity; for was it so in truth? For I ought not to prefer myself to him because I happened to be more learned than he, seeing that I took no delight therein, but sought rather to please men by it; and that not to instruct, but only to please. Wherefore also didst Thou break my bones with the rod of Thy correction.

Away with those, then, from my soul, who say unto it, 'It makes a difference from whence a man's joy is derived. That mendicant rejoiced in drunkenness; thou longedst to rejoice in glory.' What glory, O Lord? That which is not in Thee. For even as his was no true joy, so was mine no true glory; and it subverted my soul more. He would digest his drunkenness that same night, but many a night had I slept with mine, and risen again with it, and was to sleep again and again to rise with it, I know not how oft. It does indeed 'make a difference whence a man's joy is derived.' I know it is so, and that the joy of a faithful hope is incomparably beyond such vanity. Yea, and at that time was he beyond me, for he truly was the happier man; not only for that he was thoroughly steeped in mirth, I torn to pieces with cares, but he, by giving good wishes, had gotten wine, I, by lying, was following after pride. Much to this effect said I then to my dear friends, and I often marked in them how it fared with me; and I found that it went ill with me, and fretted, and doubled that very ill. And if any prosperity smiled upon me, I loathed to seize it, for almost before I could grasp it it flew away.

These things we, who lived like friends together, jointly deplored, but chiefly and most familiarly did I discuss them with Alypius and Nebridius, of whom Alypius was born in the same town as myself, his parents being of the highest rank there, but he being younger than I. For he had studied under me, first, when I taught in our own town, and afterwards at Carthage, and esteemed me highly, because I appeared to him good and learned; and I esteemed him for his innate love of virtue, which, in one of no great age,

was sufficiently eminent. But the vortex of Carthaginian customs (amongst whom these frivolous spectacles are hotly followed) had inveigled him into the madness of the Circensian games. But while he was miserably tossed about therein, I was professing rhetoric there, and had a public school. As yet he did not give ear to my teaching, on account of some ill-feeling that had arisen between me and his father. I had then found how fatally he doted upon the circus, and was deeply grieved that he seemed likely— if, indeed, he had not already done so—to cast away his so great promise. Yet had I no means of advising, or by a sort of restraint reclaiming him, either by the kindness of a friend or by the authority of a master. For I imagined that his sentiments towards me were the same as his father's; but he was not such. Disregarding, therefore, his father's will in that matter, he commenced to salute me, and, coming into my lecture-room, to listen for a little and depart.

But it slipped my memory to deal with him so that he should not, through a blind and headstrong desire of empty pastimes, undo so great a wit. But Thou, O Lord, who governest the helm of all Thou hast created, hadst not forgotten him, who was one day to be amongst Thy sons, the President of Thy sacrament; and that his amendment might plainly be attributed to Thyself, Thou broughtest it about through me, but I knowing nothing of it. For one day, when I was sitting in my accustomed place, with my scholars before me, he came in, saluted me, sat himself down, and fixed his attention on the subject I was then handling. It so happened that I had a passage in hand, which while I was explaining, a simile borrowed from the Circensian games occurred to me, as likely to make what I wished to convey pleasanter and plainer, imbued with a biting jibe at those whom that madness had enthralled. Thou knowest, O our God, that I had no thought at that time of curing Alypius of that plague. But he took it to himself, and thought that I would not have said it but for his sake. And what any other man would have made a ground of offence against me, this worthy young man took as a reason for being offended at himself, and for loving me more fervently. For Thou hast said it long ago, and written in

Thy book, 'Rebuke a wise man, and he will love thee.' But I had not rebuked him, but Thou, who makest use of all consciously or unconsciously in that order which Thyself knowest (and that order is right), wroughtest out of my heart and tongue burning coals, by which Thou mightest set on fire and cure the hopeful mind thus languishing. Let him be silent in Thy praises who meditates not on Thy mercies, which from my inmost parts confess unto Thee. For he upon that speech rushed out from that so deep pit, wherein he was wilfully plunged, and was blinded by its miserable pastimes; and he roused his mind with a resolute moderation; whereupon all the filth of the Circensian pastimes[29] flew off from him, and he did not approach them further. Upon this, he prevailed with his reluctant father to let him be my pupil. He gave in and consented. And Alypius, beginning again to hear me, was involved in the same superstition as I was, loving in the Manichæans that ostentation of continency[30] which he believed to be true and unfeigned. It was, however, a senseless and seducing continency, ensnaring precious souls, not able as yet to reach the height of virtue, and easily beguiled with the veneer of what was but a shadowy and feigned virtue.

He, not relinquishing that worldly way which his parents had bewitched him to pursue, had gone before me to Rome, to study law, and there he was carried away in an extraordinary manner with an incredible eagerness after the gladiatorial shows. For, being utterly opposed to and detesting such spectacles, he was one day met by chance by divers of his acquaintance and fellow-students returning from dinner, and they with a friendly violence drew him, vehemently objecting and resisting, into the amphitheatre, on a day of these cruel and deadly shows, he thus protesting: 'Though you drag my body to that place, and there place me, can you force me to give my mind and lend my eyes to these shows? Thus shall I be absent while present, and so shall overcome both you and them.' They hearing this, dragged him on nevertheless, desirous, perchance, to see whether he could do as he said. When they had arrived thither, and had taken their places as they could, the whole place became excited with the inhuman sports. But he, shutting up the doors of his eyes, forbade his mind to roam abroad after such naughtiness; and would that he had shut his ears also! For, upon the fall of one in the fight, a mighty cry from the whole audience stirring him strongly, he, overcome by curiosity, and prepared as it were to despise and rise superior to it, no matter what it were, opened his eyes, and was struck with a deeper wound in his soul than the other, whom he desired to see, was in his body; and he fell more miserably than he on whose fall that mighty clamour was raised, which entered through his ears, and unlocked his eyes, to make way for the striking and beating down of his soul, which was bold rather than valiant hitherto; and so much the weaker in that it presumed on itself, which ought to have depended on Thee. For, directly he saw that blood, he therewith imbibed a sort of savageness; nor did he turn away, but fixed his eye, drinking in madness unconsciously, and was delighted with the guilty contest, and drunken with the bloody pastime. Nor was he now the same he came in, but was one of the throng he came unto, and a true companion of those who had brought him thither. Why need I say more? He looked, shouted, was excited, carried away with him the madness which would stimulate him to return, not only with those who first enticed him, but also before them, yea, and to draw in others. And from all this didst Thou, with a most powerful and most merciful hand, pluck him, and taughtest him not to repose confidence in himself, but in Thee—but not till long after.

But this was all being stored up in his memory for a medicine hereafter. As was that also, that when he was yet studying under me at Carthage, and was meditating at noon-day in the market-place upon what he had to recite (as scholars are wont to be exercised), Thou sufferedst him to be apprehended as a thief by the officers of the market-place. For no other reason, I apprehend, didst Thou, O our God, suffer it, but that he who was in the future to prove so great a man should now begin to learn that, in judging of causes, man should not with a reckless credulity readily be condemned by man. For as he was walking up and down alone before the judgment-seat with his tablets and pen, lo, a young man, one of the scholars, the real thief, privily bringing a hatchet, got in without Alypius' seeing him as far as the leaden bars which protect the silversmiths' shops, and began to cut away the lead. But the noise of the hatchet being heard, the silversmiths below began to make a stir, and sent to take in custody whomsoever they should find. But the thief, hearing their voices, ran away, leaving his hatchet, fearing to be taken with it. Now Alypius, who had not seen him come in, caught sight of him as he went out, and noted with what speed he made off. And, being curious to know the reasons, he entered the place, where, finding the hatchet, he stood wondering and pondering, when behold, those that were sent caught him alone, hatchet in hand, the noise whereof had startled them and brought them thither. They lay hold of him and drag him away, and, gathering the tenants of the market-place about them, boast of having taken a notorious thief, and thereupon he was being led away to appear before the judge.

But thus far was he to be instructed. For immediately, O Lord, Thou camest to the succour of his innocency, whereof Thou wert the sole witness. For, as he was being led either to prison or to punishment, they were met by a certain architect, who had the chief charge of the public buildings. They were specially glad to come across him, by whom they used to be suspected of stealing the goods lost out of the market-place, as though at last to convince him by whom these thefts were committed. He, however, had at divers times seen Alypius at the house of a certain senator, whom he was wont to visit to pay his respects; and, recognizing him at once, he took him aside by the hand, and inquiring of him the cause of so great a misfortune, heard the whole affair, and commanded all the rabble then present (who were very uproarious and full of threatenings) to go with him. And they came to the house of the young man who had committed the deed. There, before the door, was a lad so young as not to refrain from disclosing the whole through the fear of injuring his master. For he had followed his master to the market-place. Whom, so soon as Alypius recognized, he intimated it to the architect; and he, showing the hatchet to the lad, asked him to whom it belonged. 'To us,' quoth he immediately; and on being

further interrogated, he disclosed everything. Thus, the crime being transferred to that house, and the rabble shamed, which had begun to triumph
over Alypius, he, the future dispenser of Thy word, and an examiner of
numerous causes in Thy Church, went away better experienced and
instructed.

Him, therefore, had I lighted upon at Rome, and he clung to me by a
most strong tie, and accompanied me to Milan, both that he might not
leave me, and that he might practise something of the law he had studied,
more with a view of pleasing his parents than himself. There had he thrice
sat as assessor with an uncorruptness wondered at by others, he rather
wondering at those who could prefer gold to integrity. His character was
tested, also, not only by the bait of covetousness, but by the spur of fear.
At Rome, he was assessor to the Count of the Italian Treasury. There was
at that time a most potent senator, to whose favours many were indebted,
of whom also many stood in fear. He would fain, by his usual power, have
a thing granted him which was forbidden by the laws. This Alypius
resisted; a bribe was promised, he scorned it with all his heart; threats were
employed, he trampled them under foot,—all men being astonished at so
rare a spirit, which neither coveted the friendship nor feared the enmity of
a man at once so powerful and so greatly famed for his innumerable means
of doing good or ill. Even the judge whose councillor Alypius was, although
also unwilling that it should be done, yet did not openly refuse it, but put
the matter off upon Alypius, alleging that it was he who would not permit
him to do it; for verily, had the judge done it, Alypius would have decided
otherwise. With this one thing in the way of learning was he very nearly
led away,—that he might have books copied for him at prætorian prices.
But, consulting justice, he changed his mind for the better, esteeming
equity, whereby he was hindered, more gainful than the power whereby he
was permitted. These are little things, but 'He that is faithful in that which
is least, is faithful also in much.' Nor can that possibly be void which
proceedeth out of the mouth of Thy Truth. 'If, therefore, ye have not been
faithful in the unrighteous mammon, who will commit to your trust the

true riches? And if ye have not been faithful in that which is another man's, who shall give you that which is your own?' He, being such, did at that time cling to me, and wavered in purpose, as I did, what course of life was to be taken.

Nebridius also, who had left his native country near Carthage, and Carthage itself, where he had usually lived, leaving behind his fine paternal estate, his house, and his mother, who intended not to follow him, had come to Milan, for no other reason than that he might live with me in a most ardent search after truth and wisdom. Like me he sighed, like me he wavered, an ardent seeker after true life, and a most acute examiner of the most abstruse questions. So were there three begging mouths, sighing out their wants one to the other, and waiting upon Thee, that Thou mightest give them their meat in due season. And in all the bitterness which by Thy mercy followed our worldly pursuits, as we contemplated the end, why this suffering should be ours, darkness came upon us; and we turned away groaning and exclaiming, 'How long shall these things be?' And this we often said; and saying so, we did not relinquish them, for as yet we had discovered nothing certain to which, when relinquished, we might betake ourselves.

And I, puzzling over and reviewing these things, most marvelled at the length of time from that my nineteenth year, wherein I began to be inflamed with the desire of wisdom, resolving, when I had found her, to forsake all the empty hopes and lying insanities of vain desires. And behold, I was now getting on to my thirtieth year, sticking in the same mire, eager for the enjoyment of things present, which fly away and destroy me, whilst I say, 'To-morrow I shall discover it; behold, it will appear plainly, and I shall seize it; behold, Faustus will come and explain everything! O ye great men, ye Academicians, it is then true that nothing certain for the ordering of life can be attained! Nay, let us search the more diligently, and let us not despair. Lo, the things in the ecclesiastical books, which appeared to us absurd aforetime, do not appear so now, and may be otherwise and honestly interpreted. I will set my feet upon that step, where, as a child, my parents placed me, until the clear truth be discovered. But where and when shall it be sought? Ambrose has no leisure—we have no leisure to read. Where are we to find the books? Whence or when procure them? From whom borrow them? Let set times be appointed, and certain hours be set apart for the health of the soul. Great hope has risen upon us the Catholic faith doth not teach what we conceived, and vainly accused it of. Her learned ones hold it as an abomination to believe that God is limited by the form of a human body. And do we doubt to "knock," in order that the rest may be "opened"? The mornings are taken up by our scholars; how do we employ the rest of the day? Why do we not set about this? But when, then, pay our respects to our great friends, of whose favours we stand in need? When prepare what our scholars buy from us? When recreate ourselves, relaxing our minds from the pressure of care?

'Perish everything, and let us dismiss these empty vanities, and betake ourselves solely to the search after truth! Life is miserable, death uncertain. If it creeps upon us suddenly, in what state shall we depart hence, and where shall we learn what we have neglected here? Or rather shall we not suffer the punishment of this negligence? What if death itself should cut off and put an end to all care and feeling? This also, then, must be inquired into. But God forbid that it should be so. It is not without reason, it is no empty thing, that the so eminent height of the authority of the Christian faith is diffused throughout the entire world. Never would such and so great things be wrought for us, if, by the death of the body, the life of the soul were destroyed. Why, therefore, do we delay to abandon our hopes of this world, and give ourselves wholly to seek after God and the blessed life? But stay! Even those things are enjoyable; and they possess some and no little sweetness. We must not abandon them lightly, for it would be a shame to return to them again. Behold, now is it a great matter to obtain some post of honour! And what more could we desire? We have crowds of influential friends, though we have nothing else, and if we make haste a presidentship may be offered us; and a wife with some money, that she increase not our expenses; and this shall be the height of desire. Many men, who are great and worthy of imitation, have applied themselves to the study of wisdom in the marriage state.'

Whilst I talked of these things, and these winds veered about and tossed my heart hither and thither, the time passed on; but I was slow to turn to the Lord, and from day to day deferred to live in Thee, and deferred not daily to die in myself. Being enamoured of a happy life, I yet feared it in its own abode, and, fleeing from it, sought after it. I conceived that I should be too unhappy were I deprived of the embracements of a woman;[31] and of Thy merciful medicine to cure that infirmity I thought not, not having tried it. As regards continency, I imagined it to be under the control of our own strength (though in myself I found it not), being so foolish as not to know what is written, that none can be continent unless Thou give it, and that Thou wouldst give it, if with heartfelt groaning I should knock at Thine ears, and should with firm faith cast my care upon Thee.

It was in truth Alypius who prevented me from marrying, alleging that thus we could by no means live together, having so much undistracted leisure in the love of wisdom, as we had long desired. For he himself was so chaste in this matter that it was wonderful—all the more, too, that in his early youth he had entered upon that path, but had not clung to it; rather had he, feeling sorrow and disgust at it, lived from that time to the present most continently. But I opposed him with the examples of those who as married men had loved wisdom, found favour with God, and walked faithfully and lovingly with their friends. From the greatness of whose spirit I fell far short, and, enthralled with the disease of the flesh and its deadly sweetness, dragged my chain along, fearing to be loosed, and, as if it pressed my wound, rejected his kind expostulations, as it were the hand of one who would unchain me. Moreover, it was by me that the serpent spake unto Alypius himself, weaving and laying in his path, by my tongue, pleasant snares, wherein his honourable and free feet might be entangled.

For when he wondered that I, for whom he had no slight esteem, stuck so fast in the bird-lime of that pleasure as to affirm whenever we discussed the matter that it would be impossible for me to lead a single life, and urged in my defence when I saw him wonder that there was a vast difference between the life that he had tried by stealth and snatches (of which he had now but a faint recollection, and might therefore, without regret, easily despise), and my sustained acquaintance with it, whereto if but the honourable name of marriage were added, he would not then be astonished at my inability to contemn that course,—then began he also to wish to be married, not as if overpowered by the lust of such pleasure, but from curiosity. For, as he said, he was anxious to know what that could be without which my life, which was so pleasing to him, seemed to me not life but a penalty. For his mind, free from that chain, was astounded at my slavery, and through that astonishment was going on to a desire of trying it, and from it to the trial itself, and thence, perchance, to fall into that bondage whereat he was so astonished, seeing he was ready to enter into 'a covenant with death;' and he that loves danger shall fall into it. For whatever the conjugal honour be in the office of well-ordering a married life, and sustaining children, influenced us but slightly. But that which did for the most part afflict me, already made a slave to it, was the habit of satisfying an insatiable lust; him about to be enslaved did an admiring wonder draw on. In this state were we, until Thou, O most High, not forsaking our lowliness, commiserating our misery, didst come to our rescue by wonderful and secret ways.

Active efforts were made to get me a wife. I wooed, I was engaged, my mother taking the greatest pains in the matter, that when I was once married, the health-giving baptism might cleanse me; for which she rejoiced that I was being daily fitted, remarking that her desires and Thy promises were being fulfilled in my faith. At which time, verily, both at my request and her own desire, with strong heartfelt cries did we daily beg of Thee that Thou wouldest by a vision disclose unto her something concerning my future marriage; but Thou wouldest not. She saw indeed certain vain and fantastic things, such as the earnestness of a human spirit, bent thereon, conjured up; and these she told me of, not with her usual confidence when Thou hadst shown her anything, but slighting them. For she could, she declared, through some feeling which she could not express in words, discern the difference betwixt Thy revelations and the dreams of her own spirit. Yet the affair was pressed on, and a maiden sued who wanted two years of the marriageable age; and, as she was pleasing, she was waited for.

And many of us friends, consulting on and abhorring the turbulent vexations of human life, had considered and now almost determined upon living at ease and separate from the turmoil of men. And this was to be obtained in this way: we were to bring whatever we could severally procure, and make a common household, so that, through the sincerity of our friendship, nothing should belong more to one than the other; but the whole, being derived from all, should as a whole belong to each, and the whole unto all. It seemed to us that this society might consist of ten persons, some of whom were very rich, especially Romanianus, our townsman, an intimate friend of mine from his childhood, whom grave business matters had then brought up to Court; who was the most earnest of us all for this project, and whose voice was of great weight in commending it, because his estate was far more ample than that of the rest. We had arranged, too, that two officers should be chosen yearly, for the providing of all necessary things, whilst the rest were left undisturbed. But when we began to reflect whether the wives which some of us had already, and others hoped to have, would permit this, all that plan, which was being so well framed, broke to pieces in our hands, and was utterly wrecked and cast aside. Thence we fell again to sighs and groans, and our steps to follow the broad and beaten ways of the world; for many thoughts were in our heart, but Thy counsel standeth for ever. Out of which counsel Thou didst mock ours, and preparedst Thine own, purposing to give us meat in due season, and to open Thy hand, and to fill our souls with blessing.

Meanwhile my sins were being multiplied, and my mistress being torn from my side as an impediment to my marriage, my heart, which clave to her, was racked, and wounded, and bleeding. And she went back to Africa, making a vow unto Thee never to know another man, leaving with me my natural son by her. But I, unhappy one, who could not imitate a woman, impatient of delay, since it was not until two years' time I was to obtain her I sought,—being not so much a lover of marriage as a slave to lust,—procured another (not a wife, though), that so by the bondage of a lasting habit the disease of my soul might be nursed up, and kept up in its vigour, or even increased, into the kingdom of marriage. Nor was that wound of mine as yet cured which had been caused by the separation from my former mistress, but after inflammation and most acute anguish it mortified and the pain became numbed, but more desperate.

Unto Thee be praise, unto Thee be glory, O Fountain of mercies! I became more wretched, and Thou nearer. Thy right hand was ever ready to pluck me out of the mire, and to cleanse me, but I was ignorant of it. Nor did anything recall me from a yet deeper abyss of carnal pleasures, but the fear of death and of Thy future judgment, which, amid all my fluctuations of opinion, never left my breast. And in disputing with my friends, Alypius and Nebridius, concerning the nature of good and evil, I held that Epicurus had, in my judgment, won the palm, had I not believed that after death there remained a life for the soul, and places of recompense, which Epicurus would not believe. And I demanded, 'Supposing us to be immortal, and to be living in the enjoyment of perpetual bodily pleasure, and that without any fear of losing it, why, then, should we not be happy, or why should we search for anything else?'—not knowing that even this very thing was a part of my great misery, that, being thus sunk and blinded, I could not discern that light of honour and beauty to be embraced for its own sake, which cannot be seen by the eye of the flesh, it being visible only to the inner man. Nor did I, unhappy one, consider out of what vein it emanated, that even these things, loathsome as they were, I with pleasure discussed with my friends. Nor could I, even in accordance with my then notions of happiness, make myself happy without friends, amid no matter how great abundance of carnal pleasures. And these friends assuredly I loved for their own sakes, and I knew myself to be loved of them again for my own sake. O crooked ways! Woe to the audacious soul which hoped that, if it forsook Thee, it would find some better thing! It hath turned and re-turned, on back, sides, and belly, and all was hard, and Thou alone rest. And behold, Thou art near, and deliverest us from our wretched wanderings, and stablishest us in Thy way, and dost comfort us, and say, 'Run; I will carry you, yea, I will lead you, and there also will I carry you.'

# BOOK VII

*He recalls the beginning of his youth, i.e. the thirty-first year of his age, in which very grave errors as to the nature of God, and the origin of evil, being distinguished, and the sacred books more accurately known, he at length arrives at a clear knowledge of God, not yet rightly apprehending Jesus Christ.*

DEAD now was that evil and abominable youth of mine, and I was passing into early manhood: as I increased in years, the fouler became I in vanity, who could not conceive of any substance but such as I saw with my own eyes. I thought not of Thee, O God, under the form of a human body. Since the time I began to hear something of wisdom, I always avoided this; and I rejoiced to have found the same in the faith of our spiritual mother, Thy Catholic Church. But what else to imagine Thee I knew not. And I, a man, and such a man, sought to conceive of Thee, the sovereign and only true God; and I did in my inmost heart believe that Thou wert incorruptible, and inviolable, and unchangeable; because, not knowing whence or how, yet most plainly did I see and feel sure that that which may be corrupted must be worse than that which cannot, and what cannot be violated did I without hesitation prefer before that which can, and deemed that which suffers no change to be better than that which is changeable. Violently did my heart cry out against all my phantasms, and with this one blow I endeavoured to beat away from the eye of my mind all that unclean crowd which fluttered around it. And lo, being scarce put off, they, in the twinkling of an eye, pressed in multitudes around me, dashed against my face, and beclouded it; so that, though I thought not of Thee under the form of a human body, yet was I constrained to image Thee to be something corporeal in space, either infused into the world, or infinitely diffused beyond it,—even that incorruptible, inviolable, and unchangeable, which I preferred to the corruptible, and violable, and changeable; since whatsoever I conceived, deprived of this space, appeared as nothing to me, yea, altogether nothing, not even a void, as if a body were removed from its place and the place should remain empty of any body at all, whether earthly, terrestrial, watery, aerial, or celestial, but should remain a void place—a spacious nothing, as it were.

I therefore being thus gross-hearted, nor clear even to myself, whatsoever was not stretched over certain spaces, nor diffused, nor crowded together, nor swelled out, or which did not or could not receive some of these dimensions, I judged to be altogether nothing. For over such forms as my eyes are wont to range did my heart then range; nor did I see that this same observation, by which I formed those same images, was not of this kind, and yet it could not have formed them had not itself been something great. In like manner did I conceive of Thee, Life of my life, as vast through infinite spaces, on every side penetrating the whole mass of the world, and beyond it, all ways, through immeasurable and boundless spaces; so that the earth should have Thee, the heaven have Thee, all things have Thee, and they bounded in Thee, but Thou nowhere. For as the body of this air which is above the earth preventeth not the light of the sun from passing through it, penetrating it, not by bursting or by cutting, but by filling it entirely, so I imagined the body, not of heaven, air, and sea only, but of the earth also, to be pervious to Thee, and in all its greatest parts as well as smallest penetrable to receive Thy presence, by a secret inspiration, both inwardly and outwardly governing all things which Thou hast created. So I conjectured, because I was unable to think of anything else; for it was untrue. For in this way would a greater part of the earth contain a greater portion of Thee, and the less a lesser; and all things should be so full of Thee, as that the body of an elephant should contain more of Thee than that of a sparrow by how much larger it is, and occupies more room; and so shouldest Thou make the portions of Thyself present unto the several portions of the world, in pieces, great to the great, little to the little. But

Thou art not such a one; nor hadst Thou as yet enlightened my darkness.

It was sufficient for me, O Lord, to oppose to those deceived deceivers and dumb praters (dumb, since Thy word sounded not forth from them) that which a long while ago, while we were at Carthage, Nebridius used to propound, at which all we who heard it were disturbed: 'What could that reputed nation of darkness, which the Manichæans are in the habit of setting up as a mass opposed to Thee, have done unto Thee hadst Thou objected to fight with it? For had it been answered, "It would have done Thee some injury," then shouldest Thou be subject to violence and corruption; but if the reply were: "It could do Thee no injury," then was no cause assigned for Thy fighting with it; and so fighting as that a certain portion and member of Thee, or offspring of Thy very substance, should be blended with adverse powers and natures not of Thy creation, and be by them corrupted and deteriorated to such an extent as to be turned from happiness into misery, and need help whereby it might be delivered and purged; and that this offspring of Thy substance was the soul, to which, being enslaved, contaminated, and corrupted, Thy word, free, pure, and entire, might bring succour; but yet also the word itself being corruptible, because it was from one and the same substance. So that should they affirm Thee, whatsoever Thou art, that is, Thy substance whereby Thou art, to be incorruptible, then were all these assertions false and execrable; but if corruptible, then that were false, and at the first utterance to be abhorred.'[32] This argument, then, was enough against those who wholly merited to be vomited forth from the surfeited stomach, since they had no means of escape without horrible sacrilege, both of heart and tongue, thinking and speaking such things of Thee.

But I also, as yet, although I said and was firmly persuaded, that Thou our Lord, the true God, who madest not only our souls but our bodies, and not our souls and bodies alone, but all creatures and all things, wert uncontaminable and inconvertible, and in no part mutable; yet understood I not readily and clearly what was the cause of evil. And yet, whatever it was, I perceived that it must be so sought out as not to constrain me by it to believe that the immutable God was mutable, lest I myself should become the thing that I was seeking out. I sought, therefore, for it free from care, certain of the untruthfulness of what these asserted, whom I shunned with my whole heart; for I perceived that through seeking after the origin of evil, they were filled with malice, in that they liked better to think that Thy Substance did suffer evil than that their own did commit it.

And I directed my attention to discern what I now heard, that free will was the cause of our doing evil, and Thy righteous judgment of our suffering it. But I was unable clearly to discern it. So, then, trying to draw the eye of my mind from that pit, I was plunged again therein, and trying often, was as often plunged back again. But this raised me towards Thy light, that I knew as well that I had a will as that I had life: when, therefore, I was willing or unwilling to do anything, I was most certain that it was none but myself that was willing and unwilling; and immediately I perceived that there was the cause of my sin. But what I did against my will I saw that I suffered rather than did, and that judged I not to be my fault, but my punishment; whereby, believing Thee to be most just, I quickly confessed myself to be not unjustly punished. But again I said: 'Who made me? Was it not my God, who is not only good, but goodness itself? Whence came I then to will to do evil, and to be unwilling to do good, that there might be cause for my just punishment? Who was it that put this in me, and implanted in me the root of bitterness, seeing I was altogether made by my most sweet God? If the devil were the author, whence is that devil? And if he also, by his own perverse will, of a good angel became a devil, whence also was the evil will in him whereby he became a devil, seeing that the angel was made altogether good by that most good Creator?' By these reflections was I again cast down and stifled; yet not plunged into that hell of error (where no man confesseth unto Thee), to think that Thou dost suffer evil, rather than that man doth it.

For I was so struggling to find out the rest, as having already found that what was incorruptible must be better than the corruptible; and Thee, therefore, whatsoever Thou wert, did I acknowledge to be incorruptible.

For never yet was, nor will be, a soul able to conceive of anything better than Thou, who art the highest and best good. But whereas most truly and certainly that which is incorruptible is to be preferred to the corruptible (like as I myself did now prefer it), then, if Thou wert not incorruptible, I could in my thoughts have reached unto something better than my God. Where, then, I saw that the incorruptible was to be preferred to the corruptible, there ought I to seek Thee, and there observe 'whence evil itself was,' that is, whence comes the corruption by which Thy substance can by no means be profaned. For corruption, truly, in no way injures our God,—by no will, by no necessity, by no unforeseen chance,—because He is God, and what He wills is good, and Himself is that good; but to be corrupted is not good. Nor art Thou compelled to do anything against Thy will in that Thy will is not greater than Thy power. But greater should it be wert Thou Thyself greater than Thyself; for the will and power of God is God Himself. And what can be unforeseen by Thee, who knowest all things? Nor is there any sort of nature but Thou knowest it. And what more should we say 'why that substance which God is should not be corruptible,' seeing that if it were so it could not be God?

And I sought 'whence is evil?' And sought in an evil way; nor saw I the evil in my very search. And I set in order before the view of my spirit the whole creation, and whatever we can discern in it, such as earth, sea, air, stars, trees, living creatures; yea, and whatever in it we do not see, as the firmament of heaven, all the angels, too, and all the spiritual inhabitants thereof. But these very beings, as though they were bodies, did my fancy dispose in such and such places, and I made one huge mass of all Thy creatures, distinguished according to the kinds of bodies,—some of them being real bodies, some what I myself had feigned for spirits. And this mass I made huge,—not as it was, which I could not know, but as large as I thought well, yet every way finite. But Thee, O Lord, I imagined on every part environing and penetrating it, though every way infinite; as if there were a sea everywhere, and on every side through immensity nothing but an infinite sea; and it contained within itself some sponge, huge, though finite, so that the sponge would in all its parts be filled from the immeasurable sea. So conceived I Thy creation to be itself finite, and filled by Thee, the Infinite. And I said, Behold God, and behold what God hath created; and God is good, yea, most mightily and incomparably better than all these; but yet He, who is good, hath created them good, and behold how He encircleth and filleth them. Where, then, is evil, and whence, and how crept it in hither? What is its root, and what its seed? Or hath it no being at all? Why, then, do we fear and shun that which hath no being? Or if we fear it needlessly, then surely is that fear evil whereby the heart is unnecessarily pricked and tormented,—and so much a greater evil, as we have naught to fear, and yet do fear. Therefore either that is evil which we fear, or the act of fearing is in itself evil. Whence, therefore, is it, seeing that God, who is good, hath made all these things good? He, indeed, the greatest and chiefest Good, hath created these lesser goods; but both Creator and created are all good. Whence is evil? Or was there some evil matter of which He made and formed and ordered it, but left something in it which He did not convert into good? But why was this? Was He powerless to change the whole lump, so that no evil should remain in it, seeing that He is omnipotent? Lastly, why would He make anything at all of it, and not rather by the same omnipotency cause it not to be at all? Or could it indeed exist contrary to His will? Or if it were from eternity, why did He permit it so to be for infinite spaces of time in the past, and was pleased so long after to make something out of it? Or if He wished now all of a sudden to do something, this rather should the Omnipotent have accomplished, that this evil matter should not be at all, and that He only should be the whole, true, chief, and infinite Good. Or if it were not good that He, who was good, should not also be the framer and creator of what was good, then that matter which was evil being removed, and brought to nothing, He might form good matter, whereof He might create all things. For He would not be omnipotent were He not able to create something good without being assisted by that matter which had not been created by Himself. Such like things did I revolve in my miserable breast, overwhelmed with most gnawing cares lest I should die ere I discovered the truth; yet was the faith of Thy Christ, our Lord and Saviour, as held in the Catholic Church, fixed firmly in my heart, unformed, indeed, as yet upon many points, and diverging from doctrinal rules, but yet my mind did not utterly leave it, but every day rather drank in more and more of it.

Now also had I repudiated the lying divinations and impious absurdities of the astrologers. Let Thy mercies, out of the depth of my soul, confess unto thee for this also, O my God. For Thou, Thou altogether,—for who else is it that calls us back from the death of all errors, but that Life which knows not how to die, and the Wisdom which, requiring no light, enlightens the minds that do, whereby the universe is governed, even to the fluttering leaves of trees?—Thou providest also for my obstinacy wherewith I struggled with Vindicianus, an acute old man, and Nebridius, a young one of remarkable talent; the former vehemently declaring, and the latter frequently, though with a certain measure of doubt, saying, 'That no art existed by which to foresee future things, but that men's surmises had oftentimes the help of luck, and that of many things which they foretold some came to pass unawares to the predicters, who lighted on it by their oft speaking.' Thou, therefore, didst provide a friend for me, who was no negligent consulter of the astrologers, and yet not thoroughly skilled in those arts, but, as I said, a curious consulter with them; and yet knowing somewhat, which he said he had heard from his father, which, how far it would tend to overthrow the estimation of that art, he knew not. This man, then, by name Firminius, having received a liberal education, and being well versed in rhetoric, consulted me, as one very dear to him, as to what I thought on some affairs of his, wherein his worldly hopes had risen, viewed with regard to his so-called constellations; and I, who had now begun to lean in this particular towards Nebridius' opinion, did not indeed decline to speculate about the matter, and to tell him what came into my irresolute mind, but still added that I was now almost persuaded that these were but empty and ridiculous follies. Upon this he told me that his father had been very curious in such books, and that he had a friend who was as interested in them as he was himself, who, with combined study and consultation, fanned the flame of their affection for these toys, insomuch that they would observe the moment when the very dumb animals which bred in their houses brought forth, and then observed the position of the heavens with regard to them, so as to gather fresh proofs of this so-called art. He said, moreover, that his father had told him, that at the time his mother was about to give birth to him (Firminius), a female servant of that friend of his father's was also great with child, which could not be hidden from her master, who took care with most diligent exactness to know of the birth of his very dogs. And so it came to pass that (the one for his wife, and the other for his servant, with the most careful observation, calculating the days and hours, and the smaller divisions of the hours) both were delivered at the same moment, so that both were compelled to allow the very selfsame constellations, even to the minutest point, the one for his son, the other for his young slave. For as soon as the women began to be in travail, they each gave notice to the other of what was fallen out in their respective houses, and had messengers ready to despatch to one another so soon as they had information of the actual birth, of which they had easily provided, each in his own province, to give instant intelligence. Thus, then, he said, the messengers of the respective parties met one another in such equal distances from either house, that neither of them could discern any difference either in the position of the stars or other most minute points. And yet Firminius, born in a high estate in his parents' house, ran his course through the prosperous paths of this world, was increased in wealth, and elevated to honours; whereas that slave—the yoke of his condition being unrelaxed—continued to serve his masters, as Firminius, who knew him, informed me.

Upon hearing and believing these things, related by so reliable a person, all that resistance of mine melted away; and first I endeavoured to reclaim Firminius himself from that curiosity, by telling him that upon inspecting his constellations, I ought, were I to foretell truly, to have seen in them parents eminent among their neighbours, a noble family in its own city, good birth, becoming education, and liberal learning. But if that servant had consulted me upon the same constellations, since they were his also, I ought again to tell him, likewise truly, to see in them the meanness of his origin, the abjectness of his condition, and everything else altogether removed from and at variance with the former. Whence, then, looking upon the same constellations, I should, if I spoke the truth, speak diverse things, or if I spoke the same, speak falsely; thence assuredly was it to be gathered, that whatever, upon consideration of the constellations, was foretold truly, was not by art, but by chance; and whatever falsely, was not from the unskilfulness of the art, but the error of chance.

An opening being thus made, I ruminated within myself on such things, that no one of those dotards (who followed such occupations, and whom I longed to assail, and with derision to confute) might urge against me that Firminius had informed me falsely, or his father him: I turned my thoughts to those that are born twins, who generally come out of the womb so near one to another, that the small distance of time between them—how much force soever they may contend that it has in the nature of things—cannot be noted by human observation, or be expressed in those figures which the astrologer is to examine that he may pronounce the truth. Nor can they be true; for, looking into the same figures, he must have foretold the same of Esau and Jacob, whereas the same did not happen to them. He must therefore speak falsely; or if truly, then, looking into the same figures, he must not speak the same things. Not then by art, but by chance, would he speak truly. For Thou, O Lord, most righteous Ruler of the universe, the inquirers and inquired of knowing it not, workest by a hidden inspiration that the consulter should hear what, according to the hidden deservings of souls, he ought to hear, out of the depth of Thy righteous judgment, to whom let not man say, 'What is this?' or 'Why that?' Let him not say so, for he is man.

And now, O my Helper, hadst Thou freed me from those fetters; and I inquired, 'Whence is evil?' and found no result. But Thou sufferedst me not to be carried away from the faith by any fluctuations of thought, whereby I believed Thee both to exist, and Thy substance to be unchange-able, and that Thou hadst a care of and wouldest judge men; and that in Christ, Thy Son, our Lord, and the Holy Scriptures, which the authority of Thy Catholic Church pressed upon me, Thou hadst planned the way of man's salvation to that life which is to come after this death. These things being safe and immovably settled in my mind, I eagerly inquired, 'Whence is evil?' What torments did my travailing heart then endure! What sighs, O my God! Yet even there were Thine ears open, and I knew it not; and when in stillness I sought earnestly, those silent contritions of my soul were strong cries unto Thy mercy. No man knoweth, but only Thou, what I endured. For what was that which was thence through my tongue poured into the ears of my most familiar friends? Did the whole tumult of my soul, for which neither time nor speech was sufficient, reach them? Yet went the whole into Thine ears, all of which I bellowed out from the sighings of my heart; and my desire was before Thee, and the light of mine eyes was not with me; for that was within, I without. Nor was that in place, but my attention was directed to things contained in place; but there did I find no resting-place, nor did they receive me in such a way as that I could say, 'It is sufficient, it is well;' nor did they let me turn back, where it might be well enough with me. For to these things was I superior, but inferior to Thee; and Thou art my true joy when I am subjected to Thee, and Thou hadst subjected to me what Thou createdst beneath me. And this was the true temperature and middle region of my safety, to continue in Thine image, and by serving Thee to have dominion over the body. But when I lifted myself proudly against Thee, and 'ran against the Lord, even on His neck, with the thick bosses' of my buckler, even these inferior things were placed above me, and pressed upon me, and nowhere was there alleviation or breathing space. They encountered my sight on every side in crowds and troops, and in thought the images of bodies obtruded themselves as I was returning to Thee, as if they would say unto me, 'Whither goest thou, unworthy and base one?' And these things had sprung forth out of my wound; for thou humblest the proud like one that is wounded, and through

my own swelling was I separated from Thee; yea, my too much swollen
face closed up mine eyes.

'But Thou, O Lord, shalt endure for ever,' yet not for ever art Thou
angry with us, because Thou dost commiserate our dust and ashes; and it
was pleasing in Thy sight to reform my deformity, and by inward stings
didst Thou disturb me, that I should be dissatisfied until Thou wert made
sure to my inward sight. And by the secret hand of Thy remedy was my
swelling lessened, and the disordered and darkened eyesight of my mind,
by the sharp anointings of healthful sorrows, was from day to day made
whole.

And Thou, willing first to show me how Thou 'resistest the proud, but
givest grace unto the humble,' and by how great an act of mercy Thou
hadst pointed out to men the path of humility, in that Thy 'Word was
made flesh' and dwelt among men,—Thou procuredst for me, by the
instrumentality of one inflated with most monstrous pride, certain books
of the Platonists, translated from Greek into Latin.[33] And therein I read, not
indeed in the same words, but to the selfsame effect, enforced by many and
divers reasons, that, 'In the beginning was the Word, and the Word was
with God, and the Word was God. The same was in the beginning with
God. All things were made by Him; and without Him was not any thing
made that was made.' That which was made by Him is 'life; and the life
was the light of men. And the light shineth in darkness; and the darkness
comprehendeth it not.' And that the soul of man, though it 'bears witness
of the light,' yet itself 'is not that light; but the Word of God, being God,
is that true light that lighteth every man that cometh into the world.' And
that 'He was in the world, and the world was made by Him, and the world
knew Him not.' But that 'He came unto His own, and His own received
Him not. But as many as received Him, to them gave He power to become
the sons of God, even to them that believe on His name.' This I did not
read there.

In like manner, I read there that God the Word was born not of flesh,
nor of blood, nor of the will of man, nor of the will of the flesh, but of God.

But that 'the Word was made flesh, and dwelt among us,' I read not there. For I discovered in those books that it was in many and divers ways said, that the Son was in the form of the Father, and 'thought it not robbery to be equal with God,' for that naturally He was the same substance. But that He emptied Himself, 'and took upon Him the form of a servant, and was made in the likeness of men: and being found in fashion as a man, He humbled Himself, and became obedient unto death, even the death of the cross. Wherefore God also hath highly exalted Him' from the dead, 'and given Him a name above every name; that at the name of Jesus every knee should bow, of things in heaven, and things in earth, and things under the earth; and that every tongue should confess that Jesus Christ is Lord, to the glory of God the Father;' those books have not. For that before all time, and above all times, Thy only-begotten Son remaineth unchangeably co-eternal with Thee; and that of 'His fulness' souls receive, that they may be blessed; and that by participation of the wisdom remaining in them they are renewed, that they may be wise, is there. But that 'in due time Christ died for the ungodly,' and that Thou sparedst not Thine only Son, but deliveredst Him up for us all, is not there. 'Because Thou hast hid these things from the wise and prudent, and hast revealed them unto babes;' that they 'that labour and are heavy laden' might 'come' unto Him and He might refresh them, because He is 'meek and lowly in heart.' 'The meek will He guide in judgment; and the meek will He teach His way;' looking upon our humility and our distress, and forgiving all our sins. But such as are puffed up with the elation of would-be sublimer learning, do not hear Him saying, 'Learn of Me; for I am meek and lowly in heart: and ye shall find rest unto your souls.' 'Because that, when they knew God, they glorified Him not as God, neither were thankful; but became vain in their imaginations, and their foolish heart was darkened. Professing themselves to be wise, they became fools.'

And therefore also did I read there, that they had changed the glory of Thy incorruptible nature into idols and divers forms,—'into an image made like to corruptible man, and to birds, and four-footed beasts, and creeping things,' namely, into that Egyptian food for which Esau lost his birthright[34]; for that Thy first-born people worshipped the head of a four-footed beast instead of Thee, turning back in heart towards Egypt, and prostrating Thy image—their own soul—before the image 'of an ox that eateth grass.' These things found I there; but I fed not on them. For it pleased Thee, O Lord, to take away the reproach of diminution from Jacob, that the elder should serve the younger; and Thou hast called the Gentiles into Thine inheritance. And I had come unto Thee from among the Gentiles, and I strained after that gold which Thou willedst Thy people to take from Egypt, seeing that wheresoever it was it was Thine. And to the Athenians Thou saidst by Thy apostle, that in Thee 'we live, and move, and have our being;' as one of their own poets has said. And verily these books came from thence. But I set not my mind on the idols of Egypt, whom they ministered to with Thy gold, 'who changed the truth of God into a lie, and worshipped and served the creature more than the Creator.'

And being thence warned to return to myself, I entered into my inward self, Thou leading me on; and I was able to do it, for Thou wert become my helper. And I entered, and with the eye of my soul (such as it was) saw above the same eye of my soul, above my mind, the Unchangeable Light. Not this common light, which all flesh may look upon, nor, as it were, a greater one of the same kind, as though the brightness of this should be much more resplendent, and with its greatness fill up all things. Not like this was that light, but different, yea, very different from all these. Nor was it above my mind as oil is above water, nor as heaven above earth; but above it was, because it made me, and I below it, because I was made by it. He who knows the Truth knows that Light; and he that knows it knoweth Eternity. Love knoweth it. O Eternal Truth, and true Love, and loved Eternity! Thou art my God; to Thee do I sigh both night and day. When I first knew Thee, Thou liftedst me up, that I might see there was that which I might see, and that yet it was not I that did see. And Thou didst beat back the infirmity of my sight, pouring forth upon me most strongly Thy beams of light, and I trembled with love and fear; and I found myself to be far off from Thee, in the region of dissimilarity, as if I heard this voice of Thine from on high: 'I am the food of strong men; grow, and thou shalt feed upon me; nor shalt thou convert me, like the food of thy flesh, into thee, but thou shalt be converted into me.' And I learned that Thou for iniquity dost correct man, and Thou dost make my soul to consume away like a spider. And I said, 'Is Truth, therefore, nothing because it is neither diffused through space, finite, nor infinite?' And Thou criedst to me from afar, 'Yea, verily, "I AM THAT I AM." ' And I heard this, as things are heard in the heart, nor was there room for doubt; and I should more readily doubt that I live than that Truth is not, which is 'clearly seen, being understood by the things that are made.'

And I viewed the other things below Thee, and perceived that they neither altogether are, nor altogether are not. They are, indeed, because they are from Thee; but are not, because they are not what Thou art. For that truly is which remains immutably. It is good, then, for me to cleave unto God, for if I remain not in Him, neither shall I in myself; but He, remaining in Himself, reneweth all things. And Thou art the Lord my God, since Thou standest not in need of my goodness.

And it was made clear unto me that those things are good which yet are corrupted, which, neither were they supremely good, nor unless they were good, could be corrupted; because if supremely good, they were incorruptible, and if not good at all, there were nothing in them to be corrupted. For corruption harms, but, unless it could diminish goodness, it could not harm. Either, then, corruption harms not, which cannot be; or, what is most certain, all which is corrupted is deprived of good. But if they be deprived of all good, they will cease to be. For if they be, and cannot be at all corrupted, they will become better, because they shall remain incorruptibly. And what more monstrous than to assert that those things which have lost all their goodness are made better? Therefore, if they shall be deprived of all good, they shall no longer be. So long, therefore, as they are, they are good; therefore whatsoever is, is good. That evil, then, which I sought whence it was, is not any substance; for were it a substance, it would be good. For either it would be an incorruptible substance, and so a chief good, or a corruptible substance, which unless it were good it could not be corrupted. I perceived, therefore, and it was made clear to me, that Thou didst make all things good, nor is there any substance at all that was not made by Thee; and because all that Thou hast made are not equal, therefore all things are; because individually they are good, and altogether very good, because our God made all things very good.

And to Thee is there nothing at all evil, and not only to Thee, but to Thy whole creation; because there is nothing without which can break in, and mar that order which Thou hast appointed it. But in the parts thereof, some things, because they harmonize not with others, are considered evil; whereas those very things harmonize with others, and are good, and in themselves are good. And all these things which do not harmonize together harmonize with the inferior part which we call earth, having its own cloudy and windy sky concordant to it. Far be it from me, then, to say, 'These things should not be.' For should I see nothing but these, I should indeed desire better; but yet, if only for these, ought I to praise Thee; for that Thou art to be praised is shown from the 'earth, dragons, and all deeps; fire, and hail; snow, and vapours; stormy winds fulfilling Thy word; mountains, and all hills; fruitful trees, and all cedars; beasts, and all cattle; creeping things, and flying fowl; kings of the earth, and all people; princes, and all judges of the earth; both young men and maidens; old men and children,' praise Thy name. But when, 'from the heavens,' these praise Thee, praise Thee, our God, 'in the heights,' all Thy 'angels,' all Thy 'hosts,' 'sun and moon,' all ye stars and light, 'the heavens of heavens,' and the 'waters that be above the heavens,' praise Thy name. I did not now desire better things, because I was thinking of all; and with a better judgment I reflected that the things above were better than those below, but that all were better than those above alone.

There is no wholeness in them whom aught of Thy creation displeaseth; no more than there was in me, when many things which Thou madest displeased me. And, because my soul dared not be displeased at my God, it would not suffer aught to be Thine which displeased it. Hence it had gone into the opinion of two substances, and resisted not, but talked foolishly. And, returning thence, it had made to itself a god, through infinite measures of all space; and imagined it to be Thee, and placed it in its heart, and again had become the temple of its own idol, which was to Thee an abomination. But after Thou hadst fomented the head of me unconscious of it, and closed mine eyes lest they should 'behold vanity,' I ceased from myself a little, and my madness was lulled to sleep; and I awoke in Thee, and saw Thee to be infinite, though in another way; and this sight was not derived from the flesh.

And I looked back on other things, and I perceived that it was to Thee they owed their being, and that they were all bounded in Thee; but in another way, not as being in space, but because Thou holdest all things in Thine hand in truth: and all things are true so far as they have a being; nor is there any falsehood, unless that which is not is thought to be. And I saw that all things harmonized, not with their places only, but with their seasons also. And that Thou, who only art eternal, didst not begin to work after innumerable spaces of times; for that all spaces of times, both those which have passed and which shall pass, neither go nor come, save through Thee, working and abiding.

And I discerned and found it no marvel, that bread which is distasteful to an unhealthy palate is pleasant to a healthy one; and that the light, which is painful to sore eyes, is delightful to sound ones. And Thy righteousness displeaseth the wicked; much more the viper and little worm, which Thou hast created good, fitting in with inferior parts of Thy creation; with which the wicked themselves also fit in, the more in proportion as they are unlike Thee, but with the superior creatures in proportion as they become like to Thee. And I inquired what iniquity was, and ascertained it not to be a substance, but a perversion of the will, bent aside from Thee, O God, the Supreme Substance, towards these lower things, and casting out its bowels, and swelling outwardly.

And I marvelled that I now loved Thee, and no phantasm instead of

Thee. And yet I did not merit to enjoy my God, but was transported to Thee by Thy beauty, and presently torn away from Thee by mine own weight, sinking with grief into these inferior things. This weight was carnal custom. Yet was there a remembrance of Thee with me; nor did I any way doubt that there was one to whom I might cleave, but that I was not yet one who could cleave unto Thee; for that the body which is corrupted presseth down the soul, and the earthly dwelling weigheth down the mind which thinketh upon many things. And most certain I was that Thy 'invisible things from the creation of the world are clearly seen, being understood by the things that are made, even Thy eternal power and Godhead.' For, inquiring whence it was that I admired the beauty of bodies whether celestial or terrestrial, and what supported me in judging correctly on things mutable, and pronouncing, 'This should be thus, this not,'— inquiring, then, whence I so judged, seeing I did so judge, I had found the unchangeable and true eternity of Truth, above my changeable mind. And thus, by degrees, I passed from bodies to the soul, which makes use of the senses of the body to perceive; and thence to its inward faculty, to which the bodily senses represent outward things, and up to which reach the capabilities of beasts; and thence, again, I passed on to the reasoning faculty, unto which whatever is received from the senses of the body is referred to be judged, which also, finding itself to be variable in me, raised itself up to its own intelligence, and from habit drew away my thoughts, withdrawing itself from the crowds of contradictory phantasms; that so it might find out that light by which it was besprinkled, when, without all doubting, it cried out, 'that the unchangeable was to be preferred before the changeable;' whence also it knew that unchangeable, which, unless it had in some way known, it could have had no sure ground for preferring it to the changeable. And thus, with the flash of a trembling glance, it arrived at *that which is*. And then I saw Thy invisible things understood by the things that are made. But I was not able to fix my gaze thereon; and my infirmity being beaten back, I was thrown again on my accustomed habits, carrying along with me naught but a loving memory thereof, and an appetite for what I had, as it were, smelt the odour of, but was not yet able to eat.

And I sought a way of acquiring strength sufficient to enjoy Thee; but I found it not until I embraced that 'Mediator between God and man, the man Christ Jesus,' 'who is over all, God blessed for ever,' calling unto me, and saying, 'I am the way, the truth, and the life,' and mingling that food which I was unable to receive with our flesh. For 'the Word was made flesh,' that Thy wisdom, by which Thou createdst all things, might provide milk for our infancy. For I did not grasp my Lord Jesus,—I, though humbled, grasped not the humble One; nor did I know what lesson that infirmity of His would teach us. For Thy Word, the Eternal Truth, pre-eminent above the higher parts of Thy creation, raises up those that are subject unto Itself; but in this lower world built for Itself a humble habitation of our clay, whereby He intended to abase from themselves such as would be subjected and bring them over unto Himself, allaying their swelling, and fostering their love; to the end that they might go on no further in self-confidence, but rather should become weak, seeing before their feet the Divinity weak by taking our 'coats of skins;'[35] and wearied, might cast themselves down upon It, and It rising, might lift them up.

But I thought differently, thinking only of my Lord Christ as of a man of excellent wisdom, to whom no man could be equalled; especially for that, being wonderfully born of a virgin, He seemed, through the divine care for us, to have attained so great authority of leadership,—for an example of contemning temporal things for the obtaining of immortality. But what mystery there was in, 'The Word was made flesh,' I could not even imagine. Only I had learnt out of what is delivered to us in writing of Him, that He did eat, drink, sleep, walk, rejoice in spirit, was sad, and discoursed; that flesh alone did not cleave unto Thy Word, but with the human soul and body. All know thus who know the unchangeableness of Thy Word, which I now knew as well as I could, nor did I at all have any doubt about it. For, now to move the limbs of the body at will, now not; now to be stirred by some affection, now not; now by signs to enunciate wise sayings, now to keep silence, are properties of a soul and mind subject to change. And should these things be falsely written of Him, all the rest would risk the imputation, nor would there remain in those books any saving faith for the human race. Since, then, they were written truthfully, I acknowledged a perfect man to be in Christ—not the body of a man only, nor with the body a sensitive soul without a rational, but a very man; whom, not only as being a form of truth, but for a certain great excellency of human nature and a more perfect participation of wisdom, I decided was to be preferred before others. But Alypius imagined the Catholics to believe that God was so clothed with flesh, that, besides God and flesh, there was no soul in Christ, and did not think that a human mind was ascribed to Him. And, because he was thoroughly persuaded that the actions which were recorded of Him could not be performed except by a vital and rational creature, he moved the more slowly towards the Christian faith. But, learning afterwards that this was the error of the Apollinarian heretics, he rejoiced in the Catholic faith, and was conformed to it. But somewhat later it was, I confess, that I learned how in the sentence, 'The Word was made flesh,' the Catholic truth can be distinguished from the falsehood of Photinus.[36] For the disapproval of heretics makes the tenets of Thy Church and sound doctrine to stand out boldly. For there must be also heresies, that the approved may be made manifest among the weak.

But having then read those books of the Platonists, and being admonished by them to search for incorporeal truth, I saw Thy invisible things, understood by those things that are made; and though repulsed, I perceived what that was, which through the darkness of my mind I was not allowed to contemplate,—assured that Thou wert, and wert infinite, and yet not diffused in space finite or infinite; and that Thou truly art, who art the same ever, varying neither in part nor motion; and that all other things are from Thee, on this most sure ground alone, that they are. Of these things was I indeed assured, yet too weak to enjoy Thee. I chattered as one well skilled; but had I not sought Thy way in Christ our Saviour, I would have proved not skilful, but ready to perish. For now, filled with my punishment, I had begun to desire to seem wise; yet mourned I not, but rather was puffed up with knowledge. For where was that charity building upon the 'foundation' of humility, 'which is Jesus Christ'? Or, when would these books teach me it? Upon these, therefore, I believe, it was Thy pleasure that I should fall before I studied Thy Scriptures, that it might be impressed on my memory how I was affected by them; and that afterwards when I was subdued by Thy books, and when my wounds were touched by Thy healing fingers, I might discern and distinguish what a difference there is between presumption and confession,—between those who saw whither they were to go, yet saw not the way, and the way which leadeth not only to behold but to inhabit the blessed country. For had I first been moulded in Thy Holy Scriptures, and hadst Thou, in the familiar use of them, grown sweet unto me, and had I afterwards fallen upon those volumes, they might perhaps have withdrawn me from the solid ground of piety; or, had I stood firm in that wholesome disposition which I had thence imbibed, I might have thought that it could have been attained by the study of those books alone.

Most eagerly, then, did I seize that venerable writing of Thy Spirit, but more especially the Apostle Paul; and those difficulties vanished away, in which he at one time appeared to me to contradict himself, and the text of his discourse not to agree with the testimonies of the Law and the Prophets. And the face of that pure speech appeared to me one and the same; and I learned to 'rejoice with trembling.' So I commenced, and found that whatsoever truth I had there read was declared here with the recommendation of Thy grace; that he who sees may not so glory as if he had not received not only that which he sees, but also that he can see (for what hath he which he hath not received?); and that he may not only be admonished to see Thee, who art ever the same, but also may be healed, to hold Thee; and that he who from afar off is not able to see, may still walk on the way by which he may reach, behold, and possess Thee. For though a man 'delight in the law of God after the inward man,' what shall he do with that other law in his members which warreth against the law of his mind, and bringeth him into captivity to the law of sin, which is in his

memories? For thou art righteous, O Lord, but we have sinned and committed iniquity, and have done wickedly, and Thy hand is grown heavy upon us, and we are justly delivered over unto that ancient sinner, the governor of death; for he induced our will to be like his will, whereby he remained not in Thy truth. What shall 'wretched man' do? 'Who shall deliver him from the body of this death,' but Thy grace only, 'through Jesus Christ our Lord,' whom Thou hast begotten co-eternal, and createdst in the beginning of Thy ways, in whom the Prince of this world found nothing worthy of death, yet killed he Him, and the handwriting which was contrary to us was blotted out? This those writings contain not. Those pages contain not the expression of this piety,—the tears of confession, Thy sacrifice, a troubled spirit, 'a broken and a contrite heart,' the salvation of the people, the espoused city, the earnest of the Holy Ghost, the cup of our redemption. No man sings there, Shall not my soul be subject unto God? For of Him cometh my salvation, for He is my God and my salvation, my defender, I shall not be further moved. No one there hears Him calling, 'Come unto me all ye that labour.' They scorn to learn of Him, because He is meek and lowly of heart; for 'Thou hast hid those things from the wise and prudent, and hast revealed them unto babes.' For it is one thing, from the mountain's wooded summit to see the land of peace, and not to find the way thither,—in vain to attempt impassable ways, opposed and waylaid by fugitives and deserters, under their captain the 'lion' and the 'dragon;' and another to keep to the way that leads thither, guarded by the host of the heavenly general, where they rob not who have deserted the heavenly army, which they shun as torture. These things did in a wonderful manner sink into my bowels, when I read that 'least of Thy apostles,'[37] and had reflected upon Thy works, and feared greatly.

# BOOK VIII

*He finally describes the thirty-second year of his age, the most memorable of his whole life, in which, being instructed by Simplicianus concerning the conversion of others, and the manner of acting, he is, after a severe struggle, renewed in his whole mind, and is converted unto God.*

O MY GOD, let me with gratitude remember and confess unto Thee Thy mercies bestowed upon me. Let my bones be steeped in Thy love, and let them say, Who is like unto Thee, O Lord? 'Thou hast loosed my bonds, I will offer unto Thee the sacrifice of thanksgiving.' And how Thou hast loosed them I will declare; and all who worship Thee when they hear these things shall say: 'Blessed be the Lord in heaven and earth, great and wonderful is His name.' Thy words had stuck fast into my breast, and I was hedged round about by Thee on every side. Of Thy eternal life I was now certain, although I had seen it 'through a glass darkly.' Yet I no longer doubted that there was an incorruptible substance, from which was derived all other substance; nor did I now desire to be more certain of Thee, but more stedfast in Thee. As for my temporal life, all things were uncertain, and my heart had to be purged from the old leaven. The 'Way,' the Saviour Himself, was pleasant unto me but as yet I disliked to pass through its straitness. And Thou didst put into my mind, and it seemed good in my eyes, to go unto Simplicianus,[38] who appeared to me a faithful servant of Thine, and Thy grace shone in him. I had also heard that from his very youth he had lived most devoted to Thee. Now he had grown into years, and by reason of so great age, passed in such zealous following of Thy ways, he appeared to me likely to have gained much experience; and so in truth he had. Out of which

122

experience I desired him to tell me (setting before him my griefs) which would be the most fitting way for one afflicted as I was to walk in Thy way.

For the Church I saw to be full, and one went this way, and another that. But it was displeasing to me that I led a secular life; yea, now that my passions had ceased to excite me as of old with hopes of honour and wealth, a very grievous burden it was to undergo so great a servitude. For, compared with Thy sweetness, and the beauty of Thy house, which I loved, those things delighted me no longer. But still very tenaciously was I held by the love of women; nor did the apostle forbid me to marry, although he exhorted me to something better, especially wishing that all men were as he himself was. But I, being weak, made choice of the more agreeable place, and because of this alone was tossed up and down in all beside, faint and languishing with withering cares, because in other matters I was compelled, though unwilling, to agree to a married life, to which I was given up and enthralled. I had heard from the mouth of truth that 'there be eunuchs, which have made themselves eunuchs for the kingdom of heaven's sake;' but, said He, 'he that is able to receive it, let him receive it.' Vain, assuredly, are all men in whom the knowledge of God is not, and who could not, out of the good things which are seen, find out Him who is good. But I was no longer in that vanity; I had surmounted it, and by the united testimony of Thy whole creation had found Thee, our Creator, and Thy Word, God with Thee, and together with Thee and the Holy Ghost one God, by whom Thou createdst all things. There is yet another kind of impious men, who 'when they knew God, they glorified Him not as God, neither were thankful.' Into this also had I fallen; but Thy right hand held me up, and bore me away, and Thou placedst me where I might recover. For Thou hast said unto man, 'Behold, the fear of the Lord, that is wisdom;' and desire not to seem wise, because, 'Professing themselves to be wise, they became fools.' But I had now found the goodly pearl, which, selling all that I had, I ought to have bought; and I hesitated.

To Simplicianus then I went,—the father of Ambrose (at that time a bishop) in receiving Thy grace, and whom he truly loved as a father. To him I narrated the windings of my error. But when I mentioned to him that I had read certain books of the Platonists, which Victorinus, sometime Professor of Rhetoric at Rome (who died a Christian, as I had been told), had translated into Latin, he congratulated me that I had not fallen upon the writings of other philosophers, which were full of fallacies and deceit, 'after the rudiments of the world,' whereas they, in many ways, led to the belief in God and His word. Then, to exhort me to the humility of Christ, hidden from the wise, and revealed to little ones, he spoke of Victorinus himself, whom, whilst he was at Rome, he had known very intimately; and of him he related that about which I will not be silent. For it contains great praise of Thy grace, which ought to be confessed unto Thee, how that most learned old man, highly skilled in all the liberal sciences, who had read, criticized, and explained so many works of the philosophers; the teacher of so many noble senators; who also, as a mark of his excellent discharge of his duties, had (which men of this world esteem a great honour) both merited and obtained a statue in the Roman Forum, he,—even to that age a worshipper of idols, and a participator in the sacrilegious rites to which almost all the nobility of Rome were wedded, and had inspired the people with the love of

> The dog Anubis, and a medley crew
> Of monster gods [who] 'gainst Neptune stand in arms,
> 'Gainst Venus and Minerva, steel-clad Mars,*

whom Rome once conquered, now worshipped, all which old Victorinus had with thundering eloquence defended so many years,—he now blushed not to be the child of Thy Christ, and an infant at Thy fountain, submitting his neck to the yoke of humility, and subduing his forehead to the reproach of the Cross.

O Lord, Lord, who hast bowed the heavens and come down, touched the mountains and they did smoke, by what means didst Thou convey Thyself into that bosom? He used to read, as Simplicianus said, the Holy Scripture, most studiously sought after and searched into all the Christian

* *Æneid*, viii. 736–8

writings, and said to Simplicianus,—not openly, but secretly, and as a friend,—'Know thou that I am a Christian.' To which he replied, 'I will not believe it, nor will I rank you among the Christians unless I see you in the Church of Christ.' Whereupon he replied derisively, 'Is it then the walls that make Christians?' And this he often said, that he already was a Christian; and Simplicianus making the same answer, the conceit of the 'walls' was by the other as often renewed. For he was fearful of offending his friends, proud demon-worshippers, from the height of whose Babylonian dignity, as from cedars of Lebanon which had not yet been broken by the Lord, he thought a storm of enmity would descend upon him. But after that, from reading and inquiry, he had derived strength, and feared lest he should be denied by Christ before the holy angels if he now was afraid to confess Him before men, and appeared to himself guilty of a great fault in being ashamed of the sacraments of the humility of Thy word, and not being ashamed of the sacrilegious rites of those proud demons, whose pride he had imitated and their rites adopted, he became bold-faced against vanity, and shame-faced toward the truth, and suddenly and unexpectedly said to Simplicianus,— as he himself informed me,—'Let us go to the church; I wish to be made a Christian.' But he, not containing himself for joy, accompanied him. And having been admitted to the first sacraments of instruction,[39] he not long after gave in his name, that he might be regenerated by baptism,—Rome marvelling, and the Church rejoicing. The proud saw, and were enraged; they gnashed with their teeth, and melted away! But the Lord God was the hope of Thy servant, and He regarded not vanities and lying madness.

Finally, when the hour arrived for him to make profession of his faith (which at Rome they who are about to approach Thy grace are wont to deliver from an elevated place, in view of the faithful people, in a set form of words[40] learnt by heart), the presbyters, he said, offered Victorinus to make his profession more privately, as the custom was to do to those who were likely, through bashfulness, to be afraid; but he chose rather to profess his salvation in the presence of the holy assembly. For it was not salvation that he taught in rhetoric, and yet he had publicly professed that.

How much less, therefore, ought he, when pronouncing Thy word, to dread Thy meek flock, who, in the delivery of his own words, had not feared the mad multitudes! So, then, when he ascended to make his profession, all, as they recognized him, whispered his name one to the other, with a voice of congratulation. And who was there amongst them that did not know him? And there ran a low murmur through the mouths of all the rejoicing multitude, 'Victorinus! Victorinus!' Sudden was the burst of exultation at the sight of him; and suddenly were they hushed, that they might hear him. He pronounced the true faith with an excellent boldness, and all desired to take him to their very heart—yea, by their love and joy they took him thither; such were the hands with which they took him.

Good God, what passed in man to make him rejoice more at the salvation of a soul despaired of, and delivered from greater danger, than if there had always been hope of him, or the danger had been less? For so Thou also, O merciful Father, dost 'joy over one sinner that repenteth, more than over ninety and nine just persons that need no repentance.' And with much joyfulness do we hear, whenever we hear, how the lost sheep is brought home again on the Shepherd's shoulders, while the angels rejoice, and the drachma is restored to Thy treasury, the neighbours rejoicing with the woman who found it; and the joy of the solemn service of Thy house constraineth to tears, when in Thy house it is read of Thy younger son that he 'was dead, and is alive again, and was lost, and is found.' For Thou rejoicest both in us and in Thy angels, holy through holy charity. For thou art ever the same; for all things which abide neither the same nor for ever, Thou ever knowest after the same manner.

What, then, passes in the soul when it more delights at finding or having restored to it the things it loves than if it had always possessed them? Yea, and other things bear witness hereunto; and all things are full of witnesses, crying out, 'So it is.' The victorious commander triumpheth; yet he would not have conquered had he not fought, and the greater the peril of the battle, the more the rejoicing of the triumph. The storm tosses the voyagers, threatens shipwreck, and every one waxes pale at the approach of death;

but sky and sea grow calm, and they rejoice much, as they feared much. A loved one is sick, and his pulse indicates danger; all who desire his safety are at once sick at heart: he recovers, though not able as yet to walk with his former strength, and there is such joy as was not before when he walked sound and strong. Yea, the very pleasures of human life—not those only which rush upon us unexpectedly, and against our wills, but those that are voluntary and designed—do men obtain by difficulties. There is no pleasure at all in eating and drinking unless the pains of hunger and thirst go before. And drunkards eat certain salt meats with the view of creating a troublesome heat, which the drink allaying causes pleasure. It is also the custom that the affianced bride should not immediately be given up, that the husband may not less esteem her whom, as betrothed, he longed not for.

This law obtains in base and accursed joy; in that joy also which is permitted and lawful; in the sincerity of honest friendship; and in Him who was dead, and lived again, had been lost and was found. The greater joy is everywhere preceded by the greater pain. What meaneth this, O Lord my God, when Thou art an everlasting joy unto Thine own self, and some things about Thee are ever rejoicing in Thee? What meaneth this, that this portion of things thus ebbs and flows, alternately offended and reconciled? Is this the fashion of them, and is this all Thou hast allotted to them, whereas, from the highest heaven to the lowest earth, from the beginning of the world to its end, from the angel to the worm, from the first movement unto the last, Thou settedst each in its right place, and appointedst each its proper seasons, everything good after its kind? Woe is me! How high art Thou in the highest, and how deep in the deepest! Thou withdrawest no whither, and scarcely do we *return* to Thee.

Haste, Lord, and act; stir us up, and call us back; inflame us, and draw us to Thee; stir us up, and grow sweet unto us; let us now love Thee, let us 'run after Thee.' Do not many men, out of a deeper hell of blindness than that of Victorinus, return unto Thee, and approach, and are enlightened, receiving that light, which they that receive, receive power from Thee to become Thy sons? But if they be less known among the people, even they that know them joy less for them. For when many rejoice together, the joy of each one is the fuller, in that they are incited and inflamed by one another. Again, because those that are known to many influence many towards salvation, and take the lead with many to follow them. And, therefore, do they also who preceded them much rejoice in regard to them, because they rejoice not in them alone. May it be averted that in Thy tabernacle the persons of the rich should be accepted before the poor, or the noble before the ignoble; since rather 'Thou hast chosen the weak things of the world to confound the things which are mighty; and base things of the world, and things which are despised, hast Thou chosen, yea, and things which are not, to bring to naught things that are.' And yet, even that 'least of the apostles,' by whose tongue Thou soundest out these words, when Paulus the proconsul—his pride overcome by the apostle's welfare—was made to pass under the easy yoke of Thy Christ, and became a provincial of the great King,—he also, instead of Saul, his former name, desired to be called Paul, in testimony of so great a victory. For the enemy is more overcome in one of whom he hath more hold, and by whom he hath hold of more. But the proud hath he more hold of by reason of their nobility; and by them of more, by reason of their authority. By how much the more welcome, then, was the heart of Victorinus esteemed, which the devil had held as an unassailable retreat, and the tongue of Victorinus, with which mighty and cutting weapon he had slain many; so much the more abundantly should Thy sons rejoice, seeing that our King hath bound the strong man, and they saw his vessels taken from him and cleansed, and made meet for Thy honour, and become serviceable for the Lord unto every good work.

But when that man of Thine, Simplicianus, related this to me about Victorinus, I burned to imitate him; and it was for this end he had related it. But when he had added this also, that in the time of the Emperor Julian, there was a law made by which Christians were forbidden to teach grammar and oratory, and he, in obedience to this law, chose rather to abandon the wordy school than Thy word, by which Thou makest eloquent the tongues

of the dumb,—he appeared to me not more brave than happy, in having thus discovered an opportunity of waiting on Thee only, which thing I was sighing for, thus bound, not with the irons of another, but my own iron will. My will was the enemy master of, and thence had made a chain for me and bound me. Because of a perverse will was lust made; and lust indulged in became custom; and custom not resisted became necessity. By which links, as it were, joined together (whence I term it a 'chain'), did a hard bondage hold me enthralled. But that new will which had begun to develope in me, freely to worship Thee, and to wish to enjoy Thee, O God, the only sure enjoyment, was not able as yet to overcome my former wilfulness, made strong by long indulgence. Thus did my two wills, one old and the other new, one carnal, the other spiritual, contend within me; and by their discord they unstrung my soul.

Thus came I to understand, from my own experience, what I had read, how that 'the flesh lusteth against the Spirit, and the Spirit against the flesh.' I verily lusted both ways; yet more in that which I approved in myself, than in that which I disapproved in myself. For in this last it was now rather not 'I,' because in much I rather suffered against my will than did it willingly. And yet it was through me that custom became more combative against me, because I had come willingly whither I willed not. And who, then, can with any justice speak against it, when just punishment follows the sinner? Nor had I now any longer my wonted excuse, that as yet I hesitated to be above the world and serve Thee, because my perception of the truth was uncertain; for now it was certain. But I, still bound to the earth, refused to be Thy soldier; and was as much afraid of being freed from all embarrassments, as we ought to fear to be embarrassed.

Thus with the baggage of the world was I sweetly burdened, as when in slumber; and the thoughts wherein I meditated upon Thee were like unto the efforts of those desiring to awake, who, still overpowered with a heavy drowsiness, are again steeped therein. And as no one desires to sleep always, and in the sober judgment of all waking is better, yet does a man generally defer to shake off drowsiness, when there is a heavy lethargy in all his limbs, and, though displeased, yet even after it is time to rise with pleasure yields to it, so was I assured that it were much better for me to give up myself to Thy charity, than to yield myself to my own cupidity; but the former course satisfied and vanquished me, the latter pleased me and fettered me. Nor had I aught to answer Thee calling to me, 'Awake, thou that sleepest, and arise from the dead, and Christ shall give thee light.' And to Thee showing me on every side, that what Thou saidst was true, I, convicted by the truth, had nothing at all to reply, but the drawling and drowsy words: 'Presently, lo, presently;' 'leave me a little while.' But 'presently, presently,' had no present; and my 'leave me a little while' went on for a long while. In vain did I 'delight in Thy law after the inner man,' when 'another law in my members warred against the law of my mind, and brought me into captivity to the law of sin which is in my members.' For the law of sin is the violence of custom, whereby the mind is drawn and held, even against its will; deserving to be so held in that it so willingly falls into it. 'O wretched man that I am! who shall deliver me from the body of this death' but Thy grace only, through Jesus Christ our Lord?

And how, then, Thou didst deliver me out of the bonds of carnal desire, wherewith I was most firmly fettered, and out of the drudgery of worldly business, will I now declare and confess unto Thy name, 'O Lord, my strength and my Redeemer.' Amid increasing anxiety, I was transacting my usual affairs, and daily sighing unto Thee. I resorted as frequently to Thy church as the business, under the burden of which I groaned, left me free to do. Alypius was with me, being after the third sitting disengaged from his legal occupation, and awaiting further opportunity of selling his counsel, as I was wont to sell the power of speaking, if it can be supplied by teaching. But Nebridius had, on account of our friendship, consented to teach under Verecundus, a citizen and a grammarian of Milan, and a very intimate friend of us all; who vehemently desired, and by the right of friendship demanded from our company, the faithful aid he greatly stood in need of. Nebridius, then, was not drawn to this by any desire of gain (for he could have made much more of his learning had he been so inclined), but, as a most sweet and kindly friend, he would not be wanting in an office of friendliness, and slight our request. But in this he acted very discreetly, taking care not to become known to those personages whom the world esteems great; thus avoiding distraction of mind, which he desired to have free and at leisure as many hours as possible, to search, or read, or hear something concerning wisdom.

Upon a certain day, then, Nebridius being away (why, I do not remember), lo, there came to the house to see Alypius and me, Pontitianus, a countryman of ours, in so far as he was an African, who held high office in the emperor's court. What he wanted with us I know not, but we sat down to talk together, and it fell out that upon a table before us, used for games, he noticed a book; he took it up, opened it, and, contrary to his expectation, found it to be the Apostle Paul,—for he imagined it to be one of those books which I was wearing myself out in teaching. At this he looked up at me smilingly, and expressed his delight and wonder that he had so unexpectedly found this book, and this only, before my eyes. For he was both a Christian and baptized, and often prostrated himself before Thee our God in the church, in constant and daily prayers. When, then, I had told him that I bestowed much pains upon these writings, a conversation ensued on his speaking of Antony,[41] the Egyptian monk, whose name was in high repute among Thy servants, though up to that time not familiar to us. When he came to know this, he lingered on that topic, imparting to us a knowledge of this man so eminent, and marvelling at our ignorance. But we were amazed, hearing Thy wonderful works most fully manifested in times so recent, and almost in our own, wrought in the true faith and the Catholic Church. We all wondered—we, that they were so great, and he, that we had never heard of them.

From this his conversation turned to the companies in the monasteries, and their manners so fragrant unto Thee, and of the fruitful deserts of the wilderness, of which we knew nothing. And there was a monastery at Milan full of good brethren, without the walls of the city, under the fostering care of Ambrose, and we were ignorant of it. He went on with his relation, and we listened intently and in silence. He then related to us how on a certain afternoon, at Triers, when the emperor was taken up with seeing the Circensian games, he and three others, his comrades, went out for a walk in the gardens close to the city walls, and there, as they chanced to walk two and two, one strolled away with him, while the other two went by themselves; and these, in their rambling, came upon a certain cottage inhabited by some of Thy servants, 'poor in spirit,' of whom 'is the kingdom of heaven,' where they found a book in which was written the life of Antony. This one of them began to read, marvel at, and be inflamed by it; and in the reading, to meditate on embracing such a life, and giving up his worldly employments to serve Thee. And these were of the body called 'Agents for Public Affairs.'[42] Then, suddenly being overwhelmed with a holy love and a sober sense of shame, in anger with himself, he cast his eyes upon his friend, exclaiming, 'Tell me, I entreat thee, what end we are striving for by all these labours of ours. What is our aim? What is our motive in doing service? Can our hopes in court rise higher than to be ministers of the emperor? And in such a position, what is there not brittle, and fraught with danger, and by how many dangers arrive we at greater danger? And when arrive we thither? But if I desire to become a friend of God, behold, I am even now made it.' Thus spake he, and in the pangs of the travail of the new life, he turned his eyes again upon the page and continued reading, and was inwardly changed where Thou sawest, and his mind was divested of the world, as soon became evident; for as he read, and the surging of his heart rolled along, he raged awhile, discerned and resolved on a better course, and now, having become Thine, he said to his friend, 'Now have I broken loose from those hopes of ours, and am determined to serve God; and this, from this hour, in this place, I enter upon. If thou art reluctant to imitate me, hinder me not.' The other replied that he would cleave to him, to share in so great a reward and so great a service. Thus both of them, being now Thine, were building a tower at the necessary cost,— of forsaking all that they had and following Thee. Then Pontitianus, and he that had walked with him through the other parts of the garden, came in search of them to the same place, and having found them, reminded them to return as the day had declined. But they, making known to him their resolution and purpose, and how such a resolve had sprung up and become confirmed in them, entreated them not to molest them, if they refused to join themselves unto them. But the others, no whit changed from their former selves, did yet (as he said) bewail themselves, and piously congratulated them, recommending themselves to their prayers; and with their hearts inclining towards earthly things, returned to the palace. But the other two, setting their affections upon heavenly things, remained in the cottage. And both of them had affianced brides, who, when they heard of this, dedicated also their virginity unto God.

Such was the story of Pontitianus. But Thou, O Lord, whilst he was speaking, didst turn me towards myself, taking me from behind my back, where I had placed myself while unwilling to exercise self-scrutiny; and Thou didst set me face to face with myself, that I might behold how foul I was, and how crooked and sordid, bespotted and ulcerous. And I beheld and loathed myself; and whither to fly from myself I discovered not. And if I sought to turn my gaze away from myself, he continued his narrative, and Thou again opposedst me unto myself and thrustedst me before my own eyes, that I might discover my iniquity, and hate it. I had known it, but acted as though I knew it not,—winked at it, and forgot it.

But now, the more ardently I loved those whose healthful affections I heard tell of, that they had given up themselves wholly to Thee to be cured, the more did I abhor myself when compared with them. For many of my years (perhaps twelve) had passed away since my nineteenth, when, on the reading of Cicero's *Hortensius*, I was roused to a desire for wisdom; and still I was delaying to reject mere worldly happiness, and to devote myself to search out that whereof not the finding alone, but the bare search, ought to have been preferred before the treasures and kingdoms of this world, though already found, and before the pleasures of the body, though encompassing me at my will. But I, miserable young man, supremely miserable even in the very outset of my youth, had entreated chastity of

Thee, and said, 'Grant me chastity and continency, but not yet.' For I was afraid lest Thou shouldest hear me soon, and soon deliver me from the disease of concupiscence, which I desired to have satisfied rather than extinguished. And I had wandered through perverse ways in a sacrilegious superstition; not indeed assured thereof, but preferring that to the others, which I did not seek religiously, but opposed maliciously.

And I had thought that I delayed from day to day to reject worldly hopes and follow Thee only, because there did not appear anything certain whereunto to direct my course. And now had the day arrived in which I was to be laid bare to myself, and my conscience was to chide me. 'Where art thou, O my tongue? Thou saidst, verily, that for an uncertain truth thou wert not willing to cast off the baggage of vanity. Behold, now it is certain, and yet doth that burden still oppress thee; whereas they who neither have so worn themselves out with searching after it, nor yet have spent ten years and more in thinking thereon, have had their shoulders unburdened, and gotten wings to fly away.' Thus was I inwardly consumed and mightily confounded with an horrible shame, while Pontitianus was relating these things. And he, having finished his story, and the business he came for, went his way. And unto myself, what said I not within myself? With what scourges of rebuke lashed I not my soul to make it follow me, struggling to go after Thee! Yet it drew back; it refused, and exercised not itself. All its arguments were exhausted and confuted. There remained a silent trembling; and it feared, as it would death, to be restrained from the flow of that custom whereby it was wasting away even to death.

In the midst, then, of this great strife of my inner dwelling, which I had strongly raised up against my soul in the chamber of my heart, troubled both in mind and countenance, I seized upon Alypius, and exclaimed: 'What is wrong with us? What is this? What heardest thou? The unlearned start up and "take" heaven, and we, with our learning, but wanting heart, see where we wallow in flesh and blood! Because others have preceded us, are we ashamed to follow, and not rather ashamed at not following?' Some such words I gave utterance to, and in my excitement flung myself from him, while he gazed upon me in silent astonishment. For I spoke not in my wonted tone, and my brow, cheeks, eyes, colour, tone of voice, all expressed my emotion more than the words. There was a little garden belonging to our lodging, of which we had the use, as of the whole house; for the master, our landlord, did not live there. Thither had the tempest within my breast hurried me, where no one might impede the fiery struggle in which I was engaged with myself, until it came to the issue that Thou knewest, though I did not. But I was mad that I might be whole, and dying that I might have life, knowing what evil thing I was, but not knowing what good thing I was shortly to become. Into the garden, then, I retired, Alypius following my steps. For his presence was no bar to my solitude; or how could he desert me so troubled? We sat down at as great a distance from the house as we could. I was disquieted in spirit, being most impatient with myself that I entered not into Thy will and covenant, O my God, which all my bones cried out unto me to enter, extolling it to the skies. And we enter not therein by ships, or chariots, or feet, no, nor by going so far as I had come from the house to that place where we were sitting. For not to go only, but to enter there, was naught else but to will to go, but to will it resolutely and thoroughly; not to stagger and sway about this way and that, a changeable and half-wounded will, wrestling, with one part falling as another rose.

Finally, in the very fever of my irresolution, I made many of those motions with my body which men sometimes desire to do, but cannot, if either they have not the limbs, or if their limbs be bound with fetters, weakened by disease, or hindered in any other way. Thus, if I tore my hair, struck my forehead, or if, entwining my fingers, I clasped my knee, this I did because I willed it. But I might have willed and not done it, if the power of motion in my limbs had not responded. So many things, then, I did, when to have the will was not to have the power, and I did not that which both with an unequalled desire I longed more to do, and which shortly when I should will I should have the power to do; because shortly when I should will, I should will thoroughly. For in such things the power was one with the will, and to will was to do, and yet was it not done; and more readily did the body obey the slightest wish of the soul in the moving its limbs at the order of the mind, than the soul obeyed itself to accomplish in the will alone this its great will.

Whence is this monstrous thing? And why is it? Let Thy mercy shine on me, that I may inquire, if so be the hiding-places of man's punishment, and the darkest contritions of the sons of Adam, may perhaps answer me. Whence is this monstrous thing? and why is it? The mind commands the body, and it obeys forthwith; the mind commands itself, and is resisted.[43] The mind commands the hand to be moved, and such readiness is there that the command is scarce to be distinguished from the obedience. Yet the mind is mind, and the hand is body. The mind commands the mind to will, and yet, though it be itself, it obeyeth not. Whence this monstrous thing? and why is it? I repeat, it commands itself to will, and would not give the command unless it willed; yet is not that done which it commandeth. But it willeth not entirely; therefore it commandeth not entirely. For so far forth it commandeth, as it willeth; and so far forth is the thing commanded not done, as it willeth not. For the will commandeth that there be a will;—not another, but itself. But it doth not command entirely, therefore that is not which it commandeth. For were it entire, it would not even command it to be, because it would already be. It is, therefore, no monstrous thing partly to will, partly to be unwilling, but an infirmity of the mind, that it doth not wholly rise, sustained by truth, pressed down by custom. And so there are two wills, because one of them is not entire; and the one is supplied with what the other needs.

Let them perish from Thy presence, O God, as 'vain talkers and deceivers' of the soul do perish, who, observing that there were two wills in deliberating, affirm that there are two kinds of minds in us,—one good, the other evil. They themselves verily are evil when they hold these evil opinions; and they shall become good when they hold the truth, and shall consent unto the truth, that Thy apostle may say unto them, 'Ye were sometimes darkness, but now are ye light in the Lord.' But they, desiring to be light,

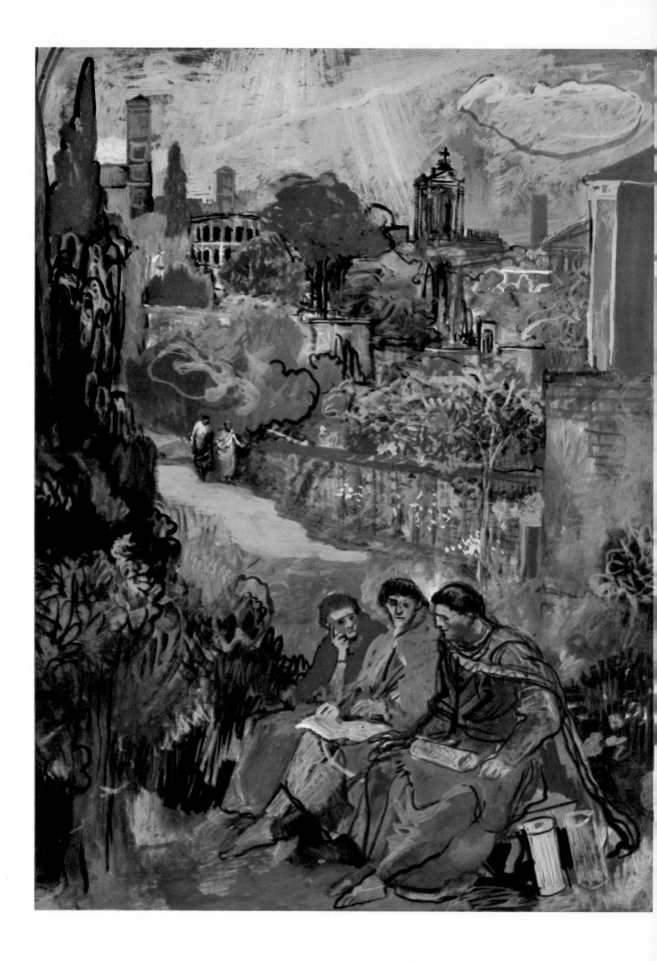

not 'in the Lord,' but in themselves, conceiving the nature of the soul to be the same as that which God is, are made more gross darkness; for that through a shocking arrogancy they went farther from Thee, 'the true Light, which lighteth every man that cometh into the world.' Take heed what you say, and blush for shame; draw near unto Him and be 'lightened,' and your faces shall not be 'ashamed.' I, when I was deliberating upon serving the Lord my God now, as I had long purposed,—I it was who willed, I who was unwilling. It was I, even I myself. I neither willed entirely nor was entirely unwilling. Therefore was I at war with myself, and destroyed by myself. And this destruction overtook me against my will, and yet showed not the presence of another mind, but the punishment of mine own. 'Now, then, it is no more I that do it, but sin that dwelleth in me,'—the punishment of a more unconfined sin, in that I was a son of Adam.

For if there be as many contrary natures as there are conflicting wills, there will not now be two natures only, but many. If any one deliberate whether he should go to their conventicle, or to the theatre, these Manichæans at once cry out, 'Behold, here are two natures,—one good, drawing this way, another bad, drawing back that way; for whence else is this indecision between conflicting wills?' But I reply that both are bad—that which draws to them, and that which draws back to the theatre. But they believe not that will to be other than good which draws to them. Supposing, then, one of us should deliberate, and through the conflict of his two wills should waver whether he should go to the theatre or to our church, would not these also waver what to answer? For either they must confess, which they are not willing to do, that the will which leads to our church is good, as well as that of those who have received and are held by the mysteries of theirs, or they must imagine that there are two evil natures and two evil minds in one man, at war one with the other; and that will not be true which they say, that there is one good and another bad; or they must be converted to the truth, and no longer deny that where any one deliberates, there is one soul fluctuating between conflicting wills.

Let them no more say, then, when they perceive two wills to be antagonistic to each other in the same man, that the contest is between two opposing minds, of two opposing substances, from two opposing principles, the one good and the other bad. For Thou, O true God, dost disprove, check, and convince them; likeas when both wills are bad, one deliberates whether he should kill a man by poison, or by the sword; whether he should take possession of this or that estate of another's, when he cannot both; whether he should purchase pleasure by prodigality, or retain his money by covetousness; whether he should go to the circus or the theatre, if both are open on the same day; or, thirdly, whether he should rob another man's house, if he have the opportunity; or, fourthly, whether he should commit adultery, if at the same time he have the means of doing so,—all these things concurring in the same point of time, and all being equally longed for, although impossible to be enacted at one time. For they rend the mind amid four, or even (among the vast variety of things men desire) more antagonistic wills, nor do they yet affirm that there are so many different substances. Thus also is it in wills which are good. For I ask them, is it a good thing to have delight in reading the apostle, or good to have delight in a sober psalm, or good to discourse on the gospel? To each of these they will answer, 'It is good.' What, then, if all equally delight us, and all at the same time? Do not different wills distract the mind, when a man is deliberating which he should rather choose? Yet are they all good, and are at variance until one be fixed upon, whither the whole united will may be borne, which before was divided into many. Thus, also, when above eternity delights us, and the pleasure of temporal good holds us down below, it is the same soul which willeth not that or this with an entire will, and is therefore torn asunder with grievous perplexities, while out of truth it prefers that, but out of custom forbears not this.

Thus was I sick and tormented, accusing myself far more severely than was my wont, tossing and turning me in my chain till that was utterly broken, whereby I now was but slightly, but still was held. And Thou, O Lord, pressedst upon me in my inward parts by a severe mercy, redoubling the lashes of fear and shame, lest I should again give way, and that same slender remaining tie not being broken off, it should recover strength, and enchain me the faster. For I said mentally, 'Lo, let it be done now, let it be done now.' And as I spoke, I all but came to a resolve. I all but did it, yet I did it not. Yet fell I not back to my old condition, but took up my position hard by, and drew breath. And I tried again, and wanted but very little of reaching it, and somewhat less, and then all but touched and grasped it; and yet came not at it, nor touched, nor grasped it, hesitating to die unto death, and to live unto life; and the worse, whereto I had been habituated, prevailed more with me than the better, which I had not tried. And the very moment in which I was to become another man, the nearer it approached me, the greater horror did it strike into me; but it did not strike me back, nor turn me aside, but kept me in suspense.

The very toys of toys, and vanities of vanities, my old mistresses, still enthralled me; they shook my fleshly garment, and whispered softly, 'Dost thou part with us? And from that moment shall we no more be with thee for ever? And from that moment shall not this or that be lawful for thee for ever?' And what did they suggest to me in the words 'this or that'? What is it that they suggested, O my God? Let Thy mercy avert it from the soul of Thy servant. What impurities did they suggest! What shame! And now I far less than half heard them, not openly showing themselves and contradicting me, but muttering, as it were, behind my back, and furtively plucking me as I was departing, to make me look back upon them. Yet they did delay me, so that I hesitated to burst and shake myself free from them, and to leap over whither I was called,—an unruly habit saying to me, 'Dost thou think thou canst live without them?'

But now it said this very faintly; for on that side towards which I had set my face, and whither I trembled to go, did the chaste dignity of Continence appear unto me, cheerful, but not dissolutely gay, honestly alluring me to come and doubt nothing, and extending her holy hands, full of a multiplicity of good examples, to receive and embrace me. There were there so many young men and maidens, a multitude of youth and every age, grave widows and ancient virgins, and Continence herself in all, not barren, but a fruitful mother of children of joys, by Thee, O Lord, her Husband. And she smiled on me with an encouraging mockery, as if to say, 'Canst not thou do what these youths and maidens can? Or can one or other do it of themselves, and not rather in the Lord their God? The Lord their God gave me unto them. Why standest thou in thine own strength, and so standest not? Cast thyself upon Him; fear not, He will not withdraw that thou shouldest fall; cast thyself upon Him without fear, He will receive thee, and heal thee.' And I blushed beyond measure, for I still heard the muttering of those toys, and hung in suspense. And she again seemed to say, 'Shut up thine ears against those unclean members of thine upon the earth, that they may be mortified. They tell thee of delights, but not as doth the law of the Lord thy God.' This controversy in my heart was naught but self against self. But Alypius, sitting close by my side, awaited in silence the result of my unwonted emotion.

But when a profound reflection had, from the secret depths of my soul, drawn together and heaped up all my misery before the sight of my heart, there arose a mighty storm, accompanied by as mighty a shower of tears. Which, that I might pour forth fully, with its natural expressions, I stole away from Alypius; for it suggested itself to me that solitude was fitter for the business of weeping. So I retired to such a distance that even his presence could not be oppressive to me. Thus was it with me at that time, and he perceived it; for something, I believe, I had spoken, wherein the sound of my voice appeared choked with weeping, and in that state had I risen up. He then remained where we had been sitting, most completely astonished. I flung myself down, how, I know not, under a certain fig-tree, giving free course to my tears, and the streams of mine eyes gushed out, an acceptable sacrifice unto Thee. And, not indeed in these words, yet to this effect, spake I much unto Thee,—'But Thou, O Lord, how long?' 'How long, Lord? Wilt Thou be angry for ever? Oh, remember not against us former iniquities;' for I felt that I was enthralled by them. I sent up these sorrowful cries,— 'How long, how long? To-morrow, and to-morrow? Why not now? Why is there not this hour an end to my uncleanness?'

I was saying these things and weeping in the most bitter contrition of my heart, when, lo, I heard the voice as of a boy or girl, I know not which, coming from a neighbouring house, chanting, and oft repeating, 'Take up and read; take up and read.' Immediately my countenance was changed, and I began most earnestly to consider whether it was usual for children in any kind of game to sing such words; nor could I remember ever to have heard the like. So, restraining the torrent of my tears, I rose up, interpreting it no other way than as a command to me from Heaven to open the book, and to read the first chapter I should light upon. For I had heard of Antony, that, accidentally coming in whilst the gospel was being read, he received the admonition as if what was read were addressed to him, 'Go and sell that thou hast, and give to the poor, and thou shalt have treasure in heaven; and come and follow me.' And by such oracle was he forthwith converted unto Thee. So quickly I returned to the place where Alypius was sitting; for there had I put down the volume of the apostles, when I rose thence. I grasped, opened, and in silence read that paragraph on which my eyes first fell,—'Not in rioting and drunkenness, not in chambering and wantonness, not in strife and envying; but put ye on the Lord Jesus Christ, and make not provision for the flesh, to fulfil the lusts thereof.' No further would I read, nor did I need; for instantly, as the sentence ended,—by a light, as it were, of security into my heart,—all the gloom of doubt vanished away.

Closing the book, then, and putting either my finger between, or some other mark, I now with a tranquil countenance made it known to Alypius. And he thus disclosed to me what was wrought in him, which I knew not. He asked to look at what I had read. I showed him; and he looked even further than I had read, and I knew not what followed. This it was, verily, 'Him that is weak in the faith, receive ye;' which he applied to himself, and discovered to me. By this admonition was he strengthened; and by a good resolution and purpose, very much in accord with his character (wherein, for the better, he was always far different from me), without any restless delay he joined me. Thence we go in to my mother. We make it known to her,—she rejoiceth. We relate how it came to pass,—she leapeth for joy, and triumpheth, and blesseth Thee, who art 'able to do exceeding abundantly above all that we ask or think;' for she perceived Thee to have given her more for me than she used to ask by her pitiful and most doleful groanings. For Thou didst so convert me unto Thyself, that I sought neither a wife, nor any other of this world's hopes,—standing in that rule of faith in which Thou, so many years before, had showed me unto her in a vision. And thou didst turn her grief into a gladness, much more plentiful than she had desired, and much dearer and chaster than she used to crave, by having grandchildren of my body.

# BOOK IX

*He speaks of his design of forsaking the profession of rhetoric; of the death of his friends, Nebridius and Verecundus, of having received baptism in the thirty-third year of his age; and of the virtues and death of his mother, Monica.*

O LORD, truly I am Thy servant; I am Thy servant, and the son of Thine handmaid: Thou hast loosed my bonds. I will offer to Thee the sacrifice of thanksgiving.' Let my heart and my tongue praise Thee, and let all my bones say, 'Lord, who is like unto Thee?' Let them so say, and answer Thou me, and 'say unto my soul, I am Thy salvation.' Who am I, and what is my nature? How evil have not my deeds been; or if not my deeds, my words; or if not my words, my will? But Thou, O Lord, art good and merciful, and Thy right hand had respect unto the profoundness of my death and removed from the bottom of my heart that abyss of corruption. And this was the result, that I willed not to do what I willed, and willed to do what Thou willest. But where, during all those years, and out of what deep and secret retreat was my free will summoned forth in a moment, whereby I gave my neck to Thy 'easy yoke,' and my shoulders to Thy 'light burden,' O Christ Jesus, 'my strength and my Redeemer'? How sweet did it suddenly become to me to be without the delights of trifles! And what at one time I feared to lose, it was now a joy to me to put away. For Thou didst cast them away from me, Thou true and highest sweetness. Thou didst cast them away, and instead of them didst enter in Thyself,—sweeter than all pleasure, though not to flesh and blood; brighter than all light, but more veiled than all mysteries; more exalted than all honour, but not to the exalted in their own conceits. Now

143

was my soul free from the gnawing cares of seeking and getting, and of wallowing and exciting the itch of lust. And I babbled unto Thee my brightness, my riches, and my health, the Lord my God.

And it seemed good to me, as before Thee, not tumultuously to snatch away, but gently to withdraw the service of my tongue from the talker's trade; that the young, who thought not on Thy law, nor on Thy peace, but on mendacious follies and forensic strifes, might no longer purchase at my mouth equipments for their vehemence. And opportunely there wanted but a few days unto the Vacation of the Vintage; and I determined to endure them, in order to leave in the usual way, and, being redeemed by Thee, no more to return for sale. Our intention then was known to Thee; but to men—excepting our own friends—was it not known. For we had determined among ourselves not to let it get abroad to any; although Thou hadst given to us, ascending from the valley of tears, and singing the song of degrees, 'sharp arrows,' and destroying coals, against the 'deceitful tongue,' which in giving counsel opposes, and in showing love consumes, as it is wont to do with its food.

Thou hadst penetrated our hearts with Thy charity, and we carried Thy words fixed, as it were, in our bowels; and the examples of Thy servant, whom of black Thou hadst made bright, and of dead, alive, crowded in the bosom of our thoughts, burned and consumed our heavy torpor, that we might not topple into the abyss; and they enkindled us exceedingly, that every breath of the deceitful tongue of the gainsayer might inflame us the more, not extinguish us. Nevertheless, because for Thy name's sake which Thou hast sanctified throughout the earth, this, our vow and purpose, might also find commenders, it looked like a vaunting of oneself not to wait for the vacation, now so near, but to leave beforehand a public profession, and one, too, under general observation; so that all who looked on this act of mine, and saw how near was the vintage-time I desired to anticipate, would talk of me a great deal as if I were trying to appear to be a great person. And what purpose would it serve that people should consider and dispute about my intention, and that our good should be evil spoken of?

Furthermore, this very summer, from too great literary labour, my lungs began to be weak, and with difficulty to draw deep breaths; showing by the pains in my chest that they were affected, and refusing too loud or prolonged speaking. This had at first been a trial to me, for it compelled me almost of necessity to lay down that burden of teaching; or, if I could be cured and become strong again, at least to leave it off for a while. But when the full desire of leisure, that I might see that Thou art the Lord, arose, and was confirmed in me, my God, Thou knowest I even began to rejoice that I had this excuse ready,—and that not a feigned one,—which might somewhat temper the offence taken by those who for their sons' good wished me never to have the freedom of sons. Full, therefore, with such joy, I bore it till that period of time had passed,—perhaps it was some twenty days,—yet they were bravely borne; for the cupidity which was wont to sustain part of this weighty business had departed, and I had remained overwhelmed had not its place been supplied by patience. Some of Thy servants, my brethren, may perchance say that I sinned in this, in that having once fully, and from my heart, entered on Thy warfare, I permitted myself to sit a single hour in the seat of falsehood. I will not contend. But hast not Thou, O most merciful Lord, pardoned and remitted this sin also, with my others, so horrible and deadly, in the holy water?

Verecundus was wasted with anxiety at that our happiness, since he, being most firmly held by his bonds, saw that he would lose our fellowship. For he was not yet a Christian, though his wife was one of the faithful; and yet hereby, being more firmly enchained than by anything else, was he held back from that journey which we had commenced. Nor, he declared, did he wish to be a Christian on any other terms than those that were impossible. However, he invited us most courteously to make use of his country house so long as we should stay there. Thou, O Lord, wilt 'recompense' him for this 'at the resurrection of the just,' seeing that Thou hast already given him 'the lot of the righteous.' For although, when we were absent at Rome, he, being overtaken with bodily sickness, and therein being made a Christian, and one of the faithful, departed this life, yet hadst Thou mercy on him, and not on him only, but on us also; lest, thinking on the exceeding kindness of our friend to us, and unable to count him in Thy flock, we should be tortured with intolerable grief. Thanks be unto Thee, our God, we are Thine. Thy exhortations, consolations and faithful promises assure us that Thou now repayest Verecundus for that country house at Cassiacum, where from the fever of the world we found rest in Thee, with the perpetual freshness of Thy Paradise, in that Thou hast forgiven him his earthly sins, in that mountain flowing with milk, that fruitful mountain,—Thine own.

He then was at that time full of grief; but Nebridius was joyous. Although he also, not being yet a Christian, had fallen into the pit of that most pernicious error of believing Thy Son to be a phantasm, yet, coming out thence, he held the same belief that we did; not as yet initiated in any of the sacraments of Thy Church, but a most earnest inquirer after truth. Whom, not long after our conversion and regeneration by Thy baptism, he being also a faithful member of the Catholic Church, and serving Thee in perfect chastity and continency amongst his own people in Africa, when his whole household had been brought to Christianity through him, didst Thou release from the flesh; and now he lives in Abraham's bosom. Whatever that may be which is signified by that bosom, there lives my Nebridius, my sweet friend, Thy son, O Lord, adopted of a freedman; there he liveth. For what other place could there be for such a soul? There liveth he, concerning which he used to ask me much,—me, an inexperienced, feeble one. Now he puts not his ear unto my mouth, but his spiritual mouth unto Thy fountain, and drinketh as much as he is able, wisdom according to his desire,—happy without end. Nor do I believe that he is so inebriated with it as to forget me, seeing Thou, O Lord, whom he drinketh, art mindful of us. Thus, then, were we comforting the sorrowing Verecundus (our friendship being untouched) concerning our conversion, and exhorting him to a faith according to his condition, I mean, his married state. And tarrying for Nebridius to follow us, which, being so near, he was just about to do, when, behold, those days passed over at last; for long and many they seemed, on account of my love of easeful liberty, that I might sing unto Thee from my very marrow. My heart said unto Thee,— I have sought Thy face; 'Thy face, Lord, will I seek.'

And the day arrived on which, in very deed, I was to be released from the Professorship of Rhetoric, from which in intention I had been already released. And done it was; and Thou didst deliver my tongue whence Thou hadst already delivered my heart; and full of joy I blessed Thee for it, and retired with all mine to the villa. What I accomplished there in writing, which was now wholly devoted to Thy service, though still, in this pause as it were, panting from the school of pride, my books testify— those in which I disputed with my friends, and those with myself alone before Thee;[44] and what with the absent Nebridius, my letters testify. And when can I find time to recount all Thy great benefits which Thou bestow-edest upon us at that time, especially as I am hasting on to still greater mercies? For my memory calls upon me, and pleasant it is to me, O Lord, to confess unto Thee, by what inward goads Thou didst subdue me, and how Thou didst make me low, bringing down the mountains and hills of my imaginations, and didst straighten my crookedness, and smooth my rough ways; and by what means Thou also didst subdue that brother of my heart, Alypius, unto the name of Thy only-begotten, our Lord and Saviour Jesus Christ, which he at first refused to have inserted in our writings. For he rather desired that they should savour of the 'cedars' of the schools, which the Lord hath now broken down, than of the wholesome herbs of the Church, hostile to serpents.

What utterances sent I up unto Thee, my God, when I read the Psalms of David, those faithful songs and sounds of devotion which exclude all swelling of spirit, when new to Thy true love, at rest in the villa with Alypius, a catechumen like myself, my mother cleaving unto us,—in woman's garb truly, but with a man's faith, with the peacefulness of age, full of motherly love and Christian piety! What utterances used I to send up unto Thee in those Psalms, and how was I inflamed towards Thee by them, and burned to rehearse them, if it were possible, throughout the whole world, against the pride of the human race! And yet they are sung throughout the whole world, and none can hide himself from Thy heat. With what vehement and bitter sorrow was I indignant at the Manichæans; whom yet again I pitied, for that they were ignorant of those sacraments, those medicaments, and were mad against the antidote which might have made them sane! I wished that they had been somewhere near me then, and, without my being aware of their presence, could have beheld my face, and heard my words, when I read the fourth Psalm in that time of my leisure,—how that psalm wrought upon me. When I called upon Thee, Thou didst hear me, O God of my righteousness; Thou hast enlarged me when I was in distress; have mercy upon me, and hear my prayer. Oh that they might have heard what I uttered on these words, without my knowing whether they heard or no, lest they should think that I spake it because of them! For, of a truth, neither should I have said the same things, nor in the way I said them, if I had perceived that I was heard and seen by them; and had I spoken them, they would not so have received them as when I spake by and for myself before Thee, out of the private feelings of my soul.

I alternately quaked with fear, and warmed with hope, and with rejoicing in Thy mercy, O Father. And all these passed forth, both by mine eyes and voice, when Thy good Spirit, turning unto us, said, O ye sons of men, how long will ye be slow of heart? 'How long will ye love vanity, and seek after leasing?' For I had loved vanity, and sought after leasing. And Thou, O Lord, hadst already magnified Thy Holy One, raising Him from the dead, and setting Him at Thy right hand, whence from on high He should send His promise, the Paraclete, 'the Spirit of Truth.' And He had already sent Him, but I knew it not; He had sent Him, because He was now magnified, rising again from the dead, and ascending into heaven. For till then 'the Holy Ghost was not yet given, because that Jesus was not yet glorified.' And the prophet cries out, How long will ye be slow of heart? How long will ye love vanity, and seek after leasing? Know this, that the Lord hath magnified His Holy One. He cries out, 'How long?' He cries out, 'Know this,' and I, so long ignorant, 'loved vanity, and sought after leasing.' And therefore I heard and trembled, because these words were spoken unto such as I remembered that I myself had been. For in those phantasms which I once held for truths was there 'vanity' and 'leasing.' And I spake many things loudly and earnestly, in the sorrow of my remembrance, which, would that they who yet 'love vanity and seek after leasing' had heard! They would perchance have been troubled, and have vomited it forth, and Thou wouldest hear them when they cried unto Thee; for by a true death in the flesh He died for us, who now maketh intercession for us with Thee.

I read further, 'Be ye angry, and sin not.' And how was I moved, O my God, who had now learned to 'be angry' with myself for the things past, so that in the future I might not sin! Yea, to be justly angry; for that it was not another nature of the race of darkness which sinned for me, as they affirm it to be who are not angry with themselves, and who treasure up to themselves wrath against the day of wrath, and of the revelation of Thy righteous judgment. Nor were my good things now without, nor were they sought after with eyes of flesh in that sun; for they that would have joy from without easily sink into oblivion, and are wasted upon those things which are seen and temporal, and in their starving thoughts do lick their very shadows.[45] Oh, if only they were wearied out with their fasting, and said, 'Who will show us any good?' And we would answer, and they hear, O Lord, The light of Thy countenance is lifted up upon us. For we are not that Light, which lighteth every man, but we are enlightened by Thee, that we, who were sometimes darkness, may be light in Thee. Oh that they could behold the internal Eternal, which having tasted I gnashed my teeth that I could not show It to them, while they brought me their heart in their eyes, roaming abroad from Thee, and said, 'Who will show us any good?' But there, where I was angry with myself in my chamber, where I was inwardly pricked, where I had offered my 'sacrifice,' slaying my old man, and beginning the resolution of a new life, putting my trust in Thee,—there hadst Thou begun to grow sweet unto me, and to 'put gladness in my heart.' And I cried out as I read this outwardly, and felt it inwardly. Nor would I be increased with worldly goods, wasting time and being wasted by time; whereas I possessed in Thy eternal simplicity other corn, and wine, and oil.

And with a loud cry from my heart, I called out in the following verse, 'Oh, in peace!' and 'the self-same!' Oh, what said he, 'I will lay me down and sleep!' For who shall hinder us, when 'shall be brought to pass the saying that is written, Death is swallowed up in victory?' And Thou art in the highest degree 'the self-same,' who changest not; and in Thee is the rest which forgetteth all labour, for there is no other beside Thee, nor ought we to seek after those many other things which are not what Thou art; but Thou, Lord, only makest me to dwell in hope. These things I read, and was inflamed; but discovered not what to do with those deaf and dead, of whom I had been a pestilent member,—a bitter and a blind declaimer against the writings behonied with the honey of heaven and luminous with Thine own light; and I was consumed on account of the enemies of this Scripture.

When shall I call to mind all that took place in those holidays? Yet neither have I forgotten, nor will I be silent about the severity of Thy scourge, and the amazing quickness of Thy mercy. Thou didst at that time torture me with toothache; and when it had become so exceeding great that I was not able to speak, it came into my heart to urge all my friends who were present to pray for me to Thee, the God of all manner of health. And I wrote it down on wax, and gave it to them to read. Presently, as with submissive desire we bowed our knees, that pain departed. But what pain? Or how did it depart? I confess to being much afraid, my Lord my God, seeing that from my earliest years I had not experienced such pain. And Thy purposes were profoundly impressed upon me; and, rejoicing in faith, I praised Thy name. And that faith suffered me not to be at rest in regard to my past sins, which were not yet forgiven me by Thy baptism.

The vintage vacation being ended, I gave the citizens of Milan notice that they might provide their scholars with another seller of words; because both of my election to serve Thee, and my inability, by reason of the

difficulty of breathing and the pain in my chest, to continue the Professorship. And by letters I notified to Thy bishop, the holy man Ambrose, my
former errors and present resolutions, with a view to his advising me which
of Thy books it was best for me to read, so that I might be readier and
fitter for the reception of such great grace. He recommended Isaiah the
Prophet; I believe, because he foreshows more clearly than others the
gospel, and the calling of the Gentiles. But I, not understanding the first
portion of the book, and imagining the whole to be like it, laid it aside,
intending to take it up hereafter, when better practised in our Lord's words.

Thence, when the time had arrived at which I was to give in my name,
having left the country, we returned to Milan.[46] Alypius also was pleased
to be born again with me in Thee, being now clothed with the humility
appropriate to Thy sacraments, and being so brave a tamer of the body, as
with unusual fortitude to tread the frozen soil of Italy with his naked feet.
We took into our company the boy Adeodatus, born of me carnally, of my
sin. Well hadst Thou made him. He was barely fifteen years, yet in wit
excelled many grave and learned men. I confess unto Thee Thy gifts, O
Lord my God, creator of all, and of exceeding power to reform our
deformities; for of me was there naught in that boy but the sin. For that
we fostered him in Thy discipline, Thou inspiredst us, none other,—Thy
gifts I confess unto Thee. There is a book of ours, which is entitled *The
Master*. It is a dialogue between him and me. Thou knowest that all things
there put into the mouth of the person in argument with me were his
thoughts in his sixteenth year. Many others more wonderful did I find in
him. That talent was a source of awe to me. And who but Thou could be
the worker of such marvels? Quickly didst Thou remove his life from the
earth; and now I recall him to mind with a sense of security, in that I fear
nothing for his childhood or youth, or for his whole self. We took him
coeval with us in Thy grace, to be educated in Thy discipline; and we were
baptized, and solicitude about our past life left us. Nor was I satiated in
those days with the wondrous sweetness of considering the depth of Thy
counsels concerning the salvation of the human race. How greatly did I

weep in Thy hymns and canticles, deeply moved by the voices of Thy sweet-speaking Church! The voices flowed into mine ears, and the truth was poured forth into my heart, whence the agitation of my piety over-flowed, and my tears ran over, and blessed was I therein.

Not long had the Church of Milan begun to employ this kind of consola-tion and exhortation, the brethren singing together with great earnestness of voice and heart. For it was about a year, or not much more, since Justina, the mother of the boy-Emperor Valentinian, persecuted Thy servant Ambrose in the interest of her heresy, to which she had been seduced by the Arians. The pious people kept guard in the church, prepared to die with their bishop, Thy servant. There my mother, Thy handmaid, bearing a chief part of those cares and watchings, lived in prayer. We, still unmelted by the heat of Thy Spirit, were yet moved by the astonished and disturbed city. At this time it was instituted that, after the manner of the Eastern Church, hymns and psalms should be sung, lest the people should pine away in the tediousness of sorrow; which custom, retained from then till now, is imitated by many, yea, by almost all of Thy congregations through-out the rest of the world.

Then didst Thou by a vision make known to Thy renowned bishop the spot where lay the bodies of Gervasius and Protasius, the martyrs (whom Thou hadst in Thy secret storehouse preserved uncorrupted for so many years), whence Thou mightest at the fitting time produce them to repress the feminine but royal fury. For when they were revealed and dug up and with due honour transferred to the Ambrosian Basilica, not only they who were troubled with unclean spirits (the devils confessing themselves) were healed, but a certain man also, who had been blind many years, a well-known citizen of that city, having asked and been told the reason of the people's tumultuous joy, rushed forth, asking his guide to lead him thither. Arrived there, he begged to be permitted to touch with his handkerchief the bier of Thy Saints, whose death is precious in Thy sight. When he had done this, and put it to his eyes, they were forthwith opened. Thence did the fame spread; thence did Thy praises burn,—shine; thence was the mind of that enemy, though not yet enlarged to the wholeness of believing, restrained from the fury of persecuting. Thanks be to Thee, O my God. Whence and whither hast Thou thus led my remembrance, that I should confess these things also unto Thee,—great, though I, forgetful, had passed them over? And yet then, when the 'savour' of Thy 'ointments' was so fragrant, did we not 'run after Thee.' And so I did the more abundantly weep at the singing of Thy hymns, formerly panting for Thee, and at last breathing in Thee, as far as the air can play in this house of grass.

Thou, who makest men to dwell of one mind in a house, didst associate with us Evodius also, a young man of our city, who, when serving as an agent for Public Affairs, was converted unto Thee and baptized prior to us; and relinquishing his secular service, prepared himself for Thine. We were together, and together were we about to dwell with a holy purpose. We sought for some place where we might be most useful in our service to Thee, and were going back together to Africa. And when we were at the Tiberine Ostia my mother died. Much I omit, having much to hasten. Receive my confessions and thanksgivings, O my God, for innumerable things concerning which I am silent. But I will not omit aught that my soul has brought forth as to that Thy handmaid who brought me forth,—in her flesh, that I might be born to this temporal light, and in her heart, that I might be born to life eternal. I will speak not of her gifts, but Thine in her; for she neither made herself nor educated herself. Thou createdst her, nor did her father nor her mother know what a being was to proceed from them. And it was the rod of Thy Christ, the discipline of Thine only Son, that trained her in Thy fear, in the house of one of Thy faithful ones, who was a sound member of Thy Church. Yet this good discipline did she not so much attribute to the diligence of her mother, as that of a certain decrepit maid-servant, who had carried about her father when an infant, as little ones are wont to be carried on the backs of elder girls. For which reason, and on account of her extreme age and very good character, was she much respected by the heads of that Christian house. Whence also was committed to her the care of her master's daughters, which she with diligence performed, and was earnest in restraining them when necessary, with a holy severity, and instructing them with a sober sagacity. For, excepting at the hours in which they were very temperately fed at their parents' table, she used not to permit them, though parched with thirst, to drink even water; thereby taking precautions against an evil custom, and adding the wholesome advice, 'You drink water only because you have not control of wine; but when you have come to be married, and made mistresses of storeroom and cellar, you will despise water, but the habit of drinking will remain.' By this method of instruction, and power of command, she restrained the longing of their tender age, and regulated the very thirst of the girls to such a becoming limit, as that what was not seemly they did not long for.

And yet—as Thine handmaid related to me, her son—there had stolen upon her a love of wine. For when she, as being a sober maiden, was as usual bidden by her parents to draw wine from the cask, the vessel being held under the opening, before she poured the wine into the bottle, she would wet the tips of her lips with a little, for more than that her inclination refused. For this she did not from any craving for drink, but out of the overflowing buoyancy of her time of life, which bubbles up with sportiveness, and is, in youthful spirits, wont to be repressed by the gravity of elders. And so unto that little, adding daily little (for 'he that contemneth small things shall fall by little and little'), she contracted such a habit as to drink off eagerly her little cup nearly full of wine. Where, then, was the sagacious old woman with her earnest restraint? Could anything prevail against a secret disease if Thy medicine, O Lord, did not watch over us? Father, mother, and nurturers absent, Thou present, who hast created, who callest, who also by those who are set over us workest some good for the salvation of our souls, what didst Thou at that time, O my God? How didst Thou heal her? How didst Thou make her whole? Didst Thou not out of another woman's soul evoke a hard and bitter insult, as a surgeon's knife from Thy secret store, and with one thrust remove all that putrefaction? For the maid-servant who used to accompany her to the cellar, falling out,

as it happens, with her little mistress, when she was alone with her, cast in
her teeth this vice, with very bitter insult, calling her a 'wine-bibber.' Stung
by this taunt, she perceived her foulness, and immediately condemned and
renounced it. Even as friends by their flattery pervert, so do enemies by
their taunts often correct us. Yet Thou renderest not unto them what Thou
dost by them, but what was proposed by them. For she, being angry,
desired to irritate her young mistress, not to cure her; and did it in secret,
either because the time and place of the dispute found them thus, or perhaps
lest she herself should be exposed to danger for disclosing it so late. But
Thou, Lord, Governor of heavenly and earthly things, who convertest to
Thy purposes the deepest torrents, and disposest the turbulent current of the
ages, healest one soul by the unsoundness of another; lest any man, when
he remarks this, should attribute it unto his own power if another, whom he
wishes to be reformed, is so through a word of his.

Being thus modestly and soberly trained, and rather made subject by
Thee to her parents, than by her parents to Thee, when she had arrived at a
marriageable age, she was given to a husband whom she served as her lord.
And she busied herself to gain him to Thee, preaching Thee unto him by
her behaviour; by which Thou madest her fair, and reverently amiable, and
admirable unto her husband. For she so bore the wronging of her bed as
never to have any dissension with her husband on account of it. For she
waited for Thy mercy upon him that by believing in Thee he might
become chaste. And besides this, as he was earnest in friendship, so was
he violent in anger; but she had learned that an angry husband should not
be resisted, neither in deed, nor even in word. But so soon as he was grown
calm and tranquil, and she saw a fitting moment, she would give him a
reason for her conduct, should he have been excited without cause. In
short, while many matrons, whose husbands were more gentle, carried the
marks of blows on their dishonoured faces, and would in private conversation blame the lives of their husbands, she would blame their tongues,
monishing them gravely, as if in jest: 'That from the hour they heard what
are called the matrimonial tablets read to them, they should think of them

as instruments whereby they were made servants; so, being always mindful of their condition, they ought not to set themselves in opposition to their lords.' And when they, knowing what a furious husband she endured, marvelled that it had never been reported, nor appeared by any indication, that Patricius had beaten his wife, or that there had been any domestic strife between them, even for a day, and asked her in confidence the reason of this, she taught them her rule, which I have mentioned above. They who observed it experienced the wisdom of it, and rejoiced; those who observed it not were kept in subjection, and suffered.

Her mother-in-law, also, being at first prejudiced against her by the whisperings of evil-disposed servants, she so conquered by submission, persevering in it with patience and meekness, that she voluntarily disclosed to her son the tongues of the meddling servants, whereby the domestic peace between herself and her daughter-in-law had been agitated, begging him to punish them for it. When, therefore, he had—in conformity with his mother's wish, and with a view to the discipline of his family, and to ensure the future harmony of its members—corrected with stripes those discovered, according to the will of her who had discovered them, she promised a similar reward to any who, to please her, should say anything evil to her of her daughter-in-law. And, none now daring to do so, they lived together with a wonderful sweetness of mutual good-will.

This great gift Thou bestowedst also, my God, my mercy, upon that good handmaid of Thine, out of whose womb Thou createdst me, even that, whenever she could, she showed herself such a peacemaker between any differing and discordant spirits, that when she had heard on both sides most bitter things, such as swelling and undigested discord is wont to give vent to, when the crudities of enmities are breathed out in bitter speeches to a present friend against an absent enemy, she would disclose nothing about the one unto the other, save what might avail to their reconcilement. A small good this might seem to me, did I not know to my sorrow countless persons, who, through some horrible and far-spreading infection of sin, not only disclose to enemies mutually enraged the things said in passion against each other, but add some things that were never spoken at all; whereas, to a generous man, it ought to seem a small thing not to incite or increase the enmities of men by ill-speaking, unless he endeavour likewise by kind words to extinguish them. Such a one was she,—Thou, her most intimate Instructor, teaching her in the school of her heart.

Finally, her own husband, now towards the end of his earthly existence, did she gain over unto Thee; and she had not to complain of that in him, as one of the faithful, which, before he became so, she had endured. She was also the servant of Thy servants. Whosoever of them knew her, did in her much magnify, honour, and love Thee; for that through the testimony of the fruits of a holy conversation, they perceived Thee to be present in her heart. For she had 'been the wife of one man,' had requited her parents, had guided her house piously, was 'well-reported of for good works,' had 'brought up children,' as often travailing in birth of them as she saw them swerving from Thee. Lastly, to all of us, O Lord (since of Thy favour Thou sufferest Thy servants to speak), who, before her sleeping in Thee, lived associated together, having received the grace of Thy baptism, did she devote care such as she might if she had been mother of us all; served us as if she had been child of all.

As the day now approached on which she was to depart this life (which day Thou knewest, we did not), it fell out—Thou, as I believe, by Thy secret ways arranging it—that she and I stood alone, leaning in a certain window, from which the garden of the house we occupied at Ostia could be seen; at which place, removed from the crowd, we were resting ourselves for the voyage, after the fatigues of a long journey. We then were conversing alone very pleasantly; and, 'forgetting those things which are behind, and reaching forth unto those things which are before,' we were seeking between ourselves in the presence of the Truth, which Thou art, of what nature the eternal life of the saints would be, which eye hath not seen, nor ear heard, neither hath entered into the heart of man. But yet we opened wide the mouth of our heart, after those supernal streams of Thy fountain, 'the fountain of life,' which is 'with Thee;' that being sprinkled with it according to our capacity, we might in some measure weigh so high a mystery.

And when our conversation had arrived at that point, that the very highest pleasure of the carnal senses, and that in the very brightest material light, seemed by reason of the sweetness of that life not only not worthy of comparison, but not even of mention, we, lifting ourselves with a more ardent affection towards 'the Self-same,' did gradually pass through all corporeal things, and even the heaven itself, whence sun, and moon, and stars shine upon the earth; yea, we soared higher yet by inward musing, and discoursing, and admiring Thy works; and we came to our own minds, and went beyond them, that we might advance as high as that region of unfailing plenty, where Thou feedest Israel for ever with the food of truth, and where life is that Wisdom by whom all these things are made, both which have been, and which are to come; and she is not made, but is as she hath been, and so shall ever be; yea, rather, to 'have been,' and 'to be hereafter,' are not in her, but only 'to be,' seeing she is eternal, for to 'have been' and 'to be hereafter' are not eternal. And while we were thus speaking, and straining after her, we slightly touched her with the whole effort of our heart; and we sighed, and there left bound 'the first-fruits of the Spirit;' and returned to the noise of our own mouth, where the word uttered has both beginning and end. And what is like unto Thy Word, our Lord, who remaineth in Himself without becoming old, and 'maketh all things new'?

We were saying, then, If to any man the tumult of the flesh were silenced,—silenced the phantasies of earth, waters, and air,—silenced, too, the poles; yea, the very soul be silenced to herself, and go beyond herself by not thinking of herself,—silenced fancies and imaginary revelations, every tongue, and every sign, and whatsoever exists by passing away, since, if any could hearken, all these say, 'We created not ourselves, but were created by Him who abideth for ever:' If, having uttered this, they now should be silenced, having only quickened our ears to Him who created them, and He alone speak not by them, but by Himself, that we may hear

His word, not by fleshly tongue, nor angelic voice, nor sound of thunder, nor the obscurity of a similitude, but might hear Him—Him whom in these we love—without these, likeas we two now strained ourselves, and with rapid thought touched on that Eternal Wisdom which remaineth over all. If this could be sustained, and other visions of a far different kind be withdrawn, and this one ravish, and absorb, and envelope its beholder amid these inward joys, so that his life might be eternally like that one moment of knowledge which we now sighed after, were not this 'Enter thou into the joy of Thy Lord'? And when shall that be? When we shall all rise again; but all shall not be changed.

Such things was I saying; and if not after this manner, and in these words, yet, Lord, Thou knowest, that in that day when we were talking thus, this world with all its delights grew contemptible to us, even while we spake. Then said my mother, 'Son, for myself, I have no longer any pleasure in aught in this life. What I want here further, and why I am here, I know not, now that my hopes in this world are satisfied. There was indeed one thing for which I wished to tarry a little in this life, and that was that I might see thee a Catholic Christian before I died. My God has exceeded this abundantly, so that I see thee despising all earthly felicity, made His servant,—what do I here?'

What reply I made unto her to these things I do not well remember. However, scarcely five days after, or not much more, she was prostrated by fever; and while she was sick, she one day sank into a swoon, and was for a short time unconscious of visible things. We hurried up to her; but she soon regained her senses, and gazing on me and my brother as we stood by her, she said to us inquiringly, 'Where was I?' Then looking intently at us stupefied with grief, 'Here,' saith she, 'shall you bury your mother.' I was silent, and refrained from weeping; but my brother said something, wishing her, as the happier lot, to die in her own country and not abroad. She, when she heard this, with anxious countenance arrested him with her eye, as savouring of such things, and then gazing at me, 'Behold,' saith she, 'what he saith;' and soon after to us both she saith, 'Lay this body anywhere, let not the care for it trouble you at all. This only I ask, that you will remember me at the Lord's altar, wherever you be.' And when she had given forth this opinion in such words as she could, she was silent, being in pain with her increasing sickness.

But, as I reflected on Thy gifts, O thou invisible God, which Thou instillest into the hearts of Thy faithful ones, whence such marvellous fruits do spring, I did rejoice and give thanks unto Thee, calling to mind what I knew before, how she had ever burned with anxiety respecting her burial-place, which she had provided and prepared for herself by the body of her husband. For as they had lived very peacefully together, her desire had also been (so little is the human mind capable of grasping things divine) that this should be added to that happiness, and be talked of among men, that after her wandering beyond the sea, it had been granted her that they both, so united on earth, should lie in the same grave. But when this uselessness had, through the bounty of Thy goodness, begun to be no longer in her heart, I knew not, and I was full of joy admiring what she had thus disclosed to me; though indeed in that our conversation in the window also, when she said, 'What do I here any longer?' she appeared not to desire to die in her own country. I heard afterwards, too, that at the time we were at Ostia, with a maternal confidence she one day, when I was absent, was speaking with certain of my friends on the contemning of this life, and the blessing of death; and when they—amazed at the courage which Thou hadst given to her, a woman—asked her whether she did not dread leaving her body at such a distance from her own city, she replied, 'Nothing is far to God; nor need I fear lest He should be ignorant at the end of the world of the place whence He is to raise me up.' On the ninth day, then, of her sickness, the fifty-sixth year of her age, and the thirty-third of mine, was that religious and devout soul set free from the body.

I closed her eyes; and there flowed a great sadness into my heart, and it was passing into tears, when mine eyes at the same time, by the violent control of my mind, sucked back the fountain dry, and woe was me in such a struggle! But, as soon as she breathed her last, the boy Adeodatus burst

out into wailing, but, being checked by us all, he became quiet. In like manner also my own childish feeling, which was, through the youthful voice of my heart, finding escape in tears, was restrained and silenced. For we did not consider it fitting to celebrate that funeral with tearful plaints and groanings; for on such wise are they who die unhappy, or are altogether dead, wont to be mourned. But she neither died unhappy, nor did she altogether die. For of this were we assured by the witness of her good conversation, her 'faith unfeigned,' and other sufficient grounds.

What, then, was that which did grievously pain me within, but the newly-made wound, from having that most sweet and dear habit of living together suddenly broken off? I was full of joy indeed in her testimony, when, in that her last illness, flattering my dutifulness, she called me 'kind,' and recalled, with great affection of love, that she had never heard any harsh or reproachful sound come out of my mouth against her. But yet, O my God, who madest us, how can the honour which I paid to her be compared with her slavery for me? As, then, I was left destitute of so great comfort in her, my soul was stricken, and that life torn apart as it were, which, of hers and mine together, had been made but one.

The boy then being restrained from weeping, Evodius took up the Psalter, and began to sing—the whole house responding—the Psalm, 'I will sing of mercy and judgment: unto Thee, O Lord.' But when they heard what we were doing, many brethren and religious women came together; and whilst they whose office it was were, according to custom, making ready for the funeral, I, in a part of the house where I conveniently could, together with those who thought that I ought not to be left alone, discoursed on what was suited to the occasion; and by this alleviation of truth mitigated the anguish known unto Thee—they being unconscious of it, listened intently, and thought me to be devoid of any sense of sorrow. But in Thine ears, where none of them heard, did I blame the softness of my feelings, and restrained the flow of my grief, which yielded a little unto me; but the paroxysm returned again, though not so as to burst forth into tears, nor to a change of countenance, though I knew what I repressed in my heart. And as I was exceedingly annoyed that these human things had such power over me, which in the due order and destiny of our natural condition must of necessity come to pass, with a new sorrow I sorrowed for my sorrow, and was wasted by a twofold sadness.

So, when the body was carried forth, we both went and returned without tears. For neither in those prayers which we poured forth unto Thee when the sacrifice of our redemption was offered up unto Thee for her,—the dead body being now placed by the side of the grave, as the custom there is, prior to its being laid therein,—neither in their prayers did I shed tears; yet was I most grievously sad in secret all the day, and with a troubled mind entreated Thee, as I was able, to heal my sorrow, but Thou didst not; fixing, I believe, in my memory by this one lesson the power of the bonds of all habit, even upon a mind which now feeds not upon a fallacious word. It appeared to me also a good thing to go and bathe, I having heard that the bath [*balneum*] took its name from the Greek βαλανεῖον, because it drives trouble from the mind. Lo, this also I confess unto Thy mercy, 'Father of the fatherless,' that I bathed, and felt the same as before I had done so. For the bitterness of my grief exuded not from my heart. Then I slept, and on awaking found my grief not a little mitigated; and as I lay alone upon my bed, there came into my mind those true verses of Thy Ambrose, for Thou art—

*Deus creator omnium,*
*Polique rector, vestiens*
*Diem decoro lumine,*
*Noctem sopora gratia;*
   *Artus solutos ut quies*
*Reddat laboris usui,*
*Mentesque fessas allevet,*
*Luctusque solvat anxios.**

---

* Rendered as follows in an anonymous translation printed in 1660:

| | |
|---|---|
| 'O God, the world's great Architect, | When wearied limbs new vigour gain |
| Who dost heaven's rowling orbs direct; | From rest, new labours to sustain; |
| Cloathing the day with beauteous light, | When hearts oppressed do meet relief, |
| And with sweet slumbers silent night; | And anxious minds forget their grief.' |

And then little by little did I bring back my former thoughts of Thine handmaid, her devout conversation towards Thee, her holy tenderness and attentiveness towards us, which was suddenly taken away from me; and it was pleasant to me to weep in Thy sight, for her and for me, concerning her and concerning myself. And I set free the tears which before I repressed, that they might flow at their will, spreading them beneath my heart; and it rested in them, for Thy ears were nigh me,—not those of man, who would have put a scornful interpretation on my weeping. But now in writing I confess it unto Thee, O Lord! Read it who will, and interpret how he will; and if he finds me to have sinned in weeping for my mother during so small a part of an hour,—that mother who was for a while dead to mine eyes, who had for many years wept for me, that I might live in Thine eyes,— let him not laugh at me, but rather, if he be a man of a noble charity, let him weep for my sins against Thee, the Father of all the brethren of Thy Christ.

But,—my heart being now healed of that wound, in so far as it could be convicted of a carnal affection,—I pour out unto Thee, O our God, on behalf of that Thine handmaid, tears of a far different sort, even that which flows from a spirit broken by the thoughts of the dangers of every soul that dieth in Adam. And although she, having been 'made alive' in Christ even before she was freed from the flesh, had so lived as to praise Thy name both by her faith and conversation, yet dare I not say that from the time Thou didst regenerate her by baptism, no word went forth from her mouth against Thy precepts. And it hath been declared by Thy Son, the Truth, that 'Whosoever shall say to his brother, Thou fool, shall be in danger of hell fire.' And woe even unto the praiseworthy life of man, if, putting away mercy, Thou shouldest investigate it. But because Thou dost not narrowly inquire after sins, we hope with confidence to find some place of indulgence with Thee. But whosoever recounts his true merits to Thee, what is it that he recounts to Thee but Thine own gifts? Oh, if men would know themselves to be men; and that 'he that glorieth' would 'glory in the Lord'!

I then, O my Praise and my Life, Thou God of my heart, putting aside for a little her good deeds, for which I joyfully give thanks to Thee, do now beseech Thee for the sins of my mother. Hearken unto me, through that Medicine of our wounds who hung upon the tree, and who, sitting at Thy right hand, 'maketh intercession for us.' I know that she acted mercifully, and from the heart forgave her debtors their debts; do Thou also forgive her debts, whatever she contracted during so many years since the water of salvation. Forgive her, O Lord, forgive her, I beseech Thee; 'enter not into judgment' with her. Let Thy mercy be exalted above Thy justice, because Thy words are true, and Thou hast promised mercy unto 'the merciful;' which Thou gavest them to be who wilt 'have mercy' on whom Thou wilt 'have mercy,' and wilt 'have compassion' on whom Thou hast had compassion.

And I believe Thou hast already done that which I ask Thee; but 'accept the free-will offerings of my mouth, O Lord.' For she, when the day of her dissolution was near at hand, took no thought to have her body sumptuously covered, or embalmed with spices; nor did she covet a choice monument, or desire her paternal burial-place. These things she entrusted not to us, but only desired to have her name remembered at Thy altar, which she had served without the omission of a single day; whence she knew that the holy sacrifice was dispensed, by which the handwriting that was against us is blotted out; by which the enemy was triumphed over, who, summing up our offences, and searching for something to bring against us, found nothing in Him in whom we conquer. Who will restore to Him the innocent blood? Who will repay Him the price with which He bought us, so as to take us from Him? Unto the sacrament of which our ransom did Thy handmaid bind her soul by the bond of faith. Let none separate her from Thy protection. Let not the 'lion' and the 'dragon' introduce himself by force or fraud. For she will not reply that she owes nothing, lest she be convicted and got the better of by the wily deceiver; but she will answer that her 'sins are forgiven' by Him to whom no one is able to repay that price which He, owing nothing, laid down for us.

May she therefore rest in peace with her husband, before or after whom she married none; whom she obeyed, with patience bringing forth fruit unto Thee, that she might gain him also for Thee. And inspire, O my Lord my God, inspire Thy servants my brethren, Thy sons my masters, whom with voice and heart and writings I serve, that so many of them as shall read these confessions may at Thy altar remember Monica, Thy handmaid, together with Patricius, her sometime husband, by whose flesh Thou introducedst me into this life, in what manner I know not. May they with pious affection be mindful of my parents in this transitory light, of my brethren that are under Thee our Father in our Catholic mother, and of my fellow-citizens in the eternal Jerusalem, which the wandering of Thy people sigheth for from their departure until their return. That so my mother's last entreaty to me may, through my confessions more than through my prayers, be more abundantly fulfilled to her through the prayers of many.

# BOOK X

*Having manifested what he was and what he is, he shows the great fruit of his confession; and being about to examine by what method God and the happy life may be found, he enlarges on the nature and power of memory. Then he examines his own acts, thoughts, and affections, viewed under the threefold division of temptation; and commemorates the Lord, the one mediator of God and men.*

LET me know Thee, O Thou who knowest me; let me know Thee, as I am known. O Thou strength of my soul, enter into it, and prepare it for Thyself, that Thou mayest have and hold it without 'spot or wrinkle.' This is my hope, 'therefore have I spoken;' and in this hope do I rejoice, when I rejoice soberly. Other things of this life ought the less to be sorrowed for, the more they are sorrowed for; and ought the more to be sorrowed for, the less men do sorrow for them. For behold, 'Thou desirest truth,' seeing that he who does it 'cometh to the light.' This wish I to do in confession in my heart before Thee, and in my writing before many witnesses.

And from Thee, O Lord, unto whose eyes the depths of man's conscience are naked, what in me could be hidden though I were unwilling to confess to Thee? For so should I hide Thee from myself, not myself from Thee. But now, because my groaning witnesseth that I am dissatisfied with myself, Thou shinest forth, and satisfiest, and art beloved and desired; that I may blush for myself, and renounce myself, and choose Thee, and may neither please Thee nor myself, except in Thee. To Thee then, O Lord, am I manifest, whatever I am, and with what fruit I may confess unto Thee I have spoken. Nor do I it with words and sounds of the flesh, but with the words of the soul, and that cry of reflection which Thine ear knoweth. For when I am wicked, to confess to Thee is naught but to be dissatisfied with myself; but when I am truly devout, it is naught but not to attribute it to myself, because Thou, O Lord, dost 'bless the righteous;' but first Thou justifiest him 'ungodly.' My confession, therefore, O my God, in Thy sight, is made unto Thee silently, and yet not silently. For in noise it is silent, in affection it cries aloud. For neither do I give utterance to anything that is right unto me, which Thou hast not heard from me before, nor dost Thou hear anything of the kind from me which Thyself saidst not first unto me.

What then have I to do with men, that they should hear my confessions, as if they were going to cure all my diseases? A people curious to know the lives of others, but slow to correct their own. Why do they desire to hear from me what I am, who are unwilling to hear from Thee what they are? And how can they tell, when they hear from me of myself, whether I speak the truth, seeing that no man knoweth what is in man, 'save the spirit of man which is in him'? But if they hear from Thee aught concerning themselves, they will not be able to say, 'The Lord lieth.' For what is it to hear from Thee of themselves, but to know themselves? And who is he that knoweth himself and saith, 'It is false,' unless he himself lieth? But because 'charity believeth all things' (amongst those at all events whom by union with itself it maketh one), I too, O Lord, also so confess unto Thee that men may hear, to whom I cannot prove whether I confess the truth, yet do they believe me whose ears charity openeth unto me.

But yet do Thou, my most secret Physician, make clear to me what fruit I may reap by doing it. For the confessions of my past sins,—which Thou hast 'forgiven' and 'covered,' that Thou mightest make me happy in Thee, changing my soul by faith and Thy sacrament,—when they are read and heard, stir up the heart, that it sleep not in despair and say, 'I cannot;' but that it may awake in the love of Thy mercy and the sweetness of Thy grace, by which he that is weak is strong, if by it he is made conscious of his own weakness. As for the good, they take delight in hearing of the past errors of such as are now freed from them; and they delight, not because they are errors, but because they have been and are so no longer. For what fruit, then, O Lord my God, to whom my conscience maketh her daily confession, more confident in the hope of Thy mercy than in her own innocency, —for what fruit, I beseech Thee, do I confess even to men in Thy presence by this book what I am at this time, not what I have been? For that fruit I have both seen and spoken of, but what I am at this time, at the very moment of making my confessions, divers people desire to know, both who knew me and who knew me not,—who have heard of or from me,—but their ear is not at my heart, where I am whatsoever I am. They are desirous, then, of hearing me confess what I am within, where they can neither stretch eye, nor ear, nor mind; they desire it as those willing to believe,— but will they understand? For charity, by which they are good, says unto them that I do not lie in my confessions, and she in them believes me.

But for what fruit do they desire this? Do they wish me happiness when they learn how near, by Thy gift, I come unto Thee; and to pray for me, when they learn how much I am kept back by my own weight? To such will I declare myself. For it is no small fruit, O Lord my God, that by many thanks should be given to Thee on our behalf, and that by many Thou shouldest be entreated for us. Let the fraternal soul love that in me which Thou teachest should be loved, and lament that in me which Thou teachest should be lamented. Let a fraternal and not an alien soul do this, nor that 'of strange children, whose mouth speaketh vanity, and their right hand is a right hand of falsehood,' but that fraternal one which, when it approves me, rejoices for me, but when it disapproves me, is sorry for me; because whether it approves or disapproves it loves me. To such will I declare myself; let them breathe freely at my good deeds, and sigh over my evil ones. My good deeds are Thy institutions and Thy gifts, my evil ones are my delinquencies and Thy judgments. Let them breathe freely at the one, and sigh over the other; and let hymns and tears ascend into Thy sight out of the fraternal hearts—Thy censers. And do Thou, O Lord, who takest delight in the incense of Thy holy temple, have mercy upon me according to Thy great mercy, 'for Thy name's sake;' and on no account leaving what Thou hast begun in me, do Thou complete what is imperfect in me.

This is the fruit of my confessions, not of what I was, but of what I am, that I may confess this not before Thee only, in a secret exultation with trembling, and a secret sorrow with hope, but in the ears also of the believing sons of men,—partakers of my joy, and sharers of my mortality, my fellow-citizens and the companions of my pilgrimage, those who are gone before, and those that are to follow after, and the comrades of my way. These are Thy servants, my brethren, those whom Thou wishest to be Thy sons; my masters, whom Thou hast commanded me to serve, if I desire to live with and of Thee. But this Thy word were little to me did it command in speaking, without going before in acting. This then do I both in deed and word, this I do under Thy wings, in too great danger, were it not that my soul, under Thy wings, is subject unto Thee, and my weakness known unto Thee. I am a little one, but my Father liveth for ever, and my Defender is 'sufficient' for me. For He is the same who begat me and who defends me; and Thou Thyself art all my good; even Thou, the Omnipotent, who art with me, and that before I am with Thee. To such, therefore, whom Thou commandest me to serve will I declare, not what I was, but what I now am, and what I still am. But neither do I judge myself. Thus then I would be heard.

For it is Thou, Lord, that judgest me; for although no 'man knoweth the things of a man, save the spirit of man which is in him,' yet is there something of man which 'the spirit of man which is in him' itself knoweth not. But Thou, Lord, who hast made him, knowest him wholly. I indeed, though in Thy sight I despise myself, and reckon 'myself but dust and ashes,' yet know something concerning Thee, which I know not concerning myself. And assuredly 'now we see through a glass darkly,' not yet 'face to face.' So long, therefore, as I be 'absent' from Thee, I am more 'present' with myself than with Thee; and yet know I that Thou canst not suffer violence; but for myself I know not what temptations I am able to resist, and what I am not able. But there is hope, because Thou art faithful, who wilt not suffer us to be tempted above that we are able, but wilt with the temptation also make a way to escape, that we may be able to bear it. I would therefore confess what I know concerning myself; I will confess also what I know not concerning myself. And because what I do know of myself, I know by Thee enlightening me; and what I know not of myself, so long I know not until the time when my 'darkness be as the noonday' in Thy sight.

Not with uncertain, but with assured consciousness do I love Thee, O Lord. Thou hast stricken my heart with Thy word, and I loved Thee. And also the heaven, and earth, and all that is therein, behold, on every side they say that I should love Thee; nor do they cease to speak unto all, 'so that they are without excuse.' But more profoundly wilt Thou have mercy on whom Thou wilt have mercy, and compassion on whom Thou wilt have compassion, otherwise do both heaven and earth tell forth Thy praises to deaf ears. But what is it that I love in loving Thee? Not corporeal beauty, nor the splendour of time, nor the radiance of the light, so pleasant to our eyes, nor the sweet melodies of songs of all kinds, nor the fragrant smell of flowers, and ointments, and spices, not manna and honey, not limbs pleasant to the embracements of flesh. I love not these things when I love my God; and yet I love a certain kind of light, and sound, and fragrance, and food, and embracement in loving my God, who is the light, sound, fragrance, food, and embracement of my inner man—where that light shineth unto my soul which no place can contain, where that soundeth which time snatcheth not away, where there is a fragrance which no breeze disperseth, where there is a food which no eating can diminish, and where that clingeth which no satiety can sunder. This is what I love, when I love my God.

And what is this? I asked the earth; and it answered, 'I am not He;' and whatsoever are therein made the same confession. I asked the sea and the deeps, and the creeping things that lived, and they replied, 'We are not thy God, seek higher than we.' I asked the breezy air, and the universal air with its inhabitants answered, 'Anaximenes[47] was deceived, I am not God.' I asked the heavens, the sun, moon, and stars: 'Neither,' say they, 'are we the God whom thou seekest.' And I answered unto all these things which stand about the door of my flesh, 'Ye have told me concerning my God, that ye are not He; tell me something about Him.' And with a loud voice they exclaimed, 'He made us.' My questioning was my observing of them; and their beauty was their reply. And I directed my thoughts to myself, and said, 'Who art thou?' And I answered, 'A man.' And lo, in me there appear both body and soul, the one without, the other within. By which of these should I seek my God, whom I had sought through the body from earth to heaven, as far as I was able to send messengers—the beams of mine eyes? But the better part is that which is inner; for to it, as both president and judge, did all these my corporeal messengers render the answers of heaven and earth and all things therein, who said, 'We are not God, but He made us.' These things was my inner man cognizant of by the ministry of the outer; I, the inner man, knew all this—I, the soul, through the senses of my body. I asked the vast bulk of the earth of my God, and it answered me, 'I am not He, but He made me.'

Is not this beauty visible to all whose senses are unimpaired? Why then doth it not speak the same things unto all? Animals, the very small and the great, see it, but they are unable to question it, because their senses are not endowed with reason to enable them to judge on what they report. But men can question it, so that 'the invisible things of Him . . . are clearly seen, being understood by the things that are made;' but by loving them, they are brought into subjection to them; and subjects are not able to judge. Neither do the creatures reply to such as question them, unless they can judge; nor will they alter their voice (that is, their beauty), if so be one man only sees, another both sees and questions, so as to appear one way to this man, and another to that; but appearing the same way to both, it is mute to this, it speaks to that—yea, verily, it speaks unto all; but they only understand it who compare that voice received from without with the truth within. For the truth declareth unto me, 'Neither heaven, nor earth, nor any body is thy God.' This, their nature declareth unto him that beholdeth them. 'They are a mass; a mass is less in part than in the whole.' Now, O my soul, thou art my better part, unto thee I speak; for thou animatest the mass of thy body, giving it life, which no body furnishes to a body; but thy God is even unto thee the Life of life.

What then is it that I love when I love my God? Who is He that is above the head of my soul? By my soul itself will I mount up unto Him. I will soar beyond that power of mine whereby I cling to the body, and fill the whole structure of it with life. Not by that power do I find my God; for then the horse and the mule, 'which have no understanding,' might find Him, since it is the same power by which their bodies also live. But there is another power, not that only by which I quicken, but that also by which I endow with sense my flesh, which the Lord hath made for me; bidding the eye not to hear, and the ear not to see; but that, for me to see by, and this, for me to hear by; and to each of the other senses its own proper seat and office, which being different, I, the single mind, do through them govern. I will soar also beyond this power of mine; for this the horse and mule possess, for they too discern through the body.

I will soar, then, beyond this power of my nature also, ascending by degrees unto Him who made me. And I enter the fields and roomy chambers of memory, where are the treasures of countless images, imported into it from all manner of things by the senses. There is treasured up whatsoever likewise we think, either by enlarging or diminishing, or by varying in any way whatever those things which the sense hath arrived at; yea, and whatever else hath been entrusted to it and stored up, which oblivion hath not yet engulfed and buried. When I am in this storehouse, I demand that what I wish should be brought forth, and some things immediately appear; others require to be longer sought after, and are dragged, as it were, out of some hidden receptacle; others, again, hurry forth in crowds, and while another thing is sought and inquired for, they leap into view, as if to say, 'Is it not we, perchance?' These I drive away with the hand of my heart from before the face of my remembrance, until what I wish be discovered making its appearance out of its secret cell. Other things suggest themselves without effort, and in continuous order, just as they are called for,—those in front giving place to those that follow, and in giving place are treasured up again to be forthcoming when I wish it. All of which takes place when I repeat a thing from memory.

All these things, each of which entered by its own avenue, are distinctly and under general heads there laid up: as, for example, light, and all colours and forms of bodies, by the eyes; sounds of all kinds by the ears; all smells by the passage of the nostrils; all flavours by that of the mouth; and by the sensation of the whole body is brought in what is hard or soft, hot or cold, smooth or rough, heavy or light, whether external or internal to the body. All these doth that great receptacle of memory, with its many and indescribable departments, receive, to be recalled and brought forth when required; each, entering by its own door, is laid up in it. And yet the things themselves do not enter it, but only the images of the things perceived are there ready at hand for thought to recall. And who can tell how these images are formed, notwithstanding that it is evident by which of the senses each has been fetched in and treasured up? For even while I live in darkness and silence, I can bring out colours in memory if I wish, and discern between black and white, and what others I wish; nor yet do sounds break in and disturb what is drawn in by mine eyes, and which I am considering, seeing that they also are there, and are concealed,—laid up, as it were, apart. For these too I can summon if I please, and immediately they appear. And though my tongue be at rest, and my throat silent, yet can I sing as much as I will; and those images of colours, which notwithstanding are there, do not interpose themselves and interrupt when another treasure is under consideration which flowed in through the ears. So the remaining things carried in and heaped up by the other senses, I recall at my pleasure. And I discern the scent of lilies from that of violets while smelling nothing; and I prefer honey to grape-syrup, a smooth thing to a rough, though then I neither taste nor handle, but only remember.

These things do I within, in that vast chamber of my memory. For there are nigh me heaven, earth, sea, and whatever I can think upon in them, besides those which I have forgotten. There also do I meet with myself, and recall myself,—what, when, or where I did a thing, and how I was affected when I did it. There are all which I remember, either by personal experience or on the faith of others. Out of the same supply do I myself with the past construct now this, now that likeness of things, which either I have experienced, or, from having experienced, have believed; and thence again future actions, events, and hopes, and upon all these again do I meditate as if they were present. 'I will do this or that,' say I to myself in that vast womb of my mind, filled with the images of things so many and so great, 'and this or that shall follow upon it.' 'Oh that this or that might come to pass!' 'God avert this or that!' Thus speak I to myself; and when I speak, the images of all I speak about are present, out of the same treasury of memory; nor could I say anything at all about them were the images absent.

Great is this power of memory, exceeding great, O my God,—an inner chamber large and boundless! Who has plumbed the depths thereof? Yet it is a power of mine, and appertains unto my nature; nor do I myself grasp all that I am. Therefore is the mind too narrow to contain itself. And where should that be which it doth not contain of itself? Is it outside and not in itself? How is it, then, that it doth not grasp itself? A great admiration rises upon me; astonishment seizes me. And men go forth to wonder at the heights of mountains, the huge waves of the sea, the broad flow of the rivers, the extent of the ocean, and the courses of the stars, and omit to wonder at themselves; nor do they marvel that when I spoke of all these things, I was not looking on them with my eyes, and yet could not speak of them unless those mountains, and waves, and rivers, and stars which I saw, and that ocean which I believe in, I saw inwardly in my memory, and with the same vast spaces between as when I saw them abroad. But I did not by seeing appropriate them when I looked on them with my eyes; nor are the things themselves with me, but their images. And I knew by what corporeal sense each made impression on me.

And yet are not these all that the illimitable capacity of my memory retains. Here also is all that is apprehended of the liberal sciences, and not yet forgotten—removed as it were into an inner place, which is not a place; nor are they the images which are retained, but the things themselves. For what is literature, what skill in disputation, whatsoever I know of all the many kinds of questions there are, is so in my memory, as that I have not taken in the image and left the thing without, or that it should have sounded and passed away like a voice imprinted on the ear by that trace, whereby it might be recorded, as though it sounded when it no longer did so; or as an odour while it passes away, and vanishes into wind, affects the sense of smell, whence it conveys the image of itself into the memory, which we realize in recollecting; or like food, which assuredly in the belly hath now no taste, and yet hath a kind of taste in the memory, or like anything that is by touching felt by the body, and which even when removed from us is imagined by the memory. For these things themselves are not put into it, but the images of them only are caught up, with a marvellous quickness, and laid up, as it were, in most wonderful garners, and wonderfully brought forth when we remember.

But truly when I hear that there are three kinds of questions, 'Whether a thing is?—what it is?—of what kind it is?' I do indeed hold fast the images of the sounds of which these words are composed, and I know that those sounds passed through the air with a noise, and now are not. But the things themselves which are signified by these sounds I never arrived at by any sense of the body, nor ever perceived them otherwise than by my mind; and in my memory have I laid up not their images, but themselves, which, how they entered into me, let them tell if they are able. For I examine all the gates of my flesh, but find not by which of them they entered. For the eyes say, 'If they were coloured, we announced them.' The ears say, 'If they sounded, we gave notice of them.' The nostrils say, 'If they smell, they passed in by us.' The sense of taste says, 'If they have no flavour, ask not me.' The touch says, 'If it have not body, I handled it not, and if I never handled it, I gave no notice of it.' Whence and how did these things enter into my memory? I know not how. For when I learned them, I gave not credit to the heart of another man, but perceived them in my own; and I approved them as true, and committed them to it, laying them up, as it were, whence I might fetch them when I willed. There, then, they were, even before I learned them, but were not in my memory. Where were they, then, or wherefore, when they were spoken, did I acknowledge them, and say, 'So it is, it is true,' unless as being already in the memory, though so put back and concealed, as it were, in more secret caverns, that had they not been drawn forth by the advice of another I would not, perchance, have been able to conceive of them?

Wherefore we find that to learn these things, whose images we drink not in by our senses, but perceive within as they are by themselves, without images, is nothing else but by meditation as it were to concentrate, and by observing to take care that those notions which the memory did before contain scattered and confused, be laid up at hand, as it were, in that same memory, where before they lay concealed, scattered, and neglected, and so the more easily present themselves to the mind well accustomed to observe them. And how many things of this sort does my memory retain which have been found out already, and, as I said, are, as it were, laid up ready to hand, which we are said to have learned and to have known; which, should we for small intervals of time cease to recall, they are again so submerged and slide back, as it were, into the more remote chambers, that they must be evolved thence again as if new (for other sphere they have none), and must be marshalled [*cogenda*] again that they may become known; that it to say, they must be collected [*colligenda*], as it were, from their dispersion; whence we have the word *cogitare*. For *cogo* [*I collect*] and *cogito* [*I re-collect*] have the same relation to each other as *ago* and *agito*, *facio* and *factito*. But the mind has appropriated to itself this word [cogitation], so that not that which is collected anywhere, but what is collected, that is marshalled, in the mind, is properly said to be 'cogitated.'

The memory containeth also the reasons and innumerable laws of numbers and dimensions, none of which hath any sense of the body impressed, seeing they have neither colour, nor sound, nor taste, nor smell, nor sense of touch. I have heard the sound of the words by which these things are signified when they are discussed; but the sounds are one thing,

the things another. For the sounds are one thing in Greek, another in Latin; but the things themselves are neither Greek, nor Latin, nor any other language. I have seen the lines of the craftsmen, even the finest, like a spider's web; but these are of another kind, they are not the images of those which the eye of my flesh showed me; he knoweth them who, without any idea whatsoever of a body, perceives them within himself. I have also observed the numbers of the things with which we number all the senses of the body; but those by which we number are of another kind, nor are they the images of these, and therefore they certainly are. Let him who sees not these things mock me for saying them; and I will pity him, whilst he mocks me.

All these things I retain in my memory, and how I learnt them I retain. I retain also many things which I have heard most falsely objected against them, which though they be false, yet is it not false that I have remembered them; and I remember, too, that I have distinguished between those truths and these falsehoods uttered against them; and I now see that it is one thing to distinguish these things, another to remember that I often distinguish them, when I often reflected upon them. I both remember, then, that I have often understood these things, and what I now distinguish and comprehend I store away in my memory, that hereafter I may remember that I understood it now. Therefore also I remember that I have remembered; so that if afterwards I shall call to mind that I have been able to remember these things, it will be through the power of memory that I shall call it to mind.

This same memory contains also the affections of my mind; not in the manner in which the mind itself contains them when it suffers them, but very differently according to a power peculiar to memory. For without being joyous, I remember myself to have had joy; and without being sad, I call to mind my past sadness; and that of which I was once afraid, I remember without fear; and without desire recall a former desire. Again, on the contrary, I at times remember when joyous my past sadness, and when sad my joy. Which is not to be wondered at as regards the body; for the mind is one thing, the body another. If I, therefore, when happy, recall some past bodily pain, it is not so strange a thing. But now, as this very memory itself is mind (for when we give orders to have a thing kept in memory, we say, 'See that you bear this in mind;' and when we forget a thing, we say, 'It did not enter my mind,' and, 'It slipped from my mind,' thus calling the memory itself mind), as this is so, how comes it to pass that when being joyful I remember my past sorrow, the mind has joy, the memory sorrow,—the mind, from the joy that is in it, is joyful, yet the memory, from the sadness that is in it, is not sad? Does not the memory perchance belong unto the mind? Who will say so? The memory doubtless is, so to say, the belly of the mind, and joy and sadness like sweet and bitter food, which, when entrusted to the memory, are, as it were, passed into the belly, where they can be reposited, but cannot taste. It is ridiculous to imagine these to be alike; and yet they are not utterly unlike.

But behold, out of my memory I educe it, when I affirm that there be four perturbations of the mind,—desire, joy, fear, sorrow; and whatsoever I shall be able to dispute on these, by dividing each into its peculiar species, and by defining it, there I find what I may say, and thence I educe it; yet am I not disturbed by any of these perturbations when by remembering them I call them to mind; and before I recollected and reviewed them, they were there; wherefore by remembrance could they be brought thence. Perchance, then, even as meat is in ruminating brought up out of the belly, so by calling to mind are these educed from the memory. Why, then, does not the disputant, thus recollecting, perceive in the mouth of his meditation the sweetness of joy or the bitterness of sorrow? Is the comparison unlike in this because not like in all points? For who would willingly discourse on these subjects, if, as often as we name sorrow or fear, we should be compelled to be sorrowful or fearful? And yet we could never speak of them, did we not find in our memory not merely the sounds of the names according to the images imprinted on it by the senses of the body, but the notions of the things themselves, which we never received by any door of the flesh, but which the mind itself, recognizing by the experience of its own passions, entrusted to the memory, or else which the memory itself retained without their being entrusted to it.

But whether by images or no, who can well affirm? For I name a stone, I name the sun, and the things themselves are not present to my senses, but their images are near to my memory. I name some pain of the body, yet it is not present when there is no pain; yet if its image were not in my memory, I should be ignorant what to say concerning it, nor in arguing be able to distinguish it from pleasure. I name bodily health when sound in body; the thing itself indeed is present with me, but unless its image also were in my memory, I could by no means call to mind what the sound of this name signified. Nor would sick people know, when health was named, what was said, unless the same image were retained by the power of memory, although the thing itself were absent from the body. I name numbers whereby we enumerate; and not their images, but they themselves are in my memory. I name the image of the sun, and this, too, is in my memory. For I do not recall the image of that image, but itself, for the image itself is present when I remember it. I name memory, and I know what I name. But where do I know it, except in the memory itself? Is it also present to itself by its image, and not by itself?

When I name forgetfulness, and know, too, what I name, whence should I know it if I did not remember it? I do not say the sound of the name, but the thing which it signifies; which, had I forgotten, I could not know what that sound signified. When, therefore, I remember memory, then is memory present with itself, through itself. But when I remember forgetfulness, there are present both memory and forgetfulness,—memory, whereby I remember, forgetfulness, which I remember. But what is forgetfulness but the privation of memory? How, then, is that present for me to remember, since, when it is so, I cannot remember? But if what we remember we retain in memory, yet, unless we remembered forgetfulness, we could never at the hearing of the name know the thing meant by it, then is forgetfulness retained by memory. Present, therefore, it is, lest we should forget it; and being so, we do forget. Is it to be inferred from this that forgetfulness, when we remember it, is not present to the memory through itself, but through its image; because, were forgetfulness present through itself, it would not lead us to remember, but to forget? Who now will investigate this? Who shall understand how it is?

Truly, O Lord, I labour therein, and labour in myself. I am become a troublesome soil that requires overmuch labour. For we are not now searching out the tracts of heaven, or measuring the distances of the stars, or inquiring about the weight of the earth. It is I myself—I, the mind—who remember. It is not much to be wondered at, if what I myself am not be far from me. But what is nearer to me than myself? And, behold, I am not able to comprehend the force of my own memory, though I cannot name myself without it. For what shall I say when it is plain to me that I remember forgetfulness? Shall I affirm that that which I remember is not in my memory? Or shall I say that forgetfulness is in my memory with the view of my not forgetting? Both of these are most absurd. What third view is there? How can I assert that the image of forgetfulness is retained by my memory, and not forgetfulness itself, when I remember it? And how can I assert this, seeing that when the image of anything is imprinted on the memory, the thing itself must of necessity be present first by which that image may be imprinted? For thus do I remember Carthage; thus, all the places to which I have been; thus, the faces of men whom I have seen, and things reported by the other senses; thus, the health or sickness of the body. For when these objects were present, my memory received images from them, which, when they were present, I might gaze on and reconsider in my mind, as I remembered them when they were absent. If, therefore, forgetfulness is retained in the memory through its image, and not through itself, then itself was once present, that its image might be taken. But when it was present, how did it write its image on the memory, seeing that forgetfulness by its presence blots out even what it finds already noted? And yet, in whatever way, though it be incomprehensible and inexplicable, yet most certain I am that I remember also forgetfulness itself, whereby what we do remember is blotted out.

Great is the power of memory; very wonderful is it, O my God, a profound and infinite manifoldness; and this thing is the mind, and this I myself am. What then am I, O my God? Of what nature am I? A life various and manifold, and exceeding vast. Behold, in the numberless fields, and caves, and caverns of my memory, full without number of numberless kinds of things, either through images, as all bodies are; or by the presence of the things themselves, as are the arts; or by some notion or observation, as the affections of the mind are, which, even though the mind doth not suffer, the memory retains, while whatsoever is in the memory is also in the mind: through all these do I run to and fro, and fly; I penetrate on this side and that, as far as I am able, and nowhere is there an end. So great is the power of memory, so great the power of life in man, whose life is mortal. What then shall I do, O Thou my true life, my God? I will pass even beyond this power of mine which is called memory— I will pass beyond it, that I may proceed to Thee, O Thou sweet Light. What sayest Thou to me? Behold, I am soaring by my mind towards Thee who remainest above me. I will also pass beyond this power of mine which is called memory, wishful to reach Thee whence Thou canst be reached, and to cleave unto Thee whence it is possible to cleave unto Thee. For even beasts and birds possess memory, else could they never find their lairs and nests again, nor many other things to which they are used; neither indeed could they become used to anything, but by their memory. I will pass, then, beyond memory also, that I may reach Him who has separated me from the four-footed beasts and the fowls of the air, making me wiser than they. I will pass beyond memory also, but where shall I find Thee, O Thou truly good and assured sweetness? But where shall I find Thee? If I find Thee without memory, then am I unmindful of Thee. And how now shall I find Thee, if I do not remember Thee?

For the woman who lost her drachma, and searched for it with a lamp, unless she had remembered it, would never have found it. For when it was found, whence could she know whether it were the same, had she not remembered it? I remember to have lost and found many things; and this I know thereby, that when I was searching for any of them, and was asked,

'Is this it?' 'Is that it?' I answered 'No,' until such time as that which I sought were offered to me. Which had I not remembered,—whatever it were,—though it were offered me, yet would I not find it, because I could not recognize it. And thus it is always, when we search for and find anything that is lost. Notwithstanding, if anything be by accident lost from the sight, not from the memory,—as any visible body,—the image of it is retained within, and is searched for until it be restored to sight; and when it is found, it is recognized by the image which is within. Nor do we say that we have found what we had lost unless we recognize it; nor can we recognize it unless we remember it. But this, though lost to the sight, was retained in the memory.

But how is it when the memory itself loses anything, as it happens when we forget anything and try to recall it? Where finally do we search, but in the memory itself? And there, if perchance one thing be offered for another, we refuse it, until we meet with what we seek; and when we do, we exclaim, 'This is it!' which we should not do unless we knew it again, nor should we recognize it unless we remembered it. Assuredly, therefore, we had forgotten it. Or, had not the whole of it slipped our memory, but by the part by which we had hold was the other part sought for; since the memory perceived that it did not revolve together as much as it was accustomed to do, and halting, as if from the mutilation of its old habit, demanded the restoration of that which was wanting. For example, if we see or think of some man known to us, and, having forgotten his name, endeavour to recover it, whatsoever other thing presents itself is not connected with it; because it was not used to be thought of in connection with him, and is consequently rejected, until that is present whereon the knowledge reposes fittingly as its accustomed object. And whence, save from the memory itself, does that present itself? For even when we recognize it as put in mind of it by another, it is thence it comes. For we do not believe it as something new, but, as we recall it, admit what was said to be correct. But if it were entirely blotted out of the mind, we should not, even when put in mind of it, recollect it. For we have not as yet entirely forgotten what we remember that we have forgotten. A lost notion, then, which we have entirely forgotten, we cannot even search for.

How, then, do I seek Thee, O Lord? For when I seek Thee, my God, I seek a happy life. I will seek Thee, that my soul may live. For my body liveth by my soul, and my soul liveth by Thee. How, then, do I seek a happy life, seeing that it is not mine till I can say, 'It is enough!' in that place where I ought to say it? How do I seek it? Is it by remembrance, as though I had forgotten it, knowing too that I had forgotten it? or, longing to learn it as a thing unknown, which either I had never known, or had so forgotten it as not even to remember that I had forgotten it? Is not a happy life the thing that all desire, and is there any one who altogether desires it not? But where did they acquire the knowledge of it, that they so desire it? Where have they seen it, that they so love it? Truly we have it, but how I know not. Yea, there is another way in which, when any one hath it, he is happy; and some there be that are happy in hope. These have it in an inferior kind to those that are happy in fact; and yet are they better off than they who are happy neither in fact nor in hope. And even these, had they it not in some way, would not so much desire to be happy, which that they do desire is most certain. How they come to know it, I cannot tell, but they have it by some kind of knowledge unknown to me, who am in much doubt as to whether it be in the memory; for if it be there, then have we been happy once; whether all individually, or as in that man who first sinned, in whom also we all died, and from whom we are all born with misery, I do not now ask; but I ask whether the happy life be in the memory? For did we not know it, we should not love it. We hear the name, and we all acknowledge that we desire the thing; for we are not delighted with the sound only. For when a Greek hears it spoken in Latin, he does not feel delighted, for he knows not what is spoken; but we are delighted, as he too would be if he heard it in Greek; because the thing itself is neither Greek nor Latin, which Greeks and Latins, and men of all other tongues, long so earnestly to obtain. It is then known unto all, and could they with one voice be asked whether they wished to be happy, without doubt they would all answer that they would. And this could not be unless the thing itself, of which it is the name, were retained in their memory.

But is it so as one who has seen Carthage remembers it? No. For a happy life is not visible to the eye, because it is not a body. Is it, then, as we remember numbers? No. For he that hath these in his knowledge strives not to attain further; but a happy life we have in our knowledge, and, therefore, do we love it, while yet we wish further to attain it that we may be happy. Is it, then, as we remember eloquence? No. For although some, when they hear this name, call the thing to mind, who, indeed, are not yet eloquent, and many who wish to be so, whence it appears to be in their knowledge; yet have these by their bodily perceptions noticed that others are eloquent, and been delighted with it, and long to be so,—although they would not be delighted save for some interior knowledge, nor desire to be so unless they were delighted,—but a happy life we can by no bodily perception make experience of in others. Is it, then, as we remember joy? It may be so; for my joy I remember, even when sad, like as I do a happy life when I am miserable. Nor did I ever with perception of the body either see, hear, smell, taste, or touch my joy; but I experienced it in my mind when I rejoiced; and the knowledge of it clung to my memory, so that I can call it to mind, sometimes with disdain and at others with desire, according to the difference of the things wherein I now remember that I rejoiced. For even from unclean things have I been bathed with a certain joy, which now calling to mind, I detest and execrate; at other times, from good and honest things, which, with longing, I call to mind, though perchance they be not nigh at hand, and then with sadness do I call to mind a former joy.

Where and when, then, did I experience my happy life, that I should call it to mind, and love and long for it? Nor is it I alone or a few others who wish to be happy, but truly all; which, unless by certain knowledge we knew, we should not wish with so certain a will. But how is this, that if two men be asked whether they would wish to serve as soldiers, one, it may be, would reply that he would, the other that he would not; but if they were asked whether they would wish to be happy, both of them would unhesitatingly say that they would; and this one would wish to serve, and the other not, from no other motive but to be happy? Is it, perchance, that as one joys in this, and another in that, so do all men agree in their wish for happiness, as they would agree, were they asked, in wishing to have joy,—and this joy they call a happy life? Although, then, one pursues joy in this way, and another in that, all have one goal, which they strive to attain, namely, to have joy. This life, being a thing which no one can say he has not experienced, it is on that account found in the memory, and recognized whenever the name of a happy life is heard.

Let it be far, O Lord,—let it be far from the heart of Thy servant who confesseth unto Thee; let it be far from me to think myself happy, be the joy what it may. For there is a joy which is not granted to the 'wicked,' but to those who worship Thee thankfully, whose joy Thou Thyself art. And the happy life is this,—to rejoice unto Thee, in Thee, and for Thee; this it is, and there is no other. But those who think there is another follow after another joy, and that not the true one. Their will, however, is not turned away from some shadow of joy.

It is not, then, certain that all men wish to be happy, since those who wish not to rejoice in Thee, which is the only happy life, do not verily desire the happy life. Or do all desire this, but because 'the flesh lusteth against the spirit, and the spirit against the flesh,' so that they 'cannot do the things that they would,' they fall upon that which they are able to do, and with that are content; because that which they are not able to do, they do not so will as to make them able? For I ask of every man, whether he would rather rejoice in truth or in falsehood. They will no more hesitate to say, 'in truth' than to say, 'that they wish to be happy.' For a happy life is joy in the truth. For this is joy in Thee, who art 'the truth,' O God, 'my light,' 'the health of my countenance, and my God.' All wish for this happy life; this life do all wish for, which is the only happy one; joy in the truth do all wish for. I have had experience of many who wished to deceive, but not one who wished to be deceived. Where, then, did they know this happy life, save where they knew also the truth? For they love it, too, since they would not be deceived. And when they love a happy life, which is naught else but joy in the truth, assuredly they love also the truth; which yet they would not love were there not some knowledge of it in the memory. Wherefore, then, do they not rejoice in it? Why are they not happy? Because they are more entirely occupied with other things which rather make them miserable, than that which would make them happy, which they remember so little of. For there is yet a little light in men; let them walk—let them 'walk,' that 'the darkness' seize them not.

Why, then, doth truth beget hatred, and that man of thine, preaching the truth, become an enemy unto them, whereas a happy life is loved, which is naught else but joy in the truth; unless that truth is loved in such a sort as that those who love aught else wish that to be the truth which they love, and, as they are willing to be deceived, are unwilling to be convinced that they are so? Therefore do they hate the truth for the sake of that thing which they love instead of the truth. They love truth when she shines on them, and hate her when she rebukes them. For, because they are not willing to be deceived, and wish to deceive, they love her when she reveals herself, and hate her when she reveals them. On that account shall she so requite them, that those who were unwilling to be discovered by her she both discovers against their will, and discovers not herself unto them. Thus, thus, truly thus doth the human mind, so blind and sick, so base and unseemly, desire to lie concealed, but wishes not that anything should be concealed from it. But the opposite is rendered unto it,—that itself is not concealed from the truth, but the truth is concealed from it. Yet, even while thus wretched, it prefers to rejoice in truth rather than in falsehood. Happy then will it be, when, no trouble intervening, it shall rejoice in that only truth by whom all things else are true.

Behold how I have enlarged in my memory seeking Thee, O Lord; and out of it have I not found Thee. Nor have I found aught concerning Thee, but what I have retained in memory from the time I learned Thee. For from the time I learned Thee have I never forgotten Thee. For where I found truth, there found I my God, who is the Truth itself, which from the time I learned it have I not forgotten. And thus since the time I learned Thee, Thou abidest in my memory; and there do I find Thee whensoever I call Thee to remembrance, and delight in Thee. These are my holy delights, which Thou hast bestowed upon me in Thy mercy, having respect unto my poverty.

But where in my memory abidest Thou, O Lord, where dost Thou there abide? What manner of chamber hast Thou there formed for Thyself? What sort of sanctuary hast Thou erected for Thyself? Thou hast granted this honour to my memory, to take up Thy abode in it; but in what quarter of it Thou abidest, I am considering. For in calling Thee to mind, I soared beyond those parts of it which the beasts also possess, since I found Thee not there amongst the images of corporeal things; and I arrived at those parts where I had committed the affections of my mind, nor there did I find Thee. And I entered into the very seat of my mind, which it has in my memory, since the mind remembers itself also—nor wert Thou there. For as Thou art not a bodily image, nor the affection of a living creature, as when we rejoice, condole, desire, fear, remember, forget, or aught of the kind; so neither art Thou the mind itself, because Thou art the Lord God of the mind; and all these things are changed, but Thou remainest unchangeable over all, yet vouchsafest to dwell in my memory, from the time I learned Thee. But why do I now seek in what part of it Thou dwellest, as if truly there were places in it? Thou dost dwell in it assuredly, since I have remembered Thee from the time I learned Thee, and I find Thee in it when I call Thee to mind.

Where, then, did I find Thee, so as to be able to learn Thee? For Thou wert not in my memory before I learned Thee. Where, then, did I find Thee, so as to be able to learn Thee, but in Thee above me? Place there is none; we go both 'backward' and 'forward,' and there is no place. Everywhere, O Truth, dost Thou direct all who consult Thee, and dost at once answer all, though they consult Thee on divers things. Clearly dost Thou answer, though all do not with clearness hear. All consult Thee upon whatever they wish, though they hear not always that which they wish. He is Thy best servant who does not so much look to hear that from Thee which he himself wisheth, as to wish that which he heareth from Thee.

Too late did I love Thee, O Fairness, so ancient, and yet so new! Too late did I love Thee! For behold, Thou wert within, and I without, and there did I seek Thee; I, unlovely, rushed heedlessly among the things of beauty Thou madest. Thou wert with me, but I was not with Thee. Those things kept me far from Thee, which, unless they were in Thee, were not. Thou calledst, and criedst aloud, and forcedst open my deafness. Thou didst gleam and shine, and chase away my blindness. Thou didst exhale odours, and I drew in my breath and do pant after Thee. I tasted, and do hunger and thirst. Thou didst touch me, and I burned for Thy peace.

When I shall cleave unto Thee with all my being, then shall I in nothing have pain and labour; and my life shall be a real life, being wholly full of Thee. But now since he whom Thou fillest is the one Thou liftest up, I am a burden to myself, as not being full of Thee. Joys of sorrow contend with sorrows of joy; and on which side the victory may be I know not. Woe is me! Lord, have pity on me. My evil sorrows contend with my good joys; and on which side the victory may be I know not. Woe is me! Lord, have pity on me. Woe is me! Lo, I hide not my wounds; Thou art the Physician, I the sick; Thou merciful, I miserable. Is not the life of man upon earth a temptation? Who is he that wishes for vexations and difficulties? Thou commandest them to be endured, not to be loved. For no man loves what he endures, though he may love to endure. For notwithstanding he rejoices to endure, he would rather there were naught for him to endure. In adversity, I desire prosperity; in prosperity, I fear adversity. What middle place, then, is there between these, where human life is not a temptation? Woe unto the prosperity of this world, once and again, from fear of misfortune and a corruption of joy! Woe unto the adversities of this world, once and again, and for the third time, from the desire of prosperity; and because adversity itself is a hard thing, and makes shipwreck of endurance! Is not the life of man upon earth a temptation, and that without intermission?

And my whole hope is only in Thy exceeding great mercy. Give what Thou commandest, and command what Thou wilt. Thou imposest continency upon us, 'nevertheless, when I perceived,' saith one, 'that I could not otherwise obtain her, except God gave her me; . . . that was a point of wisdom also to know whose gift she was.' For by continency are we bound up and brought into one, whence we were scattered abroad into many. For he loves Thee too little who loves aught with Thee, which he loves not for Thee, O love, who ever burnest, and art never quenched! O charity, my God, kindle me! Thou commandest continency; give what Thou commandest, and command what Thou wilt.

Verily, Thou commandest that I should be continent from the 'lust of the flesh, and the lust of the eyes, and the pride of life.' Thou hast commanded me to abstain from concubinage; and as to marriage itself, Thou hast advised something better than Thou hast allowed. And because Thou didst give it, it was done; and that before I became a dispenser of Thy sacrament. But there still exist in my memory—of which I have spoken much—the images of such things as my habits had fixed there; and these rush into my thoughts, though strengthless, when I am awake; but in sleep they do so not only so as to give pleasure, but even to obtain consent, and what very nearly resembles reality. Yea, to such an extent prevails the illusion of the image, both in my soul and in my flesh, that the false persuade me, when sleeping, unto that which the true are not able when waking. Am I not myself at that time, O Lord my God? And there is yet so much difference between myself and myself, in that instant wherein I pass back from waking to sleeping, or return from sleeping to waking! Where, then, is the reason which when waking resists such suggestions? And if the things themselves be forced on it, I remain unmoved. Is it shut up with the eyes? Or is it put to sleep with the bodily senses? But whence, then, comes it to pass, that even in slumber we often resist, and, bearing our purpose in mind, and continuing most chastely in it, yield no assent to such allurements? And there is yet so much difference that, when it happeneth otherwise, upon awaking we return to peace of conscience; and by this same diversity do we discover that it was not we that did it, while we still feel sorry that in some way it was done in us.

Is not Thy hand able, O Almighty God, to heal all the diseases of my soul, and by Thy more abundant grace to quench even the lascivious motions of my sleep? Thou wilt increase in me, O Lord, Thy gifts more and more, that my soul may follow me to Thee, disengaged from the birdlime of concupiscence; that it may not be in rebellion against itself, and even in dreams not simply not, through sensual images, commit those deformities of corruption, even to the pollution of the flesh, but that it may not even consent unto them. For it is no great thing for the Almighty, who is 'able to do . . . above all that we ask or think,' to bring it about that no such influence—not even so slight a one as a sign might restrain—should afford gratification to the chaste affection even of one sleeping; and that not only in this life, but at my present age. But what I still am in this species of my ill, have I confessed unto my good Lord; rejoicing with trembling in that which Thou hast given me, and bewailing myself for that wherein I am still imperfect; trusting that Thou wilt perfect Thy mercies in me, even to the fulness of peace, which both that which is within and that which is without shall have with Thee, when death is swallowed up in victory.

There is another evil of the day that I would were 'sufficient' unto it. For by eating and drinking we repair the daily decays of the body, until Thou destroyest both food and stomach, when Thou shalt destroy my want with an amazing satiety, and shalt clothe this corruptible with an eternal incorruption. But now is necessity sweet unto me, and against this sweetness do I fight, lest I be enthralled; and I carry on a daily war by fastings, oftentimes 'bringing my body into subjection,' and my pains are expelled by pleasure. For hunger and thirst are in some sort pains; they consume and destroy like unto a fever, unless the medicine of nourishment relieve us. The which, since it is at hand through the comfort we receive of Thy gifts, with which land and water and air serve our infirmity, our calamity is called pleasure.

This much hast Thou taught me, that I should bring myself to take food as medicine. But during the time that I am passing from the uneasiness of

want to the calmness of satiety, even in the very passage doth that snare of
concupiscence lie in wait for me. For the passage itself is pleasure, nor is
there any other way of passing thither, whither necessity compels us to
pass. And whereas health is the reason of eating and drinking, there joineth
itself as an handmaid a perilous delight, which mostly tries to precede it, in
order that I may do for her sake what I say I do, or desire to do, for health's
sake. Nor have both the same limit; for what is sufficient for health is too
little for pleasure. And oftentimes it is doubtful whether it be the necessary
care of the body which still asks nourishment, or whether a sensual snare of
desire offers its ministry. In this uncertainty does my unhappy soul rejoice,
and therein prepares an excuse as a defence, glad that it doth not appear
what may be sufficient for the moderation of health, that so under the
pretence of health it may conceal the business of pleasure. These temptations
do I daily endeavour to resist, and I summon Thy right hand to my help,
and refer my excitements to Thee, because as yet I have no resolve in this
matter.

I hear the voice of my God commanding, let not 'your hearts be over-
charged with surfeiting and drunkenness.' 'Drunkenness,' it is far from me;
Thou wilt have mercy, that it approach not near unto me. But 'surfeiting'
sometimes creepeth upon Thy servant; Thou wilt have mercy, that it may
be far from me. For no man can be continent unless Thou give it. Many
things which we pray for dost Thou give us; and what good soever we
receive before we prayed for it, do we receive from Thee, and that we
might afterwards know this did we receive it from Thee. Drunkard was I
never, but I have known drunkards to be made sober men by Thee. Thy
doing, then, was it, that they who never were such might not be so, as from
Thee it was that they who have been so heretofore might not remain so
always; and from Thee, too, was it, that both might know from whom it
was. I heard another voice of Thine, 'Go not after thy lusts, but refrain
thyself from thine appetites.' And by Thy favour have I heard this saying
likewise, which I have much delighted in, 'Neither if we eat, are we the
better; neither if we eat not, are we the worse;' which is to say, that neither

shall the one make me to abound, nor the other to be wretched. I heard also another voice, 'For I have learned, in whatsoever state I am, therewith to be content. I know both how to be abased, and I know how to abound. . . . I can do all things through Christ which strengtheneth me.' Lo! a soldier of the celestial camp—not dust as we are. But remember, O Lord, 'that we are dust,' and that of dust Thou hast created man; and he 'was lost, and is found.' Nor could he do this of his own power, seeing that he whom I so loved, saying these things through the afflatus of Thy inspiration, was of that same dust. 'I can,' saith he, 'do all things through Him which strengtheneth me.' Strengthen me, that I may be able. Give what Thou commandest, and command what Thou wilt. He confesses to have received, and when he glorieth, he glorieth in the Lord. Another have I heard entreating that he might receive,—'Take from me,' saith he, 'the greediness of the belly;' by which it appeareth, O my holy God, that Thou givest when what Thou commandest to be done is done.

Thou hast taught me, good Father, that 'unto the pure all things are pure;' but 'it is evil for that man who eateth with offence;' 'and that every creature of Thine is good, and nothing to be refused, if it be received with thanksgiving;' and that 'meat commendeth us not to God;' and that no man should 'judge us in meat or in drink;' and that he that eateth, let him not despise him that eateth not; and let not him that eateth not judge him that eateth. These things have I learned, thanks and praise be unto Thee, O my God and Master, who dost knock at my ears and enlighten my heart; deliver me out of all temptation. It is not the uncleanness of meat that I fear, but the uncleanness of lusting. I know that permission was granted unto Noah to eat every kind of flesh that was good for food; that Elias was fed with flesh; that John, endued with a wonderful abstinence, was not polluted by the living creatures (that is, the locusts) which he fed on.[48] I know, too, that Esau was deceived by a longing for lentils, and that David took blame to himself for desiring water, and that our King was tempted not by flesh but bread. And the people in the wilderness, therefore, also deserved reproof, not because they desired flesh,

but because, in their desire for food, they murmured against the Lord.

Placed, then, in the midst of these temptations, I strive daily against longing for food and drink. For it is not of such a nature as that I am able to resolve to cut it off once for all, and not touch it afterwards, as I was able to do with concubinage. The bridle of the throat, therefore, is to be held in the mean of slackness and tightness. And who, O Lord, is he who is not in some degree carried away beyond the bounds of necessity? Whoever he is, he is great; let him magnify Thy name. But I am not such a one, 'for I am a sinful man.' Yet do I also magnify Thy name; and He who hath 'overcome the world' maketh intercession to Thee for my sins, accounting me among the 'feeble members' of His body, because Thine eyes saw that of him which was imperfect; and in Thy book all shall be written.

With the attractions of odours I am not much troubled. When absent I do not seek them; when present I do not refuse them; and am prepared ever to be without them. At any rate thus I appear to myself; perchance I am deceived. For that also is a lamentable darkness wherein my capacity that is in me is concealed, so that my mind, making inquiry into herself concerning her own powers, ventures not readily to credit herself; because that which is already in it is, for the most part, concealed, unless experience reveal it. And no man ought to feel secure in this life, the whole of which is called a temptation, that he, who could be made better from worse, may not also from better be made worse. Our sole hope, our sole confidence, our sole assured promise, is Thy mercy.

The delights of the ear had more powerfully inveigled and conquered me, but Thou didst unbind and liberate me. Now, in those airs which Thy words breathe soul into, when sung with a sweet and trained voice, do I somewhat repose; yet not so as to cling to them, but so as to free myself when I wish. But with the words which are their life do they, that they may gain admission into me, strive after a place of some honour in my heart; and I can hardly assign them a fitting one. Sometimes I appear to myself to give them more respect than is fitting, as I perceive that our minds are more devoutly and earnestly elevated into a flame of piety by the holy words themselves when they are thus sung, than when they are not; and that all affections of our spirit, by their own diversity, have their appropriate measures in the voice and singing, wherewith by I know not what secret relationship they are stimulated. But the gratification of my flesh, to which the mind ought never to be given over to be enervated, often beguiles me, while the sense does not so attend on reason as to follow her patiently; but having gained admission merely for her sake, it strives even to run on before her, and be her leader. Thus in these things do I sin unknowing, but afterwards do I know it.

Sometimes, again, avoiding very earnestly this same deception, I err out of too great preciseness; and sometimes so much as to desire that every air of the pleasant songs to which David's Psalter is often used, be banished both from my ears and those of the Church itself; and that way seemed unto me safer which I remembered to have been often related to me of Athanasius, Bishop of Alexandria, who obliged the readers of the psalm to give utterance to it with so slight an inflection of voice, that it was more like speaking than singing. Notwithstanding, when I call to mind the tears I shed at the songs of Thy Church, at the outset of my recovered faith, and how even now I am moved not by the singing but by what is sung, when they are sung with a clear and skilfully modulated voice, I then acknowledge the great utility of this custom. Thus vacillate I between dangerous pleasure and tried soundness; being inclined rather (though I pronounce no irrevocable opinion upon the subject) to approve of the use of singing in the church, that so by the delights of the ear the weaker minds may be stimulated to a devotional frame. Yet when it happens to me to be more moved by the singing than by what is sung, I confess myself to have sinned criminally, and then I would rather not have heard the singing. See now the condition I am in! Weep with me, and weep for me, you who so control your inward feelings as that good results ensue. As for you who do not thus act, these things concern you not. But Thou, O Lord my God, give ear, behold and see, and have mercy upon me, and heal me,—Thou, in whose sight I am become a puzzle to myself; and 'this is my infirmity.'

There remain the delights of these eyes of my flesh, concerning which to make my confessions in the hearing of the ears of Thy temple, those fraternal and devout ears; and so to conclude the temptations of 'the lust of the flesh' which still assail me, groaning and desiring to be clothed upon with my house from heaven. The eyes delight in fair and varied forms, and bright and pleasing colours. Suffer not these to take possession of my soul; let God rather possess it, He who made these things 'very good' indeed; yet is He my good, not these. And these move me while awake, during the day; nor is rest from them granted me, as there is from the voices of melody, sometimes, in silence, from them all. For that queen of colours, the light, flooding all that we look upon, wherever I be during the day, gliding past me in manifold forms, doth soothe me when busied about other things, and not noticing it. And so strongly doth it insinuate itself, that if it be suddenly withdrawn it is looked for longingly, and if long absent doth sadden the mind.

O Thou Light, which Tobias saw, when, his eyes being closed, he taught his son the way of life; himself going before with the feet of charity, never going astray. Or that which Isaac saw, when his fleshly 'eyes were dim, so that he could not see' by reason of old age; it was permitted him, not knowingly to bless his sons, but in blessing them to know them. Or that which Jacob saw, when he too, blind through great age, with an enlightened heart, in the persons of his own sons, threw light upon the races of the future people, pre-signified in them; and laid his hands, mystically crossed, upon his grandchildren by Joseph, not as their father, looking outwardly, corrected them, but as he himself distinguished them. This is the light, the only one, and all those who see and love it are one. But that corporeal light of which I was speaking seasoneth the life of the world for her blind lovers, with a tempting and fatal sweetness. But they who know how to praise Thee for it, 'O God, the world's great Architect,'[49] take it up in Thy hymn, and are not taken up with it in their sleep. Such desire I to be. I resist seductions of the eyes, lest my feet with which I advance on Thy way be entangled; and I raise my invisible eyes to Thee, that Thou wouldst be pleased to 'pluck my feet out of the net.' Thou dost continually pluck them out, for they are ensnared. Thou never ceasest to pluck them out, but I constantly remain fast in the snares set all around me; because Thou 'that keepest Israel shall neither slumber nor sleep.'

What numberless things, made by divers arts and manufactures, both in our apparel, shoes, vessels, and every kind of work, in pictures, too, and sundry images, and these going far beyond necessary and moderate use and holy signification, have men added for the enthralment of the eyes; following outwardly what they make, forsaking inwardly Him by whom they were made, yea, and destroying that which they themselves were made! But I, O my God and my Joy, do hence also sing a hymn unto Thee, and offer a sacrifice of praise unto my Sanctifier, because those beautiful patterns, which through the medium of men's souls are conveyed into their artistic hands, emanate from that Beauty which is above our souls, which my soul sigheth after day and night. But as for the makers and followers of those outward beauties, they from thence derive the way of approving them, but not of using them. And though they see Him not, yet is He there, that they might not go astray, but keep their strength for Thee, and not dissipate it upon delicious lassitudes. And I, though I both say and perceive this, impede my course with such beauties, but Thou dost rescue me, O Lord, Thou dost rescue me; 'for Thy loving-kindness is before mine eyes.' For I am taken miserably, and Thou rescuest me mercifully; sometimes not perceiving it, in that I had come upon them hesitatingly; at other times with pain, because I was held fast by them.

In addition to this there is another form of temptation, more complex in its peril. For besides that concupiscence of the flesh which lieth in the gratification of all senses and pleasures, wherein its slaves who 'are far from Thee perish,' there pertaineth to the soul, through the same senses of the body, a certain vain and curious longing, cloaked under the name of knowledge and learning, not of having pleasure in the flesh, but of making experiments through the flesh. This longing, since it originates in an appetite for knowledge, and the sight being the chief amongst the senses in the acquisition of knowledge, is called in divine language, 'the lust of the eyes.' For seeing belongeth properly to the eyes; yet we apply this word to the other senses also, when we exercise them in the search after knowledge. For we do not say, Listen how it glows, smell how it glistens, taste how it shines, or feel how it flashes, since all these are said to be seen. And yet we say not only, See how it shineth, which the eyes alone can perceive; but also, See how it soundeth, see how it smelleth, see how it tasteth, see how hard it is. And thus the general experience of the senses, as was said before, is termed 'the lust of the eyes,' because the function of seeing, wherein the eyes hold the pre-eminence, the other senses by way of similitude take possession of, whensoever they seek out any knowledge.

But by this is it more clearly discerned, when pleasure and when curiosity is pursued by the senses; for pleasure follows after objects that are beautiful, melodious, fragrant, savoury, soft; but curiosity, for experiment's sake, seeks the contrary of these,—not with a view of undergoing uneasiness, but from the passion of experimenting upon and knowing them. For what pleasure is there to see, in a lacerated corpse, that which makes you shudder? And yet if it lie near, we flock thither, to be made sad, and to turn pale. Even in sleep they fear lest they should see it. Just as if when awake any one compelled them to go and see it, or any report of its beauty had attracted them! Thus also is it with the other senses, which it were tedious to pursue. From this malady of curiosity are all those strange sights exhibited in the theatre. Hence do we proceed to search out the secret powers of nature (which is beside our end), which to know profits not, and wherein men desire nothing but to know. Hence, too, with that same end of perverted knowledge we consult magical arts. Hence, again, even in religion itself, is God tempted, when signs and wonders are eagerly asked of Him,—not desired for any saving end, but to make trial only.

In this so vast a wilderness, replete with snares and dangers, lo, many of them have I lopped off, and expelled from my heart, as Thou, O God of my salvation, hast enabled me to do. And yet when dare I say, since so many things of this kind buzz around our daily life,—when dare I say that no such thing makes me intent to see it, or creates in me vain solicitude? It is true that the theatres never now carry me away, nor do I now care to know the courses of the stars, nor hath my soul at any time consulted departed spirits; all sacrilegious oaths I abhor. O Lord my God, to whom I owe all humble and single-hearted service, with what subtlety of suggestion does the enemy influence me to require some sign from Thee! But by our King, and by our pure and chaste country Jerusalem, I beseech Thee, that as any consenting unto such thoughts is far from me, so may it always be farther and farther. But when I entreat Thee for the salvation of any, the end I aim at is far otherwise, and Thou who doest what Thou wilt, givest and wilt give me willingly to 'follow' Thee.

Nevertheless, in how many most minute and contemptible things is our curiosity daily tempted, and who can number how often we succumb? How often, when people are narrating idle tales, do we begin by tolerating them, lest we should give offence unto the weak; and then gradually we listen willingly! I do not now-a-days go to the circus to see a dog chasing a hare; but if by chance I pass such a coursing in the fields, it possibly distracts me even from some serious thought, and draws me after it,—not that I turn the body of my beast aside, but the inclination of my mind. And except Thou, by demonstrating to me my weakness, dost speedily warn me, either through the sight itself, by some reflection to rise to Thee, or wholly to despise and pass it by, I, vain one, am absorbed by it. How is it, when sitting at home, a lizard catching flies, or a spider entangling them as they rush into her nets, oftentimes arrests me? Is the feeling of curiosity not the same because these are such tiny creatures? From them I proceed to praise Thee, the wonderful Creator and Disposer of all things; but it is not this that first attracts my attention. It is one thing to get up quickly, and another not to fall, and of such things is my life full; and my only hope is in Thy exceeding great mercy. For when this heart of ours is made the receptacle of such things, and bears crowds of this abounding vanity, then are our prayers often interrupted and disturbed thereby; and whilst in Thy presence we direct the voice of our heart to Thine ears, this so great a matter is broken off by the influx of I know not what idle thoughts.

Shall we, then, account this too amongst such things as are to be lightly esteemed, or shall anything restore us to hope, save Thy complete mercy, since Thou hast begun to change us? And Thou knowest to what extent Thou hast already changed me, Thou who first healedst me of the lust of vindicating myself, that so Thou mightest forgive all my remaining 'iniquities,' and heal all my 'diseases,' and redeem my life from corruption, and crown me with 'loving-kindness and tender mercies,' and satisfy my desire with 'good things;' who didst restrain my pride with Thy fear, and subdue my neck to Thy 'yoke.' And now I bear it, and it is 'light' unto me, because so hast Thou promised, and made it, and so in truth it was, though I knew it not, when I feared to take it up. But, O Lord,—Thou who alone reignest without pride, because Thou art the only true Lord, who hast no lord,— hath this third kind of temptation left me, or can it leave me during this life?

The desire to be feared and loved of men, with no other view than that I may experience a joy therein which is no joy, is a miserable life, and unseemly ostentation. Hence especially it arises that we do not love Thee, nor devoutly fear Thee. And therefore dost Thou resist the proud, but givest grace unto the humble; and Thou thunderest upon the ambitious designs of the world, and 'the foundations of the hills' tremble. Because now certain offices of human society render it necessary to be loved and feared of men, the adversary of our true blessedness presseth hard upon us, everywhere scattering his snares of 'well done, well done;' that while acquiring them eagerly, we may be caught unawares, and disunite our joy from Thy truth, and fix it on the deceits of men; and take pleasure in being loved and feared, not for Thy sake, but in Thy stead, by which means, being made like unto him, he may have them as his, not in harmony of love, but in the fellowship of punishment; who aspired to exalt his throne in the north, that dark and cold they might serve him, imitating Thee in perverse and distorted ways. But we, O Lord, lo, we are Thy 'little flock;' do Thou possess us, stretch Thy wings over us, and let us take refuge under them. Be Thou our glory; let us be loved for Thy sake, and Thy word feared in us. They who desire to be commended of men when Thou blamest, will not be defended of men when Thou judgest; nor will they be delivered when Thou condemnest. But when not the sinner is praised in the desires of his soul, nor he blessed who doeth unjustly, but a man is praised for some gift that Thou hast bestowed upon him, and he is more gratified at the praise for himself than that he possesses the gift for which he is praised, such a one is praised while Thou blamest. And better truly is he who praised than the one who was praised. For the gift of God in man was pleasing to the one, while the other was better pleased with the gift of man than that of God.

By these temptations, O Lord, are we daily tried; yea, unceasingly are we tried. Our daily 'furnace' is the human tongue. And in this respect also dost Thou command us to be continent. Give what Thou commandest, and command what Thou wilt. Regarding this matter, Thou knowest the groans of my heart, and the rivers of mine eyes. For I am not able to ascertain how far I am clean of this plague, and I stand in great fear of my 'secret faults,' which Thine eyes perceive, though mine do not. For in other kinds of temptations I have some sort of power of examining myself; but in this, hardly any. For, both as regards the pleasures of the flesh and an idle curiosity, I see how far I have been able to hold my mind in check when I do without them, either voluntarily or by reason of their not being at hand; for then I inquire of myself how much more or less troublesome it is to me not to have them. Riches truly which are sought for in order that they may minister to some one of these three 'lusts,' or to two, or the whole of them, if the mind be not able to see clearly whether, when it hath them it despiseth them, they may be cast on one side, that so it may prove itself. But if we desire to test our power of doing without praise, need we live ill, and that so flagitiously and immoderately as that every one who knows us shall detest us? What greater madness than this can be either said or conceived? But if praise both is wont and ought to be the companion of a good life and of good works, we should as little forego its companionship as a good life itself. But unless a thing be absent, I do not know whether I shall be contented or troubled at being without it.

What, then, do I confess unto Thee, O Lord, in this kind of temptation? What, save that I am delighted with praise, but more with the truth itself than with praise? For were I to have any choice, whether I had rather, being mad, or astray on all things, be praised by all men, or, being firm and well-assured in the truth, be blamed by all, I see which I should choose. Yet would I be unwilling that the approval of another should even add to my joy for any good I have. Yet I admit that it doth increase it, and, more than that, that dispraise doth diminish it. And when I am disquieted at this misery of mine, an excuse presents itself to me, the value of which Thou, God, knowest, for it renders me uncertain. For since it is not continency alone that Thou hast enjoined upon us, that is, from what things to hold back our love, but righteousness also, that is, upon what to bestow it, and hast wished us to love not Thee only, but also our neighbour,—often, when gratified by intelligent praise, I appear to myself to be gratified by the proficiency or towardliness of my neighbour, and again to be sorry for evil in him when I hear him dispraise either that which he understands not, or is good. For I am sometimes grieved at mine own praise, either when those things which I am displeased at in myself be praised in me, or even lesser and trifling goods are more valued than they should be. But, again, how do I know whether I am thus affected, because I am unwilling that he who praiseth me should differ from me concerning myself—not as being moved with consideration for him, but because the same good things which please me in myself are more pleasing to me when they also please another? For, in a sort, I am not praised when my judgment of myself is not praised; since either those things which are displeasing to me are praised, or those more so which are less pleasing to me. Am I then uncertain of myself in this matter?

Behold, O Truth, in Thee do I see that I ought not to be moved at my own praises for my own sake, but for my neighbour's good. And whether it be so, in truth I know not. For concerning this I know less of myself than dost Thou. I beseech Thee now, O my God, to reveal to me myself also, that I may confess unto my brethren, who are to pray for me, what I find in myself weak. Once again let me more diligently examine myself. If, in mine own praise, I am moved with consideration for my neighbour, why am I less moved if some other man be unjustly dispraised than if it be myself? Why am I more irritated at that reproach which is cast upon myself, than at that which is with equal injustice cast upon another in my presence? Am I ignorant of this also? or does it remain that I deceive myself, and do not the 'truth' before Thee in my heart and tongue? Put such madness far from me, O Lord, lest my mouth be to me the oil of sinners, to anoint my head.

'I am poor and needy,' yet better am I while in secret groanings I displease myself, and seek for Thy mercy, until what is lacking in me be renewed and made complete, even up to that peace of which the eye of the proud is ignorant. Yet the word which proceedeth out of the mouth, and actions known to men, have a most dangerous temptation from the love of praise, which, for the establishing of a certain excellency of our own, gathers together solicited suffrages. It tempts, even when within I reprove myself for it, on the very ground that it is reproved; and often man glories more vainly of the very scorn of vain-glory; wherefore it is not any longer scorn of vain-glory whereof it glories, for he does not truly contemn it when he inwardly glories.

Within also, within is another evil, arising out of the same kind of temptation; whereby they become empty who please themselves in themselves, although they please not, or displease, or aim at pleasing others. But in pleasing themselves, they much displease Thee, not merely taking pleasure in things not good as if they were good, but in Thy good things as though they were their own; or even as if in Thine, yet as though of their own merits; or even as if though of Thy grace, yet not with friendly rejoicings, but as envying that grace to others. In all these and similar perils and labours Thou perceivest the trembling of my heart, and I rather feel my wounds to be cured by Thee than not inflicted by me.

Where hast Thou not accompanied me, O Truth, teaching me both what to avoid and what to desire, when I submitted to Thee what I could perceive of sublunary things, and asked Thy counsel? With my external senses, as I could, I viewed the world, and noted the life which my body derives from me, and these my senses. Thence I advanced inwardly into the recesses of my memory,—the manifold rooms, wondrously full of multitudinous wealth; and I considered and was afraid, and could discern none of these things without Thee, and found none of them to be Thee. Nor was I myself the discoverer of these things,—I, who went over them all, and laboured to distinguish and to value everything according to its dignity, accepting some things upon the report of my senses, and questioning about others which I felt to be mixed up with myself, distinguishing and numbering the reporters themselves, and in the vast storehouse of my memory investigating some things, laying up others, taking out others. Neither was I myself when I did this (that is, that ability of mine whereby I did it), nor was it Thou, for Thou art that never-failing light which I took counsel of as to them all, whether they were what they were, and what was their worth; and I heard Thee teaching and commanding me. And this I do often; this is a delight to me, and, as far as I can get relief from necessary duties, to this gratification do I resort. Nor in all these which I review when consulting Thee, find I a secure place for my soul, save in Thee, into whom my scattered members may be gathered together, and nothing of me depart from Thee. And sometimes Thou dost introduce me to a most rare affection, inwardly, to an inexplicable sweetness, which, if it should be perfected in me, I know not to what point that life might not arrive. But by these wretched weights of mine do I relapse into these things, and am sucked in by my old customs, and am held, and sorrow much, yet am much held. To such an extent does the burden of habit press us down. In this way I can be, but will not; in that I will, but cannot,—on both ways miserable.

And thus have I reflected upon the weariness of my sins, in that threefold 'lust,' and have invoked Thy right hand to my aid. For with a wounded heart have I seen Thy brightness, and being beaten back I exclaimed, 'Who can attain unto it?' 'I am cut off from before Thine eyes.' Thou art the Truth, who presidest over all things, but I, through my covetousness, wished not to lose Thee, but with Thee wished to possess a lie; as no one wishes so to speak falsely as himself to be ignorant of the truth. So then I lost Thee, because Thou deignest not to be enjoyed with a lie.

Whom could I find to reconcile me to Thee? Was I to solicit the angels? By what prayer? By what sacraments? Many striving to return unto Thee, and not able of themselves, have, as I am told, tried this, and have fallen into a longing for curious visions, and were held worthy to be deceived. For they, being exalted, sought Thee by the pride of learning, thrusting themselves forward rather than beating their breasts, and so by correspondence of heart drew unto themselves the princes of the air, the conspirators and companions in pride, by whom, through the power of magic, they were deceived, seeking a mediator by whom they might be cleansed; but none was there. For the devil it was transforming himself into an angel of light. And he much allured proud flesh, in that he had no fleshly body. For they were mortal, and sinful; but Thou, O Lord, to whom they arrogantly sought to be reconciled, art immortal, and sinless. But a mediator between God and man ought to have something like unto God, and something like unto man; lest being in both like unto man, he should be far from God; or if in both like unto God, he should be far from man, and so should not be a mediator. That deceitful mediator, then, by whom in Thy secret judgments pride deserved to be deceived, hath one thing in common with man, that is, sin; another he would appear to have with God, and, not being clothed with mortality of flesh, would boast that he was immortal. But since 'the wages of sin is death,' this hath he in common with men, that together with them he should be condemned to death.

But the true Mediator, whom in Thy secret mercy Thou hast pointed out to the humble, and didst send, that by His example also they might learn the same humility—that 'Mediator between God and men, the man Christ Jesus,' appeared between mortal sinners and the immortal Just One—mortal with men, just with God; that because the reward of righteousness is life and peace, He might, by righteousness conjoined with God, cancel the death of justified sinners, which He willed to have in common with them. Hence He was pointed out to holy men of old; to the intent that they, through faith in His Passion to come, even as we through faith in that which is past, might be saved. For as man He was Mediator; but as the Word He was not between, because equal to God, and God with God, and together with the Holy Spirit one God.

How hast Thou loved us, O good Father, who sparedst not Thine only Son, but deliveredst Him up for us wicked ones! How hast Thou loved us, for whom He, who thought it no robbery to be equal with Thee, 'became obedient unto death, even the death of the cross;' He alone 'free among the dead,' that had power to lay down His life, and power to take it again, for us was He unto Thee both Victor and Victim, and the Victor as being the Victim; for us was He unto Thee both Priest and Sacrifice, and Priest as being the Sacrifice; of slaves making us Thy sons, by being born of Thee, and serving us. Rightly, then, is my hope strongly fixed on Him, that Thou wilt heal all my diseases by Him who sitteth at Thy right hand and maketh intercession for us; else should I utterly despair. For numerous and great are my infirmities, yea, numerous and great are they; but Thy medicine is greater. We might think that Thy Word was removed from union with man, and despair of ourselves had He not been 'made flesh and dwelt among us.'

Terrified by my sins and the load of my misery, I had resolved in my heart, and meditated flight into the wilderness; but Thou didst forbid me, and didst strengthen me, saying, therefore, Christ 'died for all, that they which live should not henceforth live unto themselves, but unto Him which died for them.' Behold, O Lord, I cast my care upon Thee, that I may live, and 'behold wondrous things out of Thy law.' Thou knowest my unskilfulness and my infirmities; teach me, and heal me. Thine only Son—He 'in whom are hid all the treasures of wisdom and knowledge'—hath redeemed me with His blood. Let not the proud speak evil of me, because I consider my ransom, and eat and drink, and distribute; and poor, desire to be satisfied from Him, together with those who eat and are satisfied, and they praise the Lord that seek Him.

# BOOK XI

*The design of his confessions being declared, he seeks from God the knowledge of the Holy Scriptures, and begins to expound the words of Genesis I. 1, concerning the creation of the world. The questions of rash disputers being refuted, 'What did God before He created the world?' That he might the better overcome his opponents, he adds a copious disquisition concerning time.*

O LORD, since eternity is Thine, art Thou ignorant of the things which I say unto Thee? Or seest Thou at the time that which cometh to pass in time? Why, therefore, do I place before Thee so many relations of things? Not surely that Thou mightest know them through me, but that I may awaken my own love and that of my readers towards Thee, that we may all say, 'Great is the Lord, and greatly to be praised.' I have already said, and shall say, for the love of Thy love do I this. For we also pray, and yet Truth says, 'Your Father knoweth what things ye have need of before ye ask Him.' Therefore do we make known unto Thee our love, in confessing unto Thee our own miseries and Thy mercies upon us, that Thou mayest free us altogether, since Thou hast begun, that we may cease to be wretched in ourselves, and that we may be blessed in Thee; since Thou hast called us, that we may be poor in spirit, and meek, and mourners, and hungering and athirst after righteousness, and merciful, and pure in heart, and peacemakers. Behold, I have told unto Thee many things, which I could and which I would, for Thou first wouldest that I should confess unto Thee, the Lord my God, for Thou art good, since Thy 'mercy endureth for ever.'

But when shall I suffice with the tongue of my pen to express all Thy exhortations, and all Thy terrors, and comforts, and guidances, whereby Thou hast led me to preach Thy Word and to dispense Thy Sacrament unto Thy people? And if I suffice to utter these things in order, the drops of time[50] are dear to me. Long time have I burned to meditate in Thy law, and in it to confess to Thee my knowledge and ignorance, the beginning of Thine enlightening, and the remains of my darkness, until infirmity be swallowed up by strength. And I would not that to aught else those hours should flow away, which I find free from the necessities of refreshing my body, and the care of my mind, and of the service which we owe to men, and which, though we owe not, even yet we pay.

O Lord my God, hear my prayer, and let Thy mercy regard my longing, since it burns not for myself alone, but because it desires to benefit brotherly charity; and Thou seest into my heart, that so it is. I would sacrifice to Thee the service of my thought and tongue; and do Thou give what I may offer unto Thee. For 'I am poor and needy,' Thou rich unto all that call upon Thee, who free from care carest for us. Circumcise from all rashness and from all lying my inward and outward lips. Let Thy Scriptures be my chaste delights. Neither let me be deceived in them, nor deceive out of them. Lord, hear and pity, O Lord my God, light of the blind, and strength of the weak; even also light of those that see, and strength of the strong, hearken unto my soul, and hear it crying 'out of the depths.' For unless Thine ears be present in the depths also, whither shall we go? whither shall we cry? 'The day is Thine, and the night also is Thine.' At Thy nod the moments flee by. Grant thereof space for our meditations amongst the hidden things of Thy law, nor close it against us who knock. For not in vain hast Thou willed that the obscure secret of so many pages should be written. Nor is it that those forests have not their harts, betaking themselves therein, and ranging, and walking, and feeding, lying down, and ruminating. Perfect me, O Lord, and reveal them unto me. Behold, Thy voice is my joy, Thy voice surpasseth the abundance of pleasures. Give that which I love, for I do love; and this hast Thou given. Abandon not Thine own gifts, nor despise Thy grass that thirsteth. Let me confess unto Thee whatsoever I shall have found in Thy books, and let me hear the voice of praise, and let me imbibe Thee, and reflect on the wonderful things of Thy law;

even from the beginning, wherein Thou madest the heaven and the earth, unto the everlasting kingdom of Thy holy city that is with Thee.

Lord, have mercy on me and hear my desire. For I think that it is not of the earth, nor of gold and silver, and precious stones, nor gorgeous apparel, nor honours and powers, nor the pleasures of the flesh, nor necessaries for the body, and this life of our pilgrimage; all which are added to those that seek Thy kingdom and Thy righteousness. Behold, O Lord my God, whence is my desire. The unrighteous have told me of delights, but not such as Thy law, O Lord. Behold whence is my desire. Behold, Father, look and see, and approve; and let it be pleasing in the sight of Thy mercy, that I may find grace before Thee, that the secret things of Thy Word may be opened unto me when I knock. I beseech, by our Lord Jesus Christ, Thy Son, 'the Man of Thy right hand, the Son of man, whom Thou madest strong for Thyself,' as Thy Mediator and ours, through whom Thou hast sought us, although not seeking Thee, but didst seek us that we might seek Thee,—Thy Word through whom Thou hast made all things, and amongst them me also,—Thy Only-begotten, through whom Thou hast called to adoption the believing people, and therein me also. I beseech Thee through Him, who sitteth at Thy right hand, and 'maketh intercession for us,' 'in whom are hid all treasures of wisdom and knowledge.' Him do I seek in Thy books. Of Him did Moses write; this saith Himself; this saith the Truth.

Let me hear and understand how in the beginning Thou didst make the heaven and the earth. Moses wrote this; he wrote and departed,—passed hence from Thee to Thee. Nor now is he before me; for if he were I would hold him, and ask him, and would adjure him by Thee that he would open unto me these things, and I would lend the ears of my body to the sounds bursting forth from his mouth. And should he speak in the Hebrew tongue, in vain would it beat on my senses, nor would aught touch my mind; but if in Latin, I should know what he said. But whence should I know whether he said what was true? But if I knew this even, should I know it from him? Verily within me, within in the chamber of my thought,

Truth, neither Hebrew, nor Greek, nor Latin, nor barbarian, without the organs of voice and tongue, without the sound of syllables, would say, 'He speaks the truth,' and I, forthwith assured of it, confidently would say unto that man of Thine, 'Thou speakest the truth.' As, then, I cannot inquire of him, I beseech Thee,—Thee, O Truth, full of whom he spake truth,—Thee, my God, I beseech, forgive my sins; and do Thou, who didst give to that Thy servant to speak these things, grant to me also to understand them.

Behold, the heaven and earth are; they proclaim that they were made, for they are changed and varied. Whereas whatsoever hath not been made, and yet hath being, hath nothing in it which there was not before; this is what it is to be changed and varied. They also proclaim that they made not themselves; 'therefore we are, because we have been made; we were not therefore before we were, so that we could have made ourselves.' And the voice of those that speak is in itself an evidence. Thou, therefore, Lord, didst make these things; Thou who art beautiful, for they are beautiful; Thou who art good, for they are good; Thou who art, for they are. Nor even so are they beautiful, nor good, nor are they, as Thou their Creator art; compared with whom they are neither beautiful, nor good, nor are at all. These things we know, thanks be to Thee. And our knowledge, compared with Thy knowledge, is ignorance.

But how didst Thou make the heaven and the earth, and what was the instrument of Thy so mighty work? For it was not as a human worker fashioning body from body, according to the fancy of his mind, in some-wise able to assign a form which it perceives in itself by its inner eye. And whence should he be able to do this, hadst not Thou made that mind? And he assigns to it already existing, and as it were having a being, a form, as clay, or stone, or wood, or gold, or such like. And whence should these things be, hadst not Thou appointed them? Thou didst make for the work-man his body,—Thou the mind commanding the limbs,—Thou the matter whereof he makes anything,—Thou the capacity whereby he may appre-hend his art, and see within what he may do without,—Thou the sense of his body, by which, as by an interpreter, he may from mind unto matter convey that which he doeth, and report to his mind what may have been done, that it within may consult the truth, presiding over itself, whether it be well done. All these things praise Thee, the Creator of all. But how dost Thou make them? How, O God, didst Thou make heaven and earth? Truly, neither in the heaven nor in the earth didst Thou make heaven and earth; nor in the air, nor in the waters, since these also belong to the heaven and the earth; nor in the whole world didst Thou make the whole world; because there was no place wherein it could be made before it was made, that it might be; nor didst Thou hold anything in Thy hand wherewith to make heaven and earth. For whence couldest Thou have what Thou hadst not made, whereof to make anything? For what is, save because Thou art? Therefore Thou didst speak and they were made, and in Thy Word Thou madest these things.

But how didst Thou speak? Was it in that manner in which the voice came from the cloud, saying, 'This is my beloved Son'? For that voice was uttered and passed away, began and ended. The syllables sounded and passed by, the second after the first, the third after the second, and thence in order, until the last after the rest, and silence after the last. Hence it is clear and plain that the motion of a creature expressed it, itself temporal, obeying Thy eternal will. And these thy words formed at the time, the outer ear conveyed to the intelligent mind, whose inner ear lay attentive to Thy eternal word. But it compared these words sounding in time with Thy eternal word in silence, and said, 'It is different, very different. These words are far beneath me, nor are they, since they flee and pass away; but the Word of my Lord remaineth above me for ever.' If, then, in sounding and fleeting words Thou didst say that heaven and earth should be made, and didst thus make heaven and earth, there was already a corporeal creature before heaven and earth by whose temporal motions that voice might take its course in time. But there was nothing corporeal before heaven and earth; or if there were, certainly Thou without a transitory voice hadst created that whence Thou wouldest make the passing voice, by which to say that the heaven and the earth should be made. For whatsoever that were of which such a voice was made, unless it were made by Thee, it could not be at all. By what word of Thine was it decreed that a body might be made, whereby these words might be made?

Thou callest us, therefore, to understand the Word, God with Thee, God, which is spoken eternally, and by it are all things spoken eternally. For what was spoken was not finished, and another spoken until all were spoken; but all things at once and for ever. For otherwise have we time and change, and not a true eternity, nor a true immortality. This I know, O my God, and give thanks. I know, I confess to Thee, O Lord, and whosoever is not unthankful to certain truth, knows and blesses Thee with me. We know, O Lord, we know; since in proportion as anything is not what it was, and is what it was not, in that proportion does it die and arise. Not anything, therefore, of Thy Word giveth place and cometh into place again, because it is truly immortal and eternal. And, therefore, unto the Word co-eternal with Thee, Thou dost at once and for ever say all that Thou dost say; and whatever Thou sayest shall be made, is made; nor dost Thou make otherwise than by speaking; yet all things are not made both together and everlasting which Thou makest by speaking.

Why is this, I beseech Thee, O Lord my God? I see it, however; but how I shall express it, I know not, unless that everything which begins to be and ceases to be, then begins and ceases when in Thy eternal Reason it is known that it ought to begin or cease where nothing beginneth or ceaseth. The same is Thy Word, which is also 'the Beginning,' because also It speaketh unto us. Thus, in the gospel He speaketh through the flesh; and this sounded outwardly in the ears of men, that it might be believed and sought inwardly, and that it might be found in the eternal Truth, where the good and only Master teacheth all His disciples. There, O Lord, I hear Thy voice, the voice of one speaking unto me, since He speaketh unto us who teacheth us. But He that teacheth us not, although He speaketh, speaketh not to us. Moreover, who teacheth us, unless it be the immutable Truth? For even when we are admonished through a changeable creature, we are led to the

Truth immutable. There we learn truly while we stand and hear Him, and rejoice greatly 'because of the Bridegroom's voice,' restoring us to that whence we are. And, therefore, the Beginning, because unless It remained, there would not, where we strayed, be whither to return. But when we return from error, it is by knowing that we return. But that we may know, He teacheth us, because He is the Beginning and speaketh unto us.

In this Beginning, O God, hast Thou made heaven and earth,—in Thy Word, in Thy Son, in Thy Power, in Thy Wisdom, in Thy Truth, wondrously speaking and wondrously making. Who shall comprehend? who shall relate it? What is that which shines through me, and strikes my heart without injury, and I both shudder and burn? I shudder inasmuch as I am unlike it; and I burn inasmuch as I am like it. It is Wisdom itself that shines through me, clearing my cloudiness, which again overwhelms me, fainting from it, in the darkness and amount of my punishment. For my strength is brought down in need, so that I cannot endure my blessings, until Thou, O Lord, who hast been gracious to all mine iniquities, heal also all mine infirmities; because Thou shalt also redeem my life from corruption, and crown me with Thy loving-kindness and mercy, and shalt satisfy my desire with good things because my youth shall be renewed like the eagle's. For by hope we are saved; and through patience we await Thy promises. Let him that is able hear Thee discoursing within. I will with confidence cry out from Thy oracle, How wonderful are Thy works, O Lord, in Wisdom hast Thou made them all. And this Wisdom is the Beginning, and in that Beginning hast Thou made heaven and earth.

Lo, are they not full of their ancient way, who say to us, 'What was God doing before He made heaven and earth? For if,' say they, 'He were unoccupied, and did nothing, why does He not for ever also, and from henceforth, cease from working, as in times past He did? For if any new motion has arisen in God, and a new will, to form a creature which He had never before formed, however can that be a true eternity where there ariseth a will which was not before? For the will of God is not a creature, but before the creature; because nothing could be created unless the will of the Creator were before it. The will of God, therefore, pertaineth to His very Substance. But if anything hath arisen in the Substance of God which was not before, that Substance is not truly called eternal. But if it was the eternal will of God that the creature should be, why was not the creature also from eternity?'

Those who say these things do not as yet understand Thee, O Thou Wisdom of God, Thou light of souls; not as yet do they understand how these things be made which are made by and in Thee. They even endeavour to comprehend things eternal; but as yet their heart flieth about in the past and future motions of things, and is still wavering. Who shall hold it and fix it, that it may rest a little, and by degrees catch the glory of that ever-standing eternity, and compare it with the times which never stand, and see that it is incomparable; and that a long time cannot become long, save from the many motions that pass by, which cannot at the same instant be prolonged; but that in the Eternal nothing passeth away, but that the whole is present; but no time is wholly present; and let him see that all time past is forced on by the future, and that all the future followeth from the past, and that all, both past and future, is created and issues from that which is always present? Who will hold the heart of man, that it may stand still, and see how the still-standing eternity, itself neither future nor past, uttereth the times future and past? Can my hand accomplish this, or the hand of my mouth by persuasion bring about a thing so great?

Behold, I answer to him who asks, 'What was God doing before He made heaven and earth?' I answer not, as a certain person is reported to have done facetiously (avoiding the pressure of the question), 'He was preparing hell,' saith he, 'for those who pry into mysteries.' It is one thing to perceive, another to laugh,—these things I answer not. For more willingly would I have answered, 'I know not what I know not,' than that I should make him a laughing-stock who asketh deep things, and gain praise as one who answereth false things. But I say that Thou, our God, art the Creator of every creature; and if by the term 'heaven and earth' every creature is understood, I boldly say, 'That before God made heaven and earth, He made not anything. For if He did, what did He make unless the creature?' And would that I knew whatever I desire to know to my advantage, as I know that no creature was made before any creature was made.

But if the roving thought of any one should wander through the images of bygone time, and wonder that Thou, the God Almighty, and All-creating, and All-sustaining, the Architect of heaven and earth, didst for innumerable ages refrain from so great a work before Thou wouldest make it, let him awake and consider that he wonders at false things. For whence could innumerable ages pass by which Thou didst not make, since Thou art the Author and Creator of all ages? Or what times should those be which were not made by Thee? Or how should they pass by if they had not been? Since, therefore, Thou art the Creator of all times, if any time was before Thou madest heaven and earth, why is it said that Thou didst refrain from working? For that very time Thou madest, nor could times pass by before Thou madest times. But if before heaven and earth there was no time, why is it asked, What didst Thou then? For there was no 'then' when time was not.

Nor dost Thou by time precede time; else wouldest not Thou precede all times. But in the excellency of an ever-present eternity, Thou precedest all times past, and survivest all future times, because they are future, and when they have come they will be past; but 'Thou art the same, and Thy years shall have no end.' Thy years neither go nor come; but ours both go and come, that all may come. All Thy years stand at once, since they do stand; nor were they when departing excluded by coming years, because they pass not away; but all these of ours shall be when all shall cease to be. Thy years are one day, and Thy day is not daily, but to-day; because Thy to-day yields not with to-morrow, for neither doth it follow yesterday. Thy to-day is eternity; therefore didst Thou beget the Co-eternal, to whom Thou saidst, 'This day have I begotten Thee.' Thou hast made all time; and before all times Thou art, nor in any time was there not time.

At no time, therefore, hadst Thou not made anything, because Thou hadst made time itself. And no times are co-eternal with Thee, because

Thou remainest for ever; but should these continue, they would not be times. For what is time? Who can easily and briefly explain it? Who even in thought can comprehend it, even to the pronouncing of a word concerning it? But what in speaking do we refer to more familiarly and knowingly than time? And certainly we understand when we speak of it; we understand also when we hear it spoken of by another. What, then, is time? If no one ask of me, I know; if I wish to explain to him who asks, I know not. Yet I say with confidence, that I know that if nothing passed away, there would not be past time; and if nothing were coming, there would not be future time; and if nothing were, there would not be present time. Those two times, therefore, past and future, how are they, when even the past now is not, and the future is not as yet? But should the present be always present, and should it not pass into time past, time truly it could not be, but eternity. If, then, time present—if it be time—only comes into existence because it passes into time past, how do we say that even this is, whose cause of being is that it shall not be—namely, so that we cannot truly say that time is, unless because it tends not to be?

And yet we say that 'time is long and time is short;' nor do we speak of this save of time past and future. A long time past, for example, we call a hundred years ago; in like manner a long time to come, a hundred years hence. But a short time past we call, say, ten days ago; and a short time to come, ten days hence. But in what sense is that long or short which is not? For the past is not now, and the future is not yet. Therefore let us not say, 'It is long;' but let us say of the past, 'It hath been long,' and of the future, 'It will be long.' O my Lord, my light, shall not even here Thy truth deride man? For that past time which was long, was it long when it was already past, or when it was as yet present? For then it might be long when there was that which could be long, but when past it no longer was; wherefore that could not be long which was not at all. Let us not, therefore, say, 'Time past hath been long;' for we shall not find what may have been long, seeing that since it was past it is not; but let us say 'that present time was long, because when it was present it was long.' For it had not as yet passed away so as not to be, and therefore there was that which could be long. But after it passed, that ceased also to be long which ceased to be.

Let us therefore see, O human soul, whether present time can be long; for to thee is it given to perceive and to measure periods of time. What wilt thou reply to me? Is a hundred years when present a long time? See, first, whether a hundred years can be present. For if the first year of these is current, that is present, but the other ninety and nine are future, and therefore they are not as yet. But if the second year is current, one is already past, the other present, the rest future. And thus, if we fix on any middle year of this hundred as present, those before it are past, those after it are future; wherefore a hundred years cannot be present. See at least whether that year itself which is current can be present. For if its first month be current, the rest are future; if the second, the first hath already passed, and the remainder are not yet. Therefore neither is the year which is current as a whole present; and if it is not present as a whole, then the year is not present. For twelve months make the year, of which each individual month which is current is itself present, but the rest are either past or future. Although neither is that month which is current present, but one day only: if the first, the rest being to come, if the last, the rest being past; if any of the middle, then between past and future.

Behold, the present time, which alone we found could be called long, is abridged to the space scarcely of one day. But let us discuss even that, for there is not one day present as a whole. For it is made up of four-and-twenty hours of night and day, whereof the first hath the rest future, the last hath them past, but any one of the intervening hath those before it past, those after it future. And that one hour passeth away in fleeting particles. Whatever of it hath flown away is past, whatever remaineth is future. If any portion of time be conceived which cannot now be divided into even the minutest particles of moments, this only is that which may be called present; which, however, flies so rapidly from future to past, that it cannot be extended by any delay. For if it be extended, it is divided into the past and future; but the present hath no space. Where, therefore, is the

time which we may call long? Is it future? Indeed we do not say, 'It is long,' because it is not yet, so as to be long; but we say, 'It will be long.' When, then, will it be? For if even then, since as yet it is future, it will not be long, because what may be long is not as yet; but it shall be long, when from the future, which as yet is not, it shall already have begun to be, and will have become present, so that there could be that which may be long; then doth the present time cry out in the words above that it cannot be long.

And yet, O Lord, we perceive intervals of times, and we compare them with themselves, and we say some are longer, others shorter. We even measure by how much shorter or longer this time may be than that; and we answer, 'That this is double or treble, while that is but once, or only as much as that.' But we measure times passing when we measure them by perceiving them; but past times, which now are not, or future times, which as yet are not, who can measure them? Unless, perchance, any one will dare to say, that that can be measured which is not. When, therefore, time is passing, it can be perceived and measured; but when it has passed, it cannot, since it is not.

I ask, Father, I do not affirm. O my God, rule and guide me. Who is there who can say to me that there are not three times (as we learned when boys, and as we have taught boys), the past, present, and future, but only present, because these two are not? Or are they also; but when from future it becometh present, cometh it forth from some secret place, and when from the present it becometh past, doth it retire into anything secret? For where have they, who have foretold future things, seen these things, if as yet they are not? For that which is not cannot be seen. And they who relate things past could not relate them as true, did they not perceive them in their mind. Which things, if they were not, they could in no wise be discerned. There are therefore things both future and past.

Suffer me, O Lord, to seek further; O my Hope, let not my purpose be confounded. For if there are times past and future, I desire to know where they are. But if as yet I do not succeed, I still know, wherever they are, that they are not there as future or past, but as present. For if there also they be future, they are not as yet there; if even there they be past, they are no longer there. Wheresoever, therefore, they are, whatsoever they are, they are only so as present. Although past things are related as true, they are drawn out from the memory,—not the things themselves, which have passed, but the words conceived from the images of the things which they have formed in the mind as footprints in their passage through the senses. My childhood, indeed, which no longer is, is in time past, which now is not; but when I call to mind its image, and speak of it, I behold it in the present, because it is as yet in my memory. Whether there be a like cause of foretelling future things, that of things which as yet are not the images may be perceived as already existing, I confess, my God, I know not. This certainly I know, that we generally think before on our future actions, and that this premeditation is present; but that the action whereon we premeditate is not yet, because it is future; which when we shall have entered upon, and have begun to do that which we were premeditating, then shall that action be, because then it is not future, but present.

In whatever manner, therefore, this secret preconception of future things may be, nothing can be seen, save what is. But what now is is not future, but present. When, therefore, they say that things future are seen, it is not themselves, which as yet are not (that is, which are future); but their causes or their signs perhaps are seen, the which already are. Therefore, to those already beholding them, they are not future, but present, from which future things conceived in the mind are foretold. Which conceptions again now are, and they who foretell those things behold these conceptions present before them. Let now so multitudinous a variety of things afford me some example. I behold daybreak; I foretell that the sun is about to rise. That which I behold is present; what I foretell is future,—not that the sun is future, which already is; but his rising, which is not yet. Yet even its rising I could not predict unless I had an image of it in my mind, as now I have while I speak. But that dawn which I see in the sky is not the rising of the sun, although it may go before it, nor that imagination in my mind; which two are seen as present, that the other which is future may be foretold.

Future things, therefore, are not as yet; and if they are not as yet, they are not. And if they are not, they cannot be seen at all; but they can be foretold from things present which now are, and are seen.

Thou, therefore, Ruler of Thy creatures, what is the method by which Thou teachest souls those things which are future? For Thou hast taught Thy prophets. What is that way by which Thou, to whom nothing is future, dost teach future things; or rather of future things dost teach present? For what is not, of a certainty cannot be taught. Too far is this way from my view; it is too mighty for me, I cannot attain unto it; but by Thee I shall be enabled, when Thou shalt have granted it, sweet light of my hidden eyes.

But what now is manifest and clear is, that neither are there future nor past things. Nor is it fitly said, 'There are three times, past, present, and future;' but perchance it might be fitly said, 'There are three times; a present of things past, a present of things present, and a present of things future.' For these three do somehow exist in the soul, and otherwise I see them not: present of things past, memory; present of things present, sight; present of things future, expectation. If of these things we are permitted to speak, I see three times, and I grant there are three. It may also be said, 'There are three times, past, present, and future,' as usage falsely has it. See, I trouble not, nor gainsay, nor reprove; provided always that which is said may be understood, that neither the future, nor that which is past, now is. For there are but few things which we speak properly, many things improperly; but what we may wish to say is understood.

I have just now said, then, that we measure times as they pass, that we may be able to say that this time is twice as much as that one, or that this is only as much as that, and so of any other of the parts of time which we are able to tell by measuring. Wherefore, as I said, we measure times as they pass. And if any one should ask me, 'Whence dost thou know?' I can answer, 'I know, because we measure; nor can we measure things that are not; and things past and future are not.' But how do we measure present time, since it hath not space? It is measured while it passeth; but when it shall have passed, it is not measured; for there will not be aught that can be measured. But whence, in what way, and whither doth it pass while it is being measured? Whence, but from the future? Which way, save through the present? Whither, but into the past? From that, therefore, which as yet is not, through that which hath no space, into that which now is not. But what do we measure, unless time in some space? For we say not single, and double, and triple, and equal, or in any other way in which we speak of time, unless with respect to the spaces of times. In what space, then, do we measure passing time? Is it in the future, whence it passeth over? But what yet we measure not, is not. Or is it in the present, by which it passeth? But no space, we do not measure. Or in the past, whither it passeth? But that which is not now, we measure not.

My soul yearns to know this most entangled enigma. Forbear to shut up, O Lord my God, good Father,—through Christ I beseech Thee,—forbear to shut up these things, both usual and hidden, from my desire, that it may be hindered from penetrating them; but let them dawn through Thy enlightening mercy, O Lord. Of whom shall I inquire concerning these things? And to whom shall I with more advantage confess my ignorance than to Thee, to whom these my studies, so vehemently kindled towards Thy Scriptures, are not troublesome? Give that which I love; for I do love, and this hast Thou given me. Give, Father, who truly knowest to give good gifts unto Thy children. Give, since I have undertaken to know, and trouble is before me until Thou dost open it. Through Christ, I beseech Thee, in His name, Holy of Holies, let no man interrupt me. For I believed, and therefore do I speak. This is my hope; for this do I live, that I may contemplate the delights of the Lord. Behold, Thou hast made my days old, and they pass away, and in what manner I know not. And we speak as to time and time, times and times,—'How long is the time since he said this?' 'How long the time since he did this?' and, 'How long the time since I saw that?' and, 'This syllable hath double the time of that single short syllable.' These words we speak, and these we hear; and we are understood, and we understand. They are most manifest and most usual, and the same things again lie hid too deeply, and the discovery of them is new.

I have heard from a learned man that the motions of the sun, moon, and stars constituted time, and I assented not. For why should not rather the motions of all bodies be time? What if the lights of heaven should cease, and a potter's wheel run round, would there be no time by which we might measure those revolutions, and say either that it turned with equal pauses, or, if it were moved at one time more slowly, at another more quickly, that some revolutions were longer, others less so? Or while we were saying this, should we not also be speaking in time? Or should there in our words be some syllables long, others short, but because those sounded in a longer time, these in a shorter? God grant to men to see in a small thing ideas common to things great and small. Both the stars and luminaries of heaven are 'for signs and for seasons, and for days and years.' No doubt they are; but neither should I say that the circuit of that wooden wheel was a day, nor yet should he say that therefore there was no time.

I desire to know the power and nature of time, by which we measure the motions of bodies, and say (for example) that this motion is twice as long as that. For, I ask, since 'day' declares not the stay only of the sun upon the earth, according to which day is one thing, night another, but also its entire circuit from east even to east,—according to which we say, 'So many days have passed' (the nights being included when we say 'so many days,' and their spaces not counted apart),—since, then, the day is finished by the motion of the sun, and by his circuit from east to east, I ask, whether the motion itself is the day, or the period in which that motion is completed, or both? For if the first be the day, then would there be a day although the sun should finish that course in so small a space of time as an hour. If the second, then that would not be a day if from one sunrise to another there were but so short a period as an hour, but the sun must go round four-and-twenty times to complete a day. If both, neither could that be called a day if the sun should run his entire round in the space of an hour; nor that, if, while the sun stood still, so much time should pass as the sun is accustomed to accomplish his whole course in from morning to morning. I shall not therefore now ask, what that is which is called day, but what time is, by which we, measuring the circuit of the sun, should say that it was accomplished in half the space of time it was wont, if it had been completed in so small a space as twelve hours; and comparing both times, we should call that single, this double time, although the sun should run his course from east to east sometimes in that single, sometimes in that double time. Let no man then tell me that the motions of the heavenly bodies are times, because, when at the prayer of one the sun stood still in order that he might achieve his victorious battle, the sun stood still, but time went on. For in such space of time as was sufficient was that battle fought and ended. I see that time, then, is a certain extension. But do I see it, or do I seem to see it? Thou, O Light and Truth, wilt show me.

Dost Thou command that I should assent, if any one should say that time is 'the motion of a body'? Thou dost not command me. For I hear that no body is moved but in time. This Thou sayest; but that the very motion of a body is time, I hear not; Thou sayest it not. For when a body is moved, I by time measure how long it may be moving from the time in which it began to be moved till it left off. And if I saw not whence it began, and it continued to be moved, so that I see not when it leaves off, I cannot measure unless, perchance, from the time I began until I cease to see. But if I look long, I only proclaim that the time is long, but not how long it may be; because when we say, 'How long,' we speak by comparison, as, 'This is as long as that,' or, 'This is double as long as that,' or any other thing of the kind. But if we were able to note down the distances of places whence and whither cometh the body which is moved, or its parts, if it moved as in a wheel, we can say in how much time the motion of the body or its part, from this place unto that, was performed. Since, then, the motion of a body is one thing, that by which we measure how long it is another, who cannot see which of these is rather to be called time? For, although a body be sometimes moved, sometimes stand still, we measure not its motion only, but also its standing still, by time; and we say, 'It stood still as much as it moved;' or, 'It stood still twice or thrice as long as it moved;' and if any other space which our measuring hath either determined or imagined, more or less, as we are accustomed to say. Time, therefore, is not the motion of a body.

And I confess unto Thee, O Lord, that I am as yet ignorant as to what time is, and again I confess unto Thee, O Lord, that I know that I speak these things in time, and that I have already long spoken of time, and that very 'long' is not long save by the stay of time. How, then, know I this, when I know not what time is? Or is it, perchance, that I know not in what wise I may express what I know? Alas for me, that I do not at least know the extent of my own ignorance! Behold, O my God, before Thee I lie not. As I speak, so is my heart. Thou shalt light my candle; Thou, O Lord my God, wilt enlighten my darkness.

Doth not my soul pour out unto Thee truly in confession that I do measure times? But do I thus measure, O my God, and know not what I measure? I measure the motion of a body by time; and the time itself do I not measure? But, in truth, could I measure the motion of a body, how long it is, and how long it is in coming from this place to that, unless I should measure the time in which it is moved? How, therefore, do I measure this very time itself? Or do we by a shorter time measure a longer, as by the space of a cubit the space of a crossbeam? For thus, indeed, we seem by the space of a short syllable to measure the space of a long syllable, and to say that this is double. Thus we measure the spaces of stanzas by the spaces of the verses, and the spaces of the verses by the spaces of the feet, and the spaces of the feet by the spaces of the syllables, and the spaces of long by the spaces of short syllables; not measuring by pages (for in that manner we measure spaces, not times), but when in uttering the words they pass by, and we say, 'It is a long stanza, because it is made up of so many verses; long verses, because they consist of so many feet; long feet, because they are prolonged by so many syllables; a long syllable, because double a short one.' But neither thus is any certain measure of time obtained; since it is possible that a shorter verse, if it be pronounced more fully, may take up more time than a longer one, if pronounced more hurriedly. Thus for a stanza, thus for a foot, thus for a syllable. Whence it appeared to me that time is nothing else than protraction; but of what I know not. It is wonderful to me, if it be not of the mind itself. For what do I measure, I beseech Thee, O my God, even when I say either indefinitely, 'This time is longer than that;' or even definitely, 'This is double that'? That I measure time, I know. But I measure not the future, for it is not yet; nor do I measure the present, because it is extended by no space; nor do I measure the past, because it no longer is. What, therefore, do I measure? Is it times passing, not passed? For thus had I said.

Persevere, O my mind, and give earnest heed. God is our helper; He made us, and not we ourselves. Give heed, where truth dawns. Lo, suppose the voice of a body begins to sound, and does sound, and sounds on, and lo! it ceases,—it is now silence, and that voice is past and is no longer a voice. It was future before it sounded, and could not be measured, because as yet it was not; and now it cannot, because it no longer is. Then, therefore, while it was sounding, it might, because there was then that which might be measured. But even then it did not stand still, for it was going and passing away. Could it, then, on that account be measured the more? For, while passing, it was being extended into some space of time, in which it might be measured, since the present hath no space. If, therefore, then it might be measured, lo! suppose another voice hath begun to sound, and still soundeth, in a continued tenor without any interruption, we can measure it while it is sounding; for when it shall have ceased to sound, it will be already past, and there will not be that which can be measured. Let us measure it truly, and let us say how much it is. But as yet it sounds, nor can it be measured, save from that instant in which it began to sound, even to the end in which it left off. For the interval itself we measure from some beginning unto some end. On which account, a voice which is not yet ended cannot be measured, so that it may be said how long or how short it may be; nor can it be said to be equal to another, or single or double in respect of it, or the like. But when it is ended, it no longer is. In what manner, therefore, may it be measured? And yet we measure times; still not those which as yet are not, nor those which no longer are, nor those which are protracted by some delay, nor those which have no limits. We, therefore, measure neither future times, nor past, nor present, nor those passing by; and yet we do measure times.

*Deus Creator omnium;* this verse of eight syllables alternates between short and long syllables. The four short, then, the first, third, fifth, and seventh, are single in respect of the four long, the second, fourth, sixth, and eighth. Each of these hath a double time to every one of those. I pronounce them, report on them, and thus it is, as is perceived by common sense. By common sense, then, I measure a long by a short syllable, and I find that it has twice as much. But when one sounds after another, if the former be short, the latter long, how shall I hold the short one, and how measuring shall I apply it to the long, so that I may find out that this has twice as much, when indeed the long does not begin to sound unless the short leaves off sounding? That very long one I measure not as present, since I measure it not save when ended. But its ending is its passing away. What, then, is it that I can measure? Where is the short syllable by which I measure? Where is the long one which I measure? Both have sounded, have flown, have passed away, and are no longer; and still I measure, and I confidently answer (so far as is trusted to a practised sense), that as to space of time this syllable is single, that double. Nor could I do this, unless because they have passed, and are ended. Therefore do I not measure themselves, which now are not, but something in my memory, which remains fixed.

In thee, O my mind, I measure times. Do not overwhelm me with thy clamour. That is, do not overwhelm thyself with the multitude of thy impressions. In thee, I say, I measure times; the impression which things as they pass by make on thee, and which, when they have passed by, remains that I measure as time present, not those things which have passed by, that the impression should be made. This I measure when I measure times. Either, then, these are times, or I do not measure times. What when we measure silence, and say that this silence hath lasted as long as that voice lasts? Do we not extend our thought to the measure of a voice, as if it sounded, so that we may be able to declare something concerning the intervals of silence in a given space of time? For when both the voice and tongue are still, we go over in thought poems and verses, and any discourse, or dimensions of motions; and declare concerning the spaces of times, how much this may be in respect of that, not otherwise than if uttering them we should pronounce them. Should any one wish to utter a lengthened sound, and had with forethought determined how long it should be, that man hath in silence verily gone through a space of time, and committing it to memory, he begins to utter that speech, which sounds until it be extended to the end proposed; truly it hath sounded, and will sound. For what of it is already finished hath verily sounded, but what remains will sound; and thus does it pass on, until the present intention carry over the future into the past; the past increasing by the diminution of the future, until, by the consumption of the future, all be past.

But how is that future diminished or consumed which as yet is not? Or how doth the past, which is no longer, increase, unless in the mind which enacteth this there are three things done? For it both expects, and considers, and remembers, that that which it expecteth, through that which it considereth, may pass into that which it remembereth. Who, therefore, denieth that future things as yet are not? But yet there is already in the mind the expectation of things future. And who denies that past things are now no longer? But, however, there is still in the mind the memory of things past. And who denies that time present wants space, because it passeth away in a moment? But yet our consideration endureth, through which that which may be present may proceed to become absent. Future time, which is not, is not therefore long; but a 'long future' is 'a long expectation of the future.' Nor is time past, which is now no longer, long; but a long past is 'a long memory of the past.'

I am about to repeat a psalm that I know. Before I begin, my attention is extended to the whole; but when I have begun, as much of it as becomes past by my saying it is extended in my memory; and the life of this action of mine is divided between my memory, on account of what I have repeated, and my expectation, on account of what I am about to repeat; yet my consideration is present with me, through which that which was future may be carried over so that it may become past. Which the more it is done and repeated, by so much (expectation being shortened) the memory is enlarged, until the whole expectation be exhausted, when that whole action being ended shall have passed into memory. And what takes place in the entire psalm, takes place also in each individual part of it, and in each individual syllable: this holds in the longer action, of which that psalm is perchance a portion; the same holds in the whole life of man, of which all the actions of man are parts; the same holds in the whole age of the sons of men, of which all the lives of men are parts.

But 'because Thy loving-kindness is better than life,' behold, my life is but a distraction, and Thy right hand upheld me in my Lord, the Son of man, the Mediator between Thee, The One, and us the many,—in many distractions amid many things,—that through Him I may apprehend in whom I have been apprehended, and may be recollected from my old days, following The One, forgetting the things that are past; and not distracted, but drawn on, not to those things which shall be and shall pass away, but to those things which are before, not distractedly, but intently, I follow on for the prize of my heavenly calling, where I may hear the voice of Thy praise, and contemplate Thy delights, neither coming nor passing away. But now are my years spent in mourning. And Thou, O Lord, art my comfort, my Father everlasting. But I have been divided amid times, the order of which I know not; and my thoughts, even the inmost bowels of my soul, are mangled with tumultuous varieties, until I flow together unto Thee, purged and molten in the fire of Thy love.

And I will be immovable, and fixed in Thee, in my mould, Thy truth; nor will I endure the questions of men, who by a penal disease thirst for more than they can hold, and say, 'What did God make before He made heaven and earth?' Or, 'How came it into His mind to make anything, when He never before made anything?' Grant to them, O Lord, to think well what they say, and to see that where there is no time, they cannot say 'never.' What, therefore, He is said 'never to have made,' what else is it but to say, that in no time was it made? Let them therefore see that there could be no time without a created being, and let them cease to speak that vanity. Let them also be extended unto those things which are before, and understand that Thou, the eternal Creator of all times, art before all times, and that no times are co-eternal with Thee, nor any creature, even if there be any creature beyond all times.

O Lord my God, what is that secret place of Thy mystery, and how far thence have the consequences of my transgressions cast me? Heal my eyes, that I may enjoy Thy light. Surely, if there be a mind, so greatly abounding in knowledge and foreknowledge, to which all things past and future are so known as one psalm is well known to me, that mind is exceedingly wonderful, and very astonishing; because whatever is so past, and whatever is to come of after ages, is no more concealed from Him than was it hidden from me when singing that psalm, what and how much of it had been sung from the beginning, what and how much remained unto the end. But far be it that Thou, the Creator of the universe, the Creator of souls and bodies,—far be it that Thou shouldest know all things future and past. Far, far more wonderfully, and far more mysteriously, Thou knowest them. For it is not as the feelings of one singing known things, or hearing a known song, are—through expectation of future words, and in remembrance of those that are past—varied, and his senses divided, that anything happeneth unto Thee, unchangeably eternal, that is, the truly eternal Creator of minds.[51] As, then, Thou in the Beginning knewest the heaven and the earth without any change of Thy knowledge, so in the Beginning didst Thou make heaven and earth without any distraction of Thy action. Let him who understandeth confess unto Thee; and let him who understandeth not, confess unto Thee. Oh, how exalted art Thou, and yet the humble in heart are Thy dwelling-place; for Thou raisest up those that are bowed down, and they whose exaltation Thou art fall not.

# BOOK XII

*He continues his explanation of the First Chapter of Genesis according to the Septuagint, and by its assistance he argues, especially, concerning the double heaven, and the formless matter out of which the whole world may have been created; afterwards of the interpretations of others not disallowed, and sets forth at great length the sense of the Holy Scripture.*

My heart, O Lord, affected by the words of Thy Holy Scripture, is much busied in this poverty of my life; and therefore, for the most part, is the want of human intelligence copious in language, because inquiry speaks more than discovery, and because demanding is longer than obtaining, and the hand that knocks is more active than the hand that receives. We hold the promise; who shall break it? 'If God be for us, who can be against us?' 'Ask, and ye shall have; seek, and ye shall find; knock, and it shall be opened unto you: for every one that asketh receiveth; and he that seeketh findeth; and to him that knocketh it shall be opened.' These are Thine own promises; and who need fear to be deceived where the Truth promiseth?

The weakness of my tongue confesseth unto Thy Highness, seeing that Thou madest heaven and earth. This heaven which I see, and this earth upon which I tread (from which is this earth that I carry about me), Thou hast made. But where is that heaven of heavens, O Lord, of which we hear in the words of the Psalm, The heaven of heavens is the Lord's, but the earth hath He given to the children of men? Where is the heaven, which we behold not, in comparison of which all this, which we behold, is earth? For this corporeal whole, not as a whole everywhere, hath thus received its beautiful figure in these lower parts, of which the bottom is our earth; but compared with that heaven of heavens, even the heaven of our earth is

229

but earth; yea, each of these great bodies is not absurdly called earth, as compared with that, I know not what manner of heaven, which is the Lord's, not the sons' of men.

And truly this earth was invisible and formless, and there was I know not what profundity of the deep upon which there was no light, because it had no form. Therefore didst Thou command that it should be written, that darkness was upon the face of the deep; what else was it than the absence of light?[52] For had there been light, where should it have been save by being above all, showing itself aloft, and enlightening? Where, therefore, light was as yet not, why was it that darkness was present, unless because light was absent? Darkness therefore was upon it, because the light above was absent; as silence is there present where sound is not. And what is it to have silence there, but not to have sound there? Hast not Thou, O Lord, taught this soul which confesseth unto Thee? Hast not Thou taught me, O Lord, that before Thou didst form and separate this formless matter, there was nothing, neither colour, nor figure, nor body, nor spirit? Yet not altogether nothing; there was a certain formlessness without any shape.

What, then, should it be called, that even in some ways it might be conveyed to those of duller mind, save by some conventional word? But what, in all parts of the world, can be found nearer to a total formlessness than the earth and the deep? For, from their being of the lowest position, they are less beautiful than are the other higher parts, all transparent and shining. Why, therefore, may I not consider the formlessness of matter—which Thou hadst created without shape, whereof to make this shapely world—to be fittingly intimated unto men by the name of earth invisible and formless?

So that when herein thought seeketh what the sense may arrive at, and saith to itself, 'It is no intelligible form, such as life or justice, because it is the matter of bodies; nor perceptible by the senses, because in the invisible and formless there is nothing which can be seen and felt;'—while human thought saith these things to itself, it may endeavour either to know it by being ignorant, or by knowing it to be ignorant.

But were I, O Lord, by my mouth and by my pen to confess unto Thee the whole, whatever Thou hast taught me concerning that matter, the name of which hearing beforehand, and not understanding (they who could not understand it telling me of it), I conceived it as having innumerable and varied forms. And therefore I did not conceive it; my mind revolved in disturbed order foul and horrible 'forms,' but yet 'forms;' and I called it formless, not that it lacked form, but because it had such as, did it appear, my mind would turn from, as unwonted and incongruous, and at which human weakness would be disturbed. But even that which I did conceive was formless, not by the privation of all form, but in comparison of more beautiful forms; and true reason persuaded me that I ought altogether to remove from it all remnants of any form whatever, if I wished to conceive matter wholly without form; and I could not. For sooner could I imagine that that which should be deprived of all form was not at all, than conceive anything between form and nothing,—neither formed, nor nothing, formless, nearly nothing. And my mind hence ceased to question my spirit, filled (as it was) with the images of formed bodies, and changing and varying them according to its will; and I applied myself to the bodies themselves, and looked more deeply into their mutability, by which they cease to be what they had been, and begin to be what they were not; and this same transit from form unto form I have looked upon to be through some formless condition, not through a very nothing; but desired to know, not to guess. And if my voice and my pen should confess the whole unto Thee, whatsoever knots Thou hast untied for me concerning this question, who of my readers would endure to take in the whole? Nor yet, therefore, shall my heart cease to give Thee honour, and a song of praise, for those things which it is not able to express. For the mutability of mutable things is itself capable of all those forms into which mutable things are changed. And this mutability, what is it? Is it soul? Is it body? Is it the outer appearance of soul or body? Could it be said, 'Nothing were something,' and 'That which is, is not,' I would say that this were it; and yet in some manner was it already, since it could receive these visible and compound shapes.

And whence and in what manner was this, unless from Thee, from whom are all things, in so far as they are? But by how much the farther from Thee, so much the more unlike unto Thee; for it is not distance of place. Thou, therefore, O Lord, who art not one thing in one place, and otherwise in another, but the Self-same, and the Self-same, and the Self-same Holy, Holy, Holy, Lord God Almighty, didst in the beginning, which is of Thee, in Thy Wisdom, which was born of Thy Substance, create something, and that out of nothing. For Thou didst create heaven and earth, not out of Thyself, for then they would be equal to Thine Only-begotten, and thereby even to Thee; and in no wise would it be right that anything should be equal to Thee which was not of Thee. And aught else except Thee there was not whence Thou mightest create these things, O God, One Trinity, and Trine Unity; and, therefore, out of nothing didst Thou create heaven and earth,—a great thing and a small,—because Thou art Almighty and Good, to make all things good, even the great heaven and the small earth. Thou wast, and there was naught else from which Thou didst create heaven and earth; two such things, one near unto Thee, the other near to nothing,[53]—one to which Thou shouldest be superior, the other to which nothing should be inferior.

But that heaven of heavens was for Thee, O Lord; but the earth, which Thou hast given to the sons of men, to be seen and touched, was not such as now we see and touch. For it was invisible and 'without form,' and there was a deep over which there was not light; or, darkness was over the deep, that is, more than in the deep. For this deep of waters, now visible, has, even in its depths, a light suitable to its nature, perceptible in some manner unto fishes and creeping things in the bottom of it. But the entire deep was almost nothing, since hitherto it was altogether formless; yet there was then that which could be formed. For Thou, O Lord, hast made the world of a formless matter, which matter, out of nothing, Thou hast made almost nothing, out of which to make those great things which we, sons of men, wonder at. For very wonderful is this corporeal heaven, of which firma-ment, between water and water, the second day after the creation of light,

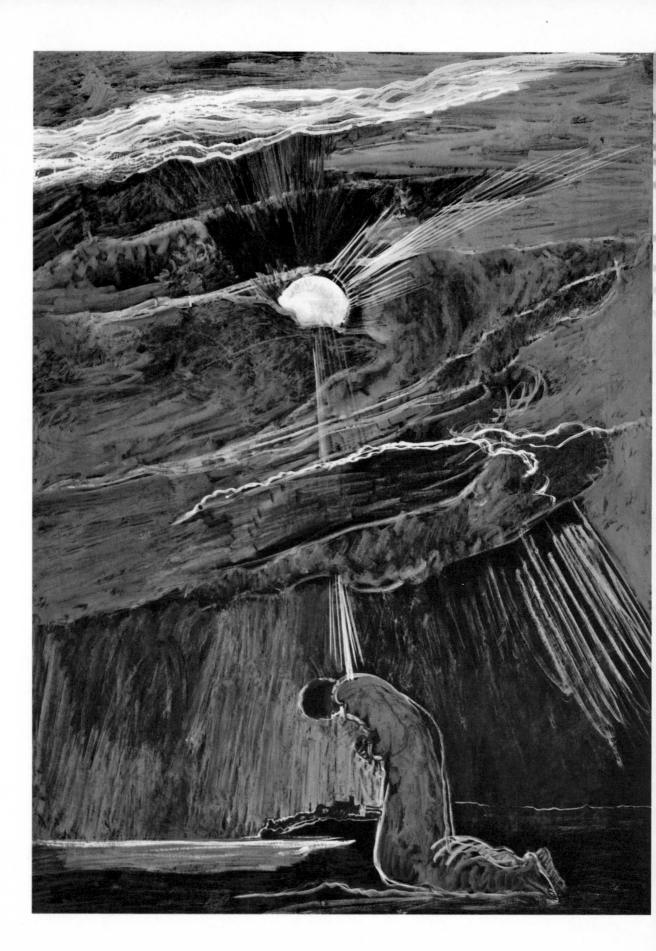

Thou saidst, Let it be made, and it was made. Which firmament Thou calledst heaven, that is, the heaven of this earth and sea, which Thou madest on the third day, by giving a visible shape to the formless matter which Thou madest before all days. For even already hadst Thou made a heaven before all days, but that was the heaven of this heaven; because in the beginning Thou hadst made heaven and earth. But the earth itself which Thou hadst made was formless matter, because it was invisible and without form, and darkness was upon the deep. Of which invisible and formless earth, of which formlessness, of which almost nothing, Thou mightest make all these things of which this changeable world consists, and yet consisteth not; whose very changeableness appears in this, that times can be observed and numbered in it. Because times are made by the change of things, while the shapes, whose matter is the invisible earth aforesaid, are varied and turned.

And therefore the Spirit, the Teacher of Thy servant, when He relates that Thou didst in the Beginning create heaven and earth, is silent as to times, silent as to days. For, doubtless, that heaven of heavens, which Thou in the Beginning didst create, is some intellectual creature, which, although in no wise co-eternal unto Thee, the Trinity, is yet a partaker of Thy eternity, and by reason of the sweetness of that most happy contemplation of Thyself, doth greatly restrain its own mutability, and without any failure, from the time in which it was created, in clinging unto Thee, surpasses all the rolling change of times. But this shapelessness—this earth invisible and without form—has not itself been numbered among the days. For where there is no shape nor order, nothing either cometh or goeth; and where this is not, there certainly are no days, nor any vicissitude of spaces of times.

Oh, let Truth, the light of my heart, not my own darkness, speak unto me! I have descended to that, and am darkened. But thence, even thence, did I love Thee. I went astray, and remembered Thee. I heard Thy voice behind me bidding me return, and scarcely did I hear it for the tumults of the unquiet ones. And now, behold, I return burning and panting after Thy fountain. Let no one prohibit me; of this will I drink, and so have life.

Let me not be my own life; for myself have I badly lived,—death was I unto myself; in Thee do I revive. Do Thou speak unto me; do Thou discourse unto me. In Thy books have I believed, and their words are very deep.

Already hast Thou told me, O Lord, with a strong voice, in my inner ear, that Thou art eternal, having alone immortality. Since Thou art not changed by any shape or motion, nor is Thy will altered by times, because no will which changes is immortal. This in Thy sight is clear to me, and let it become more and more clear, I beseech Thee; and in that manifestation let me abide more soberly under Thy wings. Likewise hast Thou said to me, O Lord, with a strong voice, in my inner ear, that Thou hast made all natures and substances, which are not what Thou Thyself art, and yet they are; and that only is not from Thee which is not, and the motion of the will from Thee who art, to that which in a less degree is, because such motion is guilt and sin; and that no one's sin doth either hurt Thee, or disturb the order of Thy rule, either first or last. This, in Thy sight, is clear to me, and let it become more and more clear, I beseech Thee; and in that manifestation let me abide more soberly under Thy wings.

Likewise hast Thou said to me, with a strong voice, in my inner ear, that that creature, whose will Thou alone art, is not co-eternal unto Thee, and which, with a most persevering purity drawing its support from Thee, doth, in no place and at no time, put forth its own mutability; and Thyself being ever present with it, unto Whom with its entire affection it holds itself, having no future to expect nor conveying into the past what it remembereth, is varied by no change, nor extended into any times. O blessed one, —if any such there be,—in clinging unto Thy Blessedness; blest in Thee, its everlasting Inhabitant and its Enlightener! Nor do I find what the heaven of heavens, which is the Lord's, can be better called than Thine house, which contemplateth Thy delight without any defection of going forth to another; a pure mind, most peacefully one, by that stability of peace of holy spirits, the citizens of Thy city 'in the heavenly places,' above these heavenly places which are seen.

Whence the soul, whose wandering has been made far away, may understand, if now she thirsts for Thee, if now her tears have become bread to
her, while it is daily said unto her 'Where is thy God?' if she now seeketh
of Thee one thing, and desireth that she may dwell in Thy house all the
days of her life. And what is her life but Thee? And what are Thy days but
Thy eternity, as Thy years which fail not, because Thou art the same? Hence,
therefore, can the soul, which is able, understand how far beyond all times
Thou art eternal; when Thy house, which has not wandered from Thee,
although it be not co-eternal with Thee, yet by continually and unfailingly
clinging unto Thee, suffers no vicissitude of times. This in Thy sight is
clear unto me, and may it become more and more clear unto me, I beseech
Thee; and in this manifestation may I abide more soberly under Thy wings.

Behold, I know not what shapelessness there is in those changes of these
last and lowest creatures. And who shall tell me, unless it be some one who,
through the emptiness of his own heart, wanders and is staggered by his
own fancies? Who, unless such a one, would tell me that (all figure being
diminished and consumed), if the formlessness only remain, through which
the thing was changed and was turned from one figure into another, that
that can exhibit the changes of times? For surely it could not be, because
without the change of motions times are not, and there is no change where
there is no figure.

Which things considered as much as Thou givest, O my God, as much
as Thou excitest me to 'knock,' and as much as Thou openest unto me
when I knock, two things I find which Thou hast made, not within the
compass of time, since neither is co-eternal with Thee. One, which is so
formed that, without any failing of contemplation, without any interval of
change, although changeable, yet not changed, it may fully enjoy Thy
eternity and unchangeableness; the other, which was so formless, that it
had not that by which it could be changed from one form into another,
either of motion or of repose, whereby it might be subject unto time. But
this Thou didst not leave to be formless, since before all days, in the beginning Thou createdst heaven and earth,—these two things of which I spoke.

But the earth was invisible and without form, and darkness was upon the deep. By which words its shapelessness is conveyed unto us,—that by degrees those minds may be drawn on which cannot wholly conceive the privation of all form without coming to nothing,—whence another heaven might be created, and another earth visible and well-formed, and water beautifully ordered, and whatever besides is, in the formation of this world, recorded to have been, not without days, created; because such things are so that in them the vicissitudes of times may take place, on account of the appointed changes of motions and of forms.

Meanwhile I conceive this, O my God, when I hear Thy Scripture speak, saying, In the beginning God made heaven and earth; but the earth was invisible and without form, and darkness was upon the deep, and not stating on what day Thou didst create these things. Thus, meanwhile, do I conceive, that it is on account of that heaven of heavens, that intellectual heaven, where to understand is to know all at once,—not 'in part,' not 'darkly,' not 'through a glass,' but as a whole, in manifestation, 'face to face;' not this thing now, that anon, but (as has been said) to know at once without any change of times; and on account of the invisible and formless earth, without any change of times; which change is wont to have 'this thing now, that anon,' because, where there is no form there can be no distinction between 'this' or 'that;'—it is, then, on account of these two,—a primitively formed, and a wholly formless; the one heaven, but the heaven of heavens, the other earth, but the earth invisible and formless;—on account of these two do I meanwhile conceive that Thy Scripture said without mention of days, 'In the beginning God created the heaven and the earth.' For immediately it added of what earth it spake. And when on the second day the firmament is recorded to have been created, and called heaven, it suggests to us of which heaven He spake before without mention of days.

Wonderful is the depth of Thy oracles, whose surface is before us, inviting the little ones, and yet wonderful is the depth, O my God, wonderful is the depth. It is awe to look into it; an awe of honour, and a tremor of love. The enemies thereof I hate vehemently. Oh, if Thou wouldst slay them with Thy two-edged sword, that they[54] be not its enemies! For thus do I love, that they should be slain unto themselves that they may live unto Thee. But behold others not reprovers, but praisers of the book of Genesis,—'The Spirit of God,' say they, 'Who by His servant Moses wrote these things, willed not that these words should be thus understood. He willed not that it should be understood as Thou sayest, but as we say.' Unto whom, O God of us all, Thyself being Judge, do I thus answer.

'Will you say that these things are false, which, with a strong voice, Truth tells me in my inner ear, concerning the very eternity of the Creator, that His substance is in no wise changed by time, nor that His will is separate from His substance? Wherefore, He willeth not one thing now, another anon, but once and for ever He willeth all things that He willeth; not again and again, nor now this, now that; nor willeth afterwards what He willeth not before, nor willeth not what before He willed. Because such a will is mutable, and no mutable thing is eternal; but our God is eternal. Likewise He tells me, tells me in my inner ear, that the expectation of future things is turned to sight when they have come; and this same sight is turned to memory when they have passed. Moreover, all thought which is thus varied is mutable, and nothing mutable is eternal; but our God is eternal.' These things I sum up and put together, and I find that my God, the eternal God, hath not made any creature by any new will, nor that His knowledge suffereth anything transitory.

What, therefore, will ye say, ye objectors? Are these things false? 'No,' they say. 'What is this? Is it false, then, that every nature already formed, or matter formable, is only from Him who is supremely good, because He is supreme?' 'Neither do we deny this,' say they. 'What then? Do you deny this, that there is a certain sublime creature, clinging with so chaste a love with the true and truly eternal God, that although it be not co-eternal with Him, yet it separateth itself not from Him, nor floweth into any variety and vicissitude of times, but resteth in the truest contemplation of Him only?' Since Thou, O God, showest Thyself unto him, and sufficest him, who loveth Thee as much as Thou commandest, and, therefore, he declineth not from Thee, nor toward himself. This is the house of God, not earthly, nor of any celestial bulk corporeal, but a spiritual house and a partaker of Thy eternity, because without blemish for ever. For Thou hast made it fast for ever and ever; Thou hast given it a law, which it shall not pass. Nor yet is it co-eternal with Thee, O God, because not without beginning, for it was made.

For although we find no time before it, for wisdom was created before all things,—not certainly that Wisdom manifestly co-eternal and equal unto Thee, our God, His Father, and by Whom all things were created, and in Whom, as the Beginning, Thou createdst heaven and earth; but truly that wisdom which has been created, namely, the intellectual nature, which, in the contemplation of light, is light. For this, although created, is also called wisdom. But as great as is the difference between the Light which enlighteneth and that which is enlightened, so great is the difference between the Wisdom that createth and that which hath been created; as between the Righteousness which justifieth, and the righteousness which has been made by justification. For we also are called Thy righteousness; for thus saith a certain servant of Thine: 'That we might be made the righteousness of God in him.' Therefore, since a certain created wisdom was created before all things, the rational and intellectual mind of that chaste city of Thine, our mother which is above, and is free, and 'eternal in the heavens' (in what heavens, unless in those that praise Thee, the 'heaven of heavens,' because this also is the 'heaven of heavens,' which is the Lord's)—although we find not time before it, because that which hath been created before all things also precedeth the creature of time, yet is the Eternity of the Creator Himself before it, from Whom, having been created, it took the beginning, although not of time,—for time as yet was not,—yet of its own very nature.

Hence comes it so to be of Thee, our God, as to be manifestly another than Thou, and not the Self-same. Since, although we find time not only not before it, but not in it (it being proper ever to behold Thy face, nor is ever turned aside from it, wherefore it happens that it is varied by no change), yet is there in it that mutability itself whence it would become dark and cold, but that, clinging unto Thee with sublime love, it shineth and gloweth from Thee like a perpetual noon. O house, full of light and splendour! I have loved thy beauty, and the place of the habitation of the glory of my Lord, thy builder and owner. Let my wandering sigh after thee; and I speak unto Him that made thee, that He may possess me also in thee, seeing He hath made me likewise. 'I have gone astray, like a lost sheep;' yet upon the shoulders of my Shepherd, thy builder, I hope that I may be brought back to thee.

'What say ye to me, O ye objectors whom I was addressing, and who yet believe that Moses was the holy servant of God, and that his books were the oracles of the Holy Ghost? Is not this house of God, not indeed co-eternal with God, yet, according to its measure, eternal in the heavens, where in vain you seek for changes of times, because you will not find them? For that surpasseth all extension, and every revolving space of time, to which it is ever good to cleave fast to God.' 'It is,' say they. 'What, therefore, of those things which my heart cried out unto my God, when within it heard the voice of His praise, what then do you contend is false? Or is it because the matter was formless, wherein, as there was no form, there was no order? But where there was no order there could not be any change of times; and yet this "almost nothing," inasmuch as it was not altogether nothing, was verily from Him, from Whom is whatever is, in what state soever anything is.' 'This also,' say they, 'we do not deny.'

With such as grant that all these things which Thy truth indicates to my mind are true, I desire to confer a little before Thee, O my God. For let those who deny these things bark and drown their own voices with their clamour as much as they please; I will endeavour to persuade them to be quiet, and to suffer Thy word to reach them. But should they be unwilling, and should they repel me, I beseech, O my God, that Thou 'be not silent to me.' Do Thou speak truly in my heart, for Thou only so speakest, and I will send them away blowing upon the dust from without, and raising it up into their own eyes; and I will myself enter into my chamber, and sing there unto Thee songs of love,—groaning with groanings unutterable in my pilgrimage, and remembering Jerusalem, with heart raised up towards it, Jerusalem my country, Jerusalem my mother, and Thyself, the Ruler over it, the Enlightener, the Father, the Guardian, the Husband, the chaste and strong delight, the solid joy, and all good things ineffable, even all at the same time, because the one supreme and true Good. And I will not be turned away until Thou collect all that I am, from this dispersion and deformity, into the peace of that very dear mother, where are the first-fruits of my spirit, whence these things are assured to me, and Thou conform and confirm it for ever, my God, my Mercy. But with reference to those who say not that all these things which are true are false, who honour Thy Holy Scripture set forth by holy Moses, placing it, as with us, on the summit of an authority to be followed, and yet who contradict us in some particulars, I thus speak: Be Thou, O our God, judge between my confessions and their contradictions.

For they say, 'Although these things be true, yet Moses regarded not those two things, when by divine revelation he said, "In the beginning God created the heaven and the earth." Under the name of heaven he did not indicate that spiritual or intellectual creature which always beholds the face of God; nor under the name of earth, that shapeless matter.' 'What then?' 'That man,' say they, 'meant as we say; this it is that he declared by those words.' 'What is that?' 'By the name of heaven and earth,' say they, 'did he first wish to set forth, universally and briefly, all this visible world, that afterwards by the enumeration of the days he might distribute, as if in detail, all those things which it pleased the Holy Spirit thus to reveal. For such men were that rude and carnal people to which he spoke, that he judged it prudent that only those works of God as were visible should be entrusted to them.' They agree, however, that the earth invisible and formless, and the darksome deep (out of which it is subsequently pointed out that all these visible things, which are known to all, were made and set in order during those 'days'), may not unsuitably be understood of this formless matter.

What, now, if another should say 'That this same formlessness and

confusion of matter was first introduced under the name of heaven and
earth, because out of it this visible world, with all those natures which most
manifestly appear in it, and which is wont to be called by the name of
heaven and earth, was created and perfected'? But what if another should
say, that 'That invisible and visible nature is not inaptly called heaven and
earth; and that consequently the universal creation, which God in His
wisdom hath made,—that is, "in the beginning,"—was comprehended under
these two words. Yet, since all things have been made, not of the substance
of God, but out of nothing (because they are not that same thing that God
is, and there is in them all a certain mutability, whether they remain, as
doth the eternal house of God, or be changed, as are the soul and body of
man), therefore, that the common matter of all things invisible and visible,
—as yet shapeless, but still capable of form,—out of which was to be
created heaven and earth (that is, the invisible and visible creature already
formed), was spoken of by the same names by which the earth invisible and
formless and the darkness upon the deep would be called; with this difference, however, that the earth invisible and formless is understood as corporeal matter, before it had any manner of form, but the darkness upon the
deep as spiritual matter, before it was restrained at all of its unlimited
fluidity, and before the enlightening of wisdom.'

Should any man wish, he may still say, 'That the already perfected and
formed natures, invisible and visible, are not signified under the name of
heaven and earth when it is read, "In the beginning God created the heaven
and the earth;" but that the yet same formless beginning of things, the
matter capable of being formed and made, was called by these names,
because contained in it there were these confused things not as yet distinguished by their qualities and forms, the which now being digested in
their own orders, are called heaven and earth, the former being the spiritual,
the latter the corporeal creature.'

All which things having been heard and considered, I am unwilling to
contend about words, for that is profitable to nothing but to the subverting
of the hearers. But the law is good to edify, if a man use it lawfully, for the

end of it 'is charity out of a pure heart, and of a good conscience, and of faith unfeigned.' And well did our Master know, upon which two commandments He hung all the Law and the Prophets. And what doth it hinder me, O my God, Thou light of my eyes in secret, while ardently confessing these things,—since by these words many things may be understood, all of which are yet true,—what, I say, doth it hinder me, should I think otherwise of what the writer thought than some other man thinketh? Indeed, all of us who read endeavour to trace out and to understand that which he whom we read wished to convey; and as we believe him to speak truly, we dare not suppose that he has spoken anything which we either know or suppose to be false. Since, therefore, each person endeavours to understand in the Holy Scriptures that which the writer understood, what hurt is it if a man understand what Thou, the light of all true-speaking minds, dost show him to be true although he whom he reads understood not this, seeing that he also understood a Truth, not, however, this Truth?

For it is true, O Lord, that Thou hast made heaven and earth; it is also true, that the Beginning is Thy Wisdom in Which Thou hast made all things. It is likewise true, that this visible world hath its own great parts, the heaven and the earth, which in a short compass comprehends all made and created natures. It is also true, that everything mutable sets before our minds a certain want of form, whereof it taketh a form, or is changed and turned. It is true, that that is subject to no times which so cleaveth to the changeless form as that, though it be mutable, it is not changed. It is true, that the formlessness, which is almost nothing, cannot have changes of times. It is true, that that of which anything is made may by a certain mode of speech be called by the name of that thing which is made of it; whence that formlessness of which heaven and earth were made might be called 'heaven and earth.' It is true, that of all things having form, nothing is nearer to the formless than the earth and the deep. It is true, that not only every created and formed thing, but also whatever is capable of creation and of form, Thou hast made, 'by whom are all things.' It is true, that everything that is formed from that which is formless was formless before it was formed.

From all these truths, of which they doubt not whose inner eye Thou hast granted to see such things, and who immovably believe Moses, Thy servant, to have spoken in the spirit of truth; from all these, then, he taketh one who saith, 'In the beginning God created the heaven and the earth,'—that is, 'In His Word, co-eternal with Himself, God made the intelligible and the sensible, or the spiritual and corporeal creature.' He taketh another, who saith, 'In the beginning God created the heaven and the earth,'—that is, 'In His Word, co-eternal with Himself, God made the universal mass of this corporeal world, with all those manifest and known natures which it containeth.' He, another, who saith, 'In the beginning God created the heaven and the earth,'—that is, 'In His Word, co-eternal with Himself, God made the formless matter of the spiritual and corporeal creature.' He, another, who saith, 'In the beginning God created the heaven and the earth,'—that is, 'In His Word, co-eternal with Himself, God made the formless matter of the corporeal creature, wherein heaven and earth lay as yet confused, which being now distinguished and formed, we, at this day, see in the mass of this world.' He, another, who saith, 'In the beginning God created heaven and earth,'—that is, 'In the very beginning of creating and working, God made that formless matter confusedly containing heaven and earth, out of which, being formed, they now stand out, and are manifest, with all the things that are in them.'

And as concerns the understanding of the following words, out of all those truths he selected one to himself, who saith, 'But the earth was invisible and without form, and darkness was upon the deep,'—that is, 'That corporeal thing, which God made, was as yet the formless matter of corporeal things, without order, without light.' He taketh another, who saith, 'But the earth was invisible and without form, and darkness was upon the deep,'—that is, 'This whole, which is called heaven and earth, was as yet formless and darksome matter, out of which the corporeal heaven and the corporeal earth were to be made, with all things therein which are known to our corporeal senses.' He, another, who saith, 'But the earth was invisible and without form, and darkness was upon the deep,'—that is, 'This whole, which is called heaven and earth, was as yet a formless and darksome matter, out of which were to be made that intelligible heaven, which is otherwise called the heaven of heavens, and the earth, namely, the whole corporeal nature, under which name may also be comprised this corporeal heaven,—that is, from which every invisible and visible creature would be created.' He, another, who saith, 'But the earth was invisible and without form, and darkness was upon the deep,'—'The Scripture called not that formlessness by the name of heaven and earth, but that formlessness itself,' saith he, 'already was, which he named the earth, invisible and formless, and the darksome deep, of which he had said before, that God had made the heaven and the earth, namely, the spiritual and corporeal creature.' He, another, who saith, 'But the earth was invisible and formless, and darkness was upon the deep,'—that is, 'There was already a formless matter, whereof the Scripture before said, that God had made heaven and earth, namely, the entire corporeal mass of the world, divided into two very great parts, the superior and the inferior, with all those familiar and known creatures which are in them.'

For, should any one endeavour to contend against these last two opinions, thus,—'If you will not admit that this formlessness of matter appears to be called by the name of heaven and earth, then there was something which God had not made out of which He could make heaven and earth; for Scripture hath not told us that God made this matter, unless we understand it to be implied in the term of heaven and earth, or of earth only, when it is said, "In the beginning God created heaven and earth," as that which follows, but the earth was invisible and formless, although it was pleasing to him so to call the formless matter, we may not yet understand any but that which God made in that text which hath been already written, "God made heaven and earth."' The maintainers of either one or the other of these two opinions which we have put last will, when they have heard these things, answer and say, 'We deny not indeed that this formless matter was created by God, the God of whom are all things, very good; for, as we say that that is a greater good which is created and formed, so we acknowledge that that is a minor good which is capable of creation and form, but yet good. But yet the Scripture hath not declared that God made this formlessness, any more than it hath declared many other things; as the "Cherubim," and "Seraphim," and those of which the apostle distinctly speaks, "Thrones," "Dominions," "Principalities," "Powers," all of which it is manifest God made. Or if in that which is said, "He made heaven and earth," all things are comprehended, what do we say of the waters upon which the Spirit of God moved? For if they are understood as incorporated in the word earth, how then can formless matter be meant in the term earth when we see the waters so beautiful? Or if it be so meant, why then is it written that out of the same formlessness the firmament was made and called heaven, and yet it is not written that the waters were made? For those waters, which we perceive flowing in so beautiful a manner, remain not formless and invisible. But if, then, they received that beauty when God said, Let the water which is under the firmament be gathered together, so that the gathering be the very formation, what will be answered concerning the waters which are above the firmament, because if formless they would not have deserved to receive a seat so honourable, nor is it written by what word they were formed? If, then, Genesis is silent as to anything that God hath made, which, however, neither sound faith nor unerring understanding doubteth that God hath made, let not any sober teaching dare to say that these waters were co-eternal with God because we find them mentioned in the book of Genesis; but when they were created, we find not. Why— truth instructing us—may we not understand that that formless matter, which the Scripture calls the earth invisible and without form, and the darksome deep, have been made by God out of nothing, and therefore that they are not co-eternal with Him, although that narrative hath failed to tell when they were made?'

These things, therefore, being heard and perceived according to my weakness of apprehension, which I confess unto Thee, O Lord, who knowest it, I see that two sorts of differences may arise when by signs anything is related, even by true reporters,—one concerning the truth of the things, the other concerning the meaning of him who reports them. For in one way we inquire, concerning the forming of the creature, what is true; but in another, what Moses, that excellent servant of Thy faith, would have wished that the reader and hearer should understand by these words. As for the first kind, let all those depart from me who imagine themselves to know as true what is false. And as for the other also, let all depart from me who imagine Moses to have spoken things that are false. But let me be united in Thee, O Lord, with them, and in Thee delight myself with them that feed on Thy truth, in the breadth of charity; and let us approach together unto the words of Thy book, and in them make search for Thy will, through the will of Thy servant by whose pen Thou hast dispensed them.

But which of us, amid so many truths which occur to inquirers in these words, understood as they are in different ways, shall so discover that one interpretation as to confidently say 'that Moses thought this,' and 'that in that narrative he wished this to be understood,' as confidently as he says 'that this is true,' whether he thought this thing or the other? For behold, O my God, I Thy servant, who in this book have vowed unto Thee a sacrifice of confession, and beseech Thee that of Thy mercy I may pay my vows unto Thee, behold, can I, as I confidently assert that Thou in Thy immutable word hast created all things, invisible and visible, with equal confidence assert that Moses meant nothing else than this when he wrote, 'In the beginning God created the heaven and the earth.' No. Because it is not as clear to me that this was in his mind when he wrote these things, as I see it to be certain in Thy truth. For his thoughts might be set upon the very beginning of the creation when he said, 'In the beginning;' and he might wish it to be understood that, in this place 'the heaven and the earth' were no formed and perfect nature, whether spiritual or corporeal, but each of them newly begun, and as yet formless. Because I see, that whichsoever of these had been said, it might have been said truly; but which of them he may have thought in these words, I do not so perceive. Although, whether it were one of these, or some other meaning which has not been mentioned by me, that this great man saw in his mind when he used these words, I make no doubt but that he saw it truly, and expressed it suitably.

Let no one now trouble me by saying, 'Moses thought not as you say, but as I say.' For should he ask me, 'Whence knowest thou that Moses thought this which you deduce from his words?' I ought to take it contentedly, and reply perhaps as I have before, or somewhat more fully should he be obstinate. But when he says, 'Moses meant not what you say, but what I say,' and yet denies not what each of us says, and that both are true, O my God, life of the poor, in whose bosom there is no contradiction, pour down into my heart Thy soothings, that I may patiently bear with such as say this to me; not because they are divine, and because they have seen in the heart of Thy servant what they say, but because they are proud, and have not known the opinion of Moses, but love their own,—not because it is true, but because it is their own. Otherwise they would equally love another true opinion, as I love what they say when they speak what is true; not because it is theirs, but because it is true, and therefore now not theirs because true. But if they therefore love that because it is true, it is now both theirs and mine, since it is common to all the lovers of truth. But because they contend that Moses meant not what I say, but what they themselves say, this I neither like nor love; because, though it were so, yet that rashness is not of knowledge, but of audacity; and not vision, but vanity brought it forth. And therefore, O Lord, are Thy judgments to be dreaded, since Thy truth is neither mine, nor his, nor another's, but of all of us, whom Thou publicly callest to have it in common, warning us terribly not to hold it as specially for ourselves, lest we be deprived of it. For whosoever claims for himself as his own that which Thou appointed to all to enjoy, and desires that to be his own which belongs to all, is forced away from what is common to all to that which is his own—that is, from truth to falsehood. For he that 'speaketh a lie, speaketh of his own.'

Hearken, O God, Thou best Judge! Truth itself, hearken to what I shall say to this gainsayer; hearken, for before Thee I say it, and before my brethren who use Thy law lawfully, to the end of charity; hearken and behold what I shall say to him, if it be pleasing unto Thee. For this brotherly and peaceful word do I return unto him: 'If we both see that that which thou sayest is true, and if we both see that what I say is true, where, I ask, do we see it? Certainly not I in thee, nor thou in me, but both in the unchangeable truth itself, which is above our minds.' When, therefore, we may not contend about the very light of the Lord our God, why do we contend about the thoughts of our neighbour, which we cannot so see as incommutable truth is seen; when, if Moses himself had appeared to us and said, 'This I meant,' not so should we see it, but believe it? Let us not, then, 'be puffed up for one against the other,' above that which is written; let us love the Lord our God with all our heart, with all our soul, and with all our mind, and our neighbour as ourself. As to which two precepts of charity, unless we believe that Moses meant whatever in these books he did mean, we shall make God a liar when we think otherwise concerning our fellow-servants' mind than He hath taught us. Behold, now, how foolish it is, in so great an abundance of the truest opinions which can be extracted from these words, rashly to affirm which of them Moses particularly meant; and with pernicious contentions to offend charity itself, on account of which he hath spoken all the things whose words we endeavour to explain!

And yet, O my God, Thou exaltation of my humility, and rest of my labour, who hearest my confessions, and forgivest my sins, since Thou commandest me that I should love my neighbour as myself, I cannot believe that Thou gavest to Moses, Thy most faithful servant, a less gift than I should wish and desire for myself from Thee, had I been born in his time, and hadst Thou placed me in that position that through the service of my heart and of my tongue those books might be distributed, which so long after were to profit all nations, and through the whole world, from so great a pinnacle of authority, were to surmount the words of all false and proud teachings. I should have wished truly had I then been Moses (for we all come from the same mass; and what is man, saving that Thou art mindful of him?). I should then, had I been at that time what he was, and

enjoined by Thee to write the book of Genesis, have wished that such a power of expression and such a method of arrangement should be given me, that they who cannot as yet understand how God creates might not reject the words as surpassing their powers; and they who are already able to do this, would find, in what true opinion soever they had by thought arrived at, that it was not passed over in the few words of Thy servant; and should another man by the light of truth have discovered another, neither should that fail to be found in those same words.

For as a fountain in a limited space is more plentiful, and affords supply for more streams over larger spaces than any one of those streams which, after a wide interval, is derived from the same fountain; so the narrative of Thy dispenser, destined to benefit many who were likely to discourse thereon, does, from a limited measure of language, overflow into streams of clear truth, whence each one may draw out for himself that truth which he can concerning these subjects,—this one that truth, that one another, by larger circumlocutions of discourse. For some, when they read or hear these words, think that God as a man or some mass gifted with immense power, by some new and sudden resolve, had, outside itself, as if at distant places, created heaven and earth, two great bodies above and below, wherein all things were to be contained. And when they hear, God said, Let it be made, and it was made, they think of words begun and ended, sounding in times and passing away, after the departure of which that came into being which was commanded to be; and whatever else of the kind their familiarity with the world would suggest. In whom, being as yet little ones, while their weakness by this humble kind of speech is carried on as if in a mother's bosom, their faith is healthfully built up, by which they have and hold as certain that God made all natures, which in wondrous variety their senses perceive on every side. Which words, if any one despising them, as if trivial, with proud weakness shall have stretched himself beyond his fostering cradle, he will, alas, fall miserably. Have pity, O Lord God, lest they who pass by trample on the unfledged bird; and send Thine angel, who may restore it to its nest, that it may live until it can fly.

But others, to whom these words are no longer a nest, but shady fruit-bowers, see the fruits concealed in them, fly around rejoicing, and chirpingly search and pluck them. For they see when they read or hear these words, O God, that all times past and future are surmounted by Thy eternal and stable abiding, and still that there is no temporal creature which Thou hast not made. And by Thy will, because it is that which Thou art, Thou hast made all things, not by any changed will, nor by a will which before was not,—not out of Thyself, in Thine own likeness, the form of all things, but out of nothing, a formless unlikeness which should be formed by Thy likeness (having recourse to Thee the One, after their settled capacity, according as it has been given to each thing in his kind), and might all be made very good; whether they remain around Thee, or, being by degrees removed in time and place, make or undergo beautiful variations. These things they see, and rejoice in the light of Thy truth, in the little degree they here may.

Again, another of these directs his attention to that which is said, 'In the beginning God made the heaven and the earth,' and beholdeth Wisdom,—the Beginning, because It also speaketh unto us. Another likewise directs his attention to the same words, and by 'beginning' understands the commencement of things created; and receives it thus,—In the beginning He made, as if it were said, He at first made. And among those who understand 'In the beginning' to mean, that 'in Thy Wisdom Thou hast created heaven and earth,' one believes that matter out of which the heaven and earth were to be created to be there called 'heaven and earth;' another, that they are natures already formed and distinct; another, one formed nature, and that a spiritual, under the name of heaven, the other formless, of corporeal matter, under the name of earth. But they who under the name of 'heaven and earth' understand matter as yet formless, out of which were to be formed heaven and earth, do not themselves understand it in one manner; but one, that matter out of which the intelligible and the sensible creature were to be completed; another, that only out of which this sensible corporeal mass was to come, holding in its vast bosom these visible and prepared natures. Nor are they who believe that the creatures already set in order and arranged are in this place called heaven and earth of one accord but the one, both the invisible and visible; the other, the visible only, in which we admire the luminous heaven and darksome earth, and the things that are therein.

But he who does not otherwise understand, 'In the beginning He made,' than if it were said, 'At first He made,' can only truly understand heaven and earth of the matter of heaven and earth, namely, of the universal, that is, intelligible and corporeal creation. For if he would have it of the universe, as already formed, it might rightly be asked of him: 'If at first God made this, what made He afterwards?' And after the universe he will find nothing; thereupon must he, though unwilling, hear, 'How is this first, if there is nothing afterwards?' But when he says that God made matter first formless, then formed, he is not absurd if he be but able to discern what precedes by eternity, what by time, what by choice, what by origin. By eternity, as God is before all things; by time, as the flower is before the fruit; by choice, as the fruit is before the flower; by origin, as sound is before the tune. Of these four, the first and last which I have referred to are with much difficulty understood; the two middle very easily. For an uncommon and too lofty vision it is to behold, O Lord, Thy Eternity, immutably making things mutable, and thereby before them. Who is so acute of mind as to be able without great labour to discover how the sound is prior to the tune, because a tune is a formed sound; and a thing not formed may exist, but that which existeth not cannot be formed? So is the matter prior to that which is made from it; not prior because it maketh it, since itself is rather made, nor is it prior by an interval of time. For we do not as to time first utter formless sounds without singing, and then adapt or fashion them into the form of a song, just as wood or silver from which a chest or vessel is made. Because such materials do by time also precede the forms of the things which are made from them; but in singing this is not so. For when it is sung, its sound is heard at the same time; seeing there is not first a formless sound, which is afterwards formed into a song. For as soon as it shall have first sounded it passeth away; nor canst thou find anything of it, which being recalled thou canst by art compose. And, therefore, the song is absorbed in its own sound, which sound of it is its matter. Because this same is formed that it may be a tune; and therefore, as I was saying, the matter of the sound is prior to the form of the tune, not before through any power of making it a tune; for neither is a sound the composer of the tune, but is sent forth from the body and is subjected to the soul of the singer, that from it he may form a tune. Nor is it first in time, for it is given forth together with the tune; nor first in choice, for a sound is not better than a tune, since a tune is not merely a sound, but a beautiful sound. But it is first in origin, because the tune is not formed that it may become a sound, but the sound is formed that it may become a tune. By this example, let him who is able to understand that the matter of things was first made, and called heaven and earth, because out of it heaven and earth were made. Not that it was made first in time, because the forms of things give rise to time, but that was formless; but now, in time, it is perceived together with its form. Nor yet can anything be related concerning that matter, unless as if it were prior in time, while it is considered last (because things formed are assuredly superior to things formless), and is preceded by the Eternity of the Creator, so that there might be out of nothing that from which something might be made.

In this diversity of true opinions let Truth itself beget concord; and may our God have mercy upon us, that we may use the law lawfully, the end of the commandment, pure charity. And by this if any one asks of me, 'Which of these was the meaning of Thy servant Moses?' these were not the utterances of my confessions, should I not confess unto Thee, 'I know not;' and yet I know that those opinions are true, with the exception of those carnal ones concerning which I have spoken what I thought well. However, these words of Thy Book affright not those little ones of good hope, treating few of high things in a humble fashion, and few things in varied ways. But let all, whom I acknowledge to see and speak the truth in these words, love one another, and equally love Thee, our God, fountain of truth,—if we thirst not for vain things, but for it; yea, let us so honour this servant of Thine, the dispenser of this Scripture, full of Thy Spirit, as to believe that when Thou revealedst Thyself to him, and he wrote these things, he intended that which in them chiefly excels both for light of truth and fruitfulness of profit.

Thus, when one shall say, 'He [Moses] meant as I do,' and another, 'Nay, but as I do,' I suppose that I am speaking more religiously when I say, 'Why not rather as both, if both be true?' And if there be a third truth, or a fourth, and if any one seek any truth altogether different in those words, why may not he be believed to have seen all these, through whom one God hath tempered the Holy Scriptures to the senses of many, about to see therein things true but different? I certainly,—and I fearlessly declare it from my heart,—were I to write anything to have the highest authority, should prefer so to write, that whatever of truth any one might apprehend concerning these matters, my words should re-echo, rather than that I should set down one true opinion so clearly on this as that I should exclude the rest, that which was false in which could not offend me. Therefore am I unwilling, O my God, to be so headstrong as not to believe that from Thee this man [Moses] hath received so much. He, surely, when he wrote those words, perceived and thought whatever truth we have been able to discover, yea, and whatever we have not been able, nor yet are able, though still it may be found in them.

Finally, O Lord, who art God, and not flesh and blood, if man doth see anything less, can anything lie hid from 'Thy good Spirit,' who shall 'lead me into the land of uprightness,' which Thou Thyself, by those words, wert about to reveal to future readers, although he through whom they were spoken, amid the many interpretations that might have been found, fixed on but one? Which, if it be so, let that which he thought on be more exalted than the rest. But to us, O Lord, either point out the same, or any other true one which may be pleasing unto Thee so that whether Thou makest known to us that which Thou didst to that man of Thine, or some other by occasion of the same words, yet Thou mayest feed us, not error deceive us. Behold, O Lord my God, how many things we have written concerning a few words,—how many, I beseech Thee! What strength of ours, what ages would suffice for all Thy books after this manner? Permit me, therefore, in these more briefly to confess unto Thee, and to select some one true, certain, and good sense, that Thou shalt inspire, although many senses offer themselves, where many, indeed, may; this being the faith of my confession, that if I should say that which Thy minister felt, rightly and profitably, this I should strive for; the which if I shall not attain, yet I may say that which Thy Truth willed through Its words to say unto me, which said also unto him what It willed.

# BOOK XIII

*Of the goodness of God explained in the creation of things, and of the trinity as found in the first words of Genesis. The story concerning the origin of the world (Gen. I.) is allegorically explained, and he applies it to those things which God works for sanctified and blessed man. Finally, he makes an end of this work, having implored eternal rest from God.*

I CALL upon Thee, my God, my mercy, who madest me, and who didst not forget me, though forgetful of Thee. I call Thee into my soul, which by the desire which Thou inspirest in it Thou preparest for Thy reception. Do not Thou forsake me calling upon Thee, who didst anticipate me before I called, and didst importunately urge with manifold calls that I should hear Thee from afar, and be converted, and call upon Thee who calledst me. For Thou, O Lord, hast blotted out all my evil deserts, that Thou mightest not repay into my hands wherewith I have fallen from Thee, and thou hast anticipated all my good deserts, that Thou mightest repay into Thy hands wherewith Thou madest me; because before I was, Thou wast, nor was I [anything] to which Thou mightest grant being. And yet behold, I am, out of Thy goodness, anticipating all this which Thou hast made me, and of which Thou hast made me. For neither hadst Thou stood in need of me, nor am I such a good as to be helpful unto Thee, my Lord and God; not that I may so serve Thee as though Thou wert fatigued in working, or lest Thy power may be less if lacking my assistance; nor that, like the land, I may so cultivate Thee that Thou wouldest be uncultivated did I cultivate Thee not; but that I may serve and worship Thee, to the end that I may have well-being from Thee, from whom it is that I am one susceptible of well-being.

For the plenitude of Thy goodness Thy creature subsists, that a good, which could profit Thee nothing, nor though of Thee was equal to Thee, might yet be, since it could be made of Thee. For what did heaven and earth, which Thou madest in the beginning, deserve of Thee? Let those spiritual and corporeal natures, which Thou in Thy wisdom madest, declare what they deserve of Thee to depend thereon,—even the inchoate and formless, each in its own kind, either spiritual or corporeal, going into excess, and into remote unlikeness unto Thee (the spiritual, though formless, more excellent than if it were a formed body; and the corporeal, though form-less, more excellent than if it were altogether nothing), and thus they as formless would depend upon Thy Word, unless by the same Word they were recalled to Thy Unity, and endued with form, and from Thee, the one sovereign Good, were all made very good. How have they deserved of Thee, that they should be even formless, since they would not be even this except from Thee?

How has corporeal matter deserved of Thee, to be even invisible and formless, since it were not even this hadst Thou not made it; and therefore since it was not, it could not deserve of Thee that it should be made? Or how could the inchoate spiritual creature deserve of Thee, that even it should flow darksomely like the deep,—unlike Thee, had it not been by the same Word turned to that by Whom it was created, and by Him so enlightened become light, although not equally, yet conformably to that Form which is equal unto Thee? For as to a body, to be is not all one with being beautiful, for then it could not be deformed; so also to a created spirit to live is not all one with living wisely, for then it would be wise unchangeably. But it is good for it always to hold fast unto Thee, lest, in turning from Thee, it lose that light which it hath obtained in turning to Thee, and relapse into a light resembling the darksome deep. For even we ourselves, who in respect of the soul are a spiritual creature, having turned away from Thee, our light, were in that life 'sometimes darkness;' and do labour amidst the remains of our darkness, until in Thy Only One we become Thy righteousness, like the mountains of God. For we have been Thy judgments, which are like the great deep.

But what Thou saidst in the beginning of the creation, 'Let there be light, and there was light,' I do not unfitly understand of the spiritual creature; because there was even then a kind of life, which Thou mightest illuminate. But as it had not deserved of Thee that it should be such a life as could be enlightened, so neither, when it already was, hath it deserved of Thee that it should be enlightened. For neither could its formlessness be pleasing unto Thee, unless it became light,—not by merely existing, but by beholding the illuminating light, and cleaving unto it; so also, that it lives, and lives happily, it owes to nothing whatsoever but to Thy grace; being converted by means of a better change unto that which can be changed neither into better nor into worse; the which Thou only art because Thou only simply art, to whom it is not one thing to live, another to live blessedly, since Thou art Thyself Thine own Blessedness.

What, therefore, could there be wanting unto Thy good, which Thou Thyself art, although these things had either never been, or had remained formless,—the which Thou madest not out of any want, but out of the plenitude of Thy goodness, restraining them and converting them to form not as though Thy joy were perfected by them? For to Thee, being perfect, their imperfection is displeasing, and therefore were they perfected by Thee, and were pleasing unto Thee; but not as if Thou wert imperfect, and wert to be perfected in their perfection. For Thy good Spirit was borne over the waters, not borne up by them as if He rested upon them. For those in whom Thy good Spirit is said to rest, He causes to rest in Himself. But Thy incorruptible and unchangeable will, which in itself is all-sufficient for itself, was borne over that life which Thou hadst made, to which to live is not all one with living happily, since, flowing in its own darkness, it liveth also; for which it remaineth to be converted unto Him by whom it was made, and to live more and more by 'the fountain of life,' and in His light to 'see light,' and to be perfected, and enlightened, and made happy.

Behold now, the Trinity appears unto me in an enigma, which Thou, O my God, art, since Thou, O Father, in the Beginning of our wisdom,— Which is Thy Wisdom, born of Thyself, equal and co-eternal unto Thee,—

that is, in Thy Son, hast created heaven and earth. Many things have we said of the heaven of heavens, and of the earth invisible and formless, and of the darksome deep, in reference to the wandering defects of its spiritual deformity, were it not converted unto Him from whom was its life, such as it was, and by His enlightening became a beauteous life, and the heaven of that heaven which was afterwards set between water and water. And under the name of God, I now held the Father, who made these things; and under the name of the Beginning, the Son, in whom He made these things; and believing, as I did, that my God was the Trinity, I sought further in His holy words, and behold, Thy Spirit was borne over the waters. Behold the Trinity, O my God, Father, Son, and Holy Ghost,—the Creator of all creation.

But what was the cause, O Thou true-speaking Light? Unto Thee do I lift up my heart, let it not teach me vain things; disperse its darkness, and tell me, I beseech Thee, by our mother charity, tell me, I beseech Thee, the reason why, after the mention of heaven, and of the earth invisible and formless, and darkness upon the deep, Thy Scripture should then at length mention Thy Spirit? Was it because it was meet that it should be spoken of Him that He was 'borne over,' and this could not be said, unless that were first mentioned 'over' which Thy Spirit may be understood to have been 'borne'? For neither was he 'borne over' the Father, nor the Son, nor could it rightly be said that He was 'borne over' if He were 'borne over' nothing. That, therefore, was first to be spoken of 'over' which He might be 'borne;' and then He, whom it was not meet to mention otherwise than as having been 'borne.' Why, then, was it not meet that it should otherwise be mentioned of Him, than as having been 'borne over'?

Hence let him that is able now follow Thy apostle with his understanding where he thus speaks, because Thy love 'is shed abroad in our hearts by the Holy Ghost, which is given unto us;' and where, 'concerning spiritual gifts,' he teacheth and showeth unto us a more excellent way of charity; and where he bows his knees unto Thee for us, that we may know the super-eminent knowledge of the love of Christ. And, therefore, from the beginning was He super-eminently 'borne above the waters.' To whom shall I tell this? How speak of the weight of lustful desires, pressing downwards to the steep abyss? and how charity raises us up again, through Thy Spirit which was 'borne over the waters'? To whom shall I tell it? How tell it? For neither are there places in which we are merged and emerge. What can be more like, and yet more unlike? They be affections, they be loves; the filthiness of our spirit flowing away downwards with the love of cares, and the sanctity of Thine raising us upwards by the love of freedom from care; that we may lift our hearts unto Thee where Thy Spirit is 'borne over the waters;' and that we may come to that pre-eminent rest, when our soul shall have passed through the waters which have no substance.

The angels fell, the soul of man fell, and they have thus indicated the abyss in that dark deep, ready for the whole spiritual creation, unless Thou hadst said from the beginning, 'Let there be light,' and there had been light, and every obedient intelligence of Thy celestial City had cleaved to Thee, and rested in Thy Spirit, which unchangeably is 'borne over' everything changeable. Otherwise, even the heaven of heavens itself would have been a darksome deep, whereas now it is light in the Lord. For even in that wretched restlessness of the spirits who fell away, and, when unclothed of the garments of Thy light, discovered their own darkness, dost Thou sufficiently disclose how noble Thou hast made the rational creature; to which nought which is inferior to Thee will suffice to yield a happy rest, and so not even herself. For Thou, O our God, shalt enlighten our darkness; from Thee are derived our garments of light, and then shall our darkness be as the noon-day. Give Thyself unto me, O my God, restore Thyself unto me; behold, I love Thee, and if it be too little, let me love Thee more strongly. I cannot measure my love so that I may come to know how much there is yet wanting in me, ere my life run into Thy embracements, and not be turned away until it be hidden in the secret place of Thy Presence. This only I know, that woe is me except in Thee,—not only without, but even also within myself; and all plenty which is not my God is poverty to me.

But was not either the Father or the Son 'borne over the waters'? If we understand this to mean in space, as a body, then neither was the Holy Spirit; but if the incommutable super-eminence of Divinity above everything mutable, then both Father, and Son, and Holy Ghost were borne 'over the waters.' Why, then, is this said of Thy Spirit only? Why is it said of Him alone? As if He had been in place who is not in place, of whom only it is written, that He is Thy gift? In Thy gift we rest; there we enjoy Thee. Our rest is our place. Love lifts us up thither, and Thy good Spirit lifteth our lowliness from the gates of death. In Thy good pleasure lies our peace. The body by its own weight gravitates towards it own place. Weight goes not downward only, but to its own place. Fire tends upwards, a stone downwards. They are propelled by their own weights, they seek their own places. Oil poured under the water is raised above the water; water poured upon oil sinks under the oil. They are propelled by their own weights, they seek their own places. Out of order, they are restless; restored to order, they are at rest. My weight is my love; by it am I borne whithersoever I am borne. By Thy Gift we are inflamed, and are borne upwards; we wax hot inwardly, and go forwards. We ascend Thy ways that be in our heart, and sing a song of degrees; we glow inwardly with Thy fire, with Thy good fire, and we go, because we go upwards to the peace of Jerusalem; for glad was I when they said unto me, 'Let us go into the house of the Lord.' There hath Thy good pleasure placed us, that we may desire no other thing than to dwell there for ever.

Happy creature, which, though in itself it was other than Thou, hath known no other state than that as soon as it was made, it was, without any interval of time, by Thy Gift, which is borne over everything mutable, raised up by that calling whereby Thou saidst, 'Let there be light, and there was light.' Whereas in us there is a difference of times, in that we were darkness, and are made light; but of that it is only said what it would have been had it not been enlightened. And this is so spoken as if it had been fleeting and darksome before; that so the cause whereby it was made to be otherwise might appear,—that is to say, being turned to the unfailing Light it might become light. Let him who is able understand this; and let him who is not, ask of Thee. Why should he trouble me, as if I could enlighten any 'man that cometh into the world'?

Which of us understandeth the Almighty Trinity? And yet which speaketh not of It, if indeed it be It? Rare is that soul which, while it speaketh of It, knows what it speaketh of. And they contend and strive, but no one without peace seeth that vision. I could wish that men would consider these three things that are in themselves. These three are far other than the Trinity; but I speak of things in which they may exercise and prove themselves, and feel how far other they be. But the three things I speak of are, To Be, to Know, and to Will. For I Am, and I Know, and I Will: I Am Knowing and Willing; and I Know myself to Be and to Will; and I Will to Be and to Know. In these three, therefore, let him who can see how inseparable a life there is,—even one life, one mind, and one essence; finally, how inseparable is the distinction, and yet a distinction. Surely a man hath it before him; let him look into himself, and see, and tell me. But when he discovers and can say anything of these, let him not then think that he has discovered that which is above these Unchangeable, which Is unchangeably, and Knows unchangeably, and Wills unchangeably. And whether on account of these three there is also, where they are, a Trinity; or whether these three be in Each, so that the three belong to Each; or whether both ways at once, wondrously, simply, and yet diversely, in Itself a limit unto Itself, yet illimitable;[55] whereby It is, and is known unto Itself, and sufficeth to Itself, unchangeably the Self-same, by the abundant magnitude of its Unity,—who can readily conceive? Who in any wise express it? Who in any way rashly pronounce thereon?

Proceed in thy confession, say to the Lord thy God, O my faith, Holy, Holy, Holy, O Lord my God, in Thy name have we been baptized, Father, Son, and Holy Ghost, in Thy name do we baptize, Father, Son, and Holy Ghost, because among us also in His Christ did God make heaven and earth, namely, the spiritual and carnal people of His Church. Yea, and our earth, before it received the 'form of doctrine,' was invisible and formless, and we were covered with the darkness of ignorance. For Thou correctest man for iniquity, and 'Thy judgments are a great deep.' But because Thy Spirit was 'borne over the waters,' Thy mercy forsook not our misery, and Thou saidst, 'Let there be light,' 'Repent ye, for the kingdom of heaven is at hand.' Repent ye, let there be light. And because our soul was troubled within us, we remembered Thee, O Lord, from the land of Jordan, and that mountain[56] equal unto Thyself, but little for our sakes; and upon our being displeased with our darkness, we turned unto Thee, 'and there was light.' And, behold, we were sometimes darkness, but now light in the Lord.

But as yet 'by faith, not by sight,' for 'we are saved by hope; but hope that is seen is not hope.' As yet deep calleth unto deep but in 'the noise of Thy waterspouts.' And as yet doth he that saith, I 'could not speak unto you as unto spiritual, but as unto carnal,' even he, as yet, doth not count himself to have apprehended, and forgetteth those things which are behind, and reacheth forth to those things which are before, and groaneth being burdened, and his soul thirsteth after the living God, as the hart after the water-brooks, and saith, 'When shall I come?' 'desiring to be clothed upon with his house which is from heaven;' and calleth upon this lower deep, saying, 'Be not conformed to this world, but be ye transformed by the renewing of your mind.' And, 'Be not children in understanding, howbeit in malice be ye children,' that in 'understanding ye may be perfect;' and 'O foolish Galatians, who hath bewitched you?' But now not in his own voice, but in Thine who sentest Thy Spirit from above; through Him who 'ascended up on high,' and set open the flood-gates of His gifts, that the force of His streams might make glad the city of God. For, for Him doth 'the friend of the bridegroom' sigh, having now the first-fruits of the Spirit laid up with Him, yet still groaning within himself, waiting for the adoption, to wit, the redemption of his body; to Him he sighs, for he is a member of the Bride; for Him is he jealous, for he is the friend of the Bridegroom; for Him is he jealous, not for himself; because in the voice of Thy 'water-spouts,' not in his own voice, doth he call on that other deep, for whom being jealous he feareth, lest that, as the serpent beguiled Eve through his subtilty, so their minds should be corrupted from the simplicity that is in our Bridegroom, Thine only Son. What a light of beauty will that be when 'we shall see Him as He is,' and those tears be passed away which 'have been my meat day and night, while they continually say unto me, Where is thy God?'

And so say I too, O my God, where art Thou? Behold where Thou art! In Thee I breathe a little, when I pour out my soul by myself in the voice of joy and praise, the sound of him that keeps holy-day. And yet it is 'cast down,' because it relapses and becomes a deep, or rather it feels that it is still a deep. Unto it doth my faith speak which Thou hast kindled to enlighten my feet in the night, 'Why art thou cast down, O my soul? and why art thou disquieted in me? hope thou in God;' His 'word is a lamp unto my feet.' Hope and endure until the night,—the mother of the wicked, —until the anger of the Lord be overpast, whereof we also were once children who were sometimes darkness, the remains whereof we carry about us in our body, dead on account of sin, 'until the day break and the shadows flee away.' 'Hope thou in the Lord.' In the morning I shall stand in Thy presence, and contemplate Thee; I shall for ever confess unto Thee. In the morning I shall stand in Thy presence, and shall see 'the health of my countenance,' my God, who also shall quicken our mortal bodies by the Spirit that dwelleth in us, because in mercy He was borne over our inner darksome and floating deep. Whence we have in this pilgrimage received 'an earnest' that we should now be light, whilst as yet we 'are saved by hope,' and are the children of light, and the children of the day,— not the children of the night nor of the darkness, which yet we have been. Betwixt whom and us, in this as yet uncertain state of human knowledge, Thou only dividest, who provest our hearts and callest the light day, and the darkness night. For who discerneth us but Thou? But what have we that we have not received of Thee? Out of the same lump vessels unto honour, of which others also are made to dishonour.

Or who but Thou, our God, made for us that firmament of authority over us in Thy divine Scripture? As it is said, For heaven shall be folded up like a scroll; and now it is extended over us like a skin. For Thy divine Scripture is of more sublime authority, since those mortals through whom Thou didst dispense it unto us underwent mortality. And Thou knowest, O Lord, Thou knowest, how Thou with skins didst clothe men when by sin they became mortal. Whence as a skin hast Thou stretched out the firmament of Thy Book; that is to say, Thy harmonious words, which by the ministry of mortals Thou hast spread over us. For by their very death is that solid firmament of authority in Thy discourses set forth by them more sublimely extended above all things that are under it, the which, while they were living here, was not so eminently extended. Thou hadst not as yet spread abroad the heaven like a skin; Thou hadst not as yet noised everywhere the report of their deaths.[57]

Let us look, O Lord, 'upon the heavens, the work of Thy fingers;' clear from our eyes that mist with which Thou hast covered them. There is that testimony of Thine which giveth wisdom unto the little ones. Perfect, O my God, Thy praise out of the mouth of babes and sucklings. Nor have we known any other books so destructive to pride, so destructive to the enemy and the defender, who resisteth Thy reconciliation in defence of his own sins. I know not, O Lord, I know not other such 'pure' words which so persuade me to confession, and make my neck submissive to Thy yoke, and invite me to serve Thee for nought. Let me understand these things, good Father. Grant this to me, placed under them; because Thou hast established these things for those placed under them.

Other 'waters' there be 'above' this 'firmament,' I believe immortal, and removed from earthly corruption. Let them praise Thy Name,—those super-celestial people, Thine angels, who have no need to look up at this firmament, or by reading to attain the knowledge of Thy Word,—let them praise Thee. For they always behold Thy face, and therein read without any syllables in time what Thy eternal will willeth. They read, they choose, they love. They are always reading; and that which they read never passeth away. For, by choosing and by loving, they read the very unchangeableness of Thy counsel. Their book is not closed, nor is the scroll folded up, because Thou Thyself art this to them, yea, and art so eternally; because Thou hast appointed them above this firmament, which Thou hast made firm over the weakness of the lower people, where they might look up and learn Thy mercy, announcing in time Thee who hast made times. 'For Thy mercy, O Lord, is in the heavens, and Thy faithfulness reacheth unto the clouds.' The clouds pass away, but the heaven remaineth. The preachers of Thy Word pass away from this life into another; but Thy Scripture is spread abroad over the people, even to the end of the world. Yea, both heaven and earth shall pass away, but Thy Words shall not pass away. Because the scroll shall be rolled together, and the grass over which it was spread shall with its goodliness pass away; but Thy Word remaineth for ever, which now appeareth unto us in the dark image of the clouds, and through the glass of the heavens, not as it is; because we also, although we be the well-beloved of Thy Son, yet it hath not yet appeared what we shall be. He looketh through the lattice of our flesh, and He is fair-speaking, and hath inflamed us, and we run after His odours. But 'when He shall appear, then shall we be like Him, for we shall see Him as He is.' As He is, O Lord, shall we see Him, although the time be not yet.

For altogether as Thou art, Thou only knowest, Who art unchangeably, and knowest unchangeably, and willest unchangeably. And Thy Essence Knoweth and Willeth unchangeably; and Thy Knowledge Is, and Willeth unchangeably; and Thy Will Is, and Knoweth unchangeably. Nor doth it appear just to Thee, that as the Unchangeable Light knoweth Itself, so should It be known by that which is enlightened and changeable. Therefore unto Thee is my soul as 'land where no water is,' because as it cannot of itself enlighten itself, so it cannot of itself satisfy itself. For so is the fountain of life with Thee, like as in Thy light we shall see light.

Who hath gathered the embittered together into one society? For they have all the same end, that of temporal and earthly happiness, on account of which they do all things, although they may fluctuate with an innumerable variety of cares. Who, O Lord, unless Thou, saidst, Let the waters be gathered together into one place, and let the dry land appear, which 'thirsteth after Thee'? For the sea also is Thine, and Thou hast made it, and Thy hands prepared the dry land. For neither is the bitterness of men's wills, but the gathering together of waters called sea; for Thou even curbest the wicked desires of men's souls, and fixest their bounds, how far they may be permitted to advance, and that their waves may be broken against each other; and thus dost Thou make it a sea, by the order of Thy dominion over all things.

But as for the souls that thirst after Thee, and that appear before Thee (being by other bounds divided from the society of the sea), them Thou waterest by a secret and sweet spring, that the earth may bring forth her fruit, and, Thou, O Lord God, so commanding, our soul may bud forth works of mercy according to their kind,—loving our neighbour in the relief of his bodily necessities, having seed in itself according to its likeness, when from our infirmity we compassionate even to the relieving of the needy; helping them in a like manner as we would that help should be brought unto us if we were in a like need; not only in the things that are easy, as in 'herb yielding seed,' but also in the protection of our assistance, in our very strength, like the tree yielding fruit; that is, a good turn in delivering him who suffers an injury from the hand of the powerful, and in furnishing him with the shelter of protection by the mighty strength of just judgment.

Thus, O Lord, thus, I beseech Thee, let there arise, as Thou makest, as Thou givest joy and ability,—let 'truth spring out of the earth, and righteousness look down from heaven,' and let there be 'lights in the firmament.' Let us break our bread to the hungry, and let us bring the houseless poor to our house. Let us clothe the naked, and despise not those of our own flesh. The which fruits having sprung forth from the earth, behold, because it is good; and let our temporary light burst forth; and let us, from this inferior fruit of action, possessing the delights of contemplation and of the Word of Life above, let us appear as lights in the world, clinging to the firmament of Thy Scripture. For therein Thou makest it plain unto us, that we may distinguish between things intelligible and things of sense, as if between the day and the night; or between souls, given, some to things intellectual, others to things of sense; so that now not Thou only in the secret of Thy judgment, as before the firmament was made, dividest between the light and the darkness, but Thy spiritual children also, placed and ranked in the same firmament (Thy grace being manifest throughout the world), may give light upon the earth, and divide between the day and night, and be for signs of times; because 'old things have passed away,' and 'behold all things are become new;' and 'because our salvation is nearer than when we believed;' and because 'the night is far spent, the day is at hand;' and because Thou wilt crown Thy year with blessing, sending the labourers of Thy goodness into Thy harvest, in the sowing of which others have laboured, sending also into another field, whose harvest shall be in the end. Thus Thou grantest the prayers of him that asketh, and blessest the years of the just; but Thou art the same, and in Thy years which fail not Thou preparest a garner for our passing years. For by an eternal counsel Thou dost in their proper seasons bestow upon the earth heavenly blessings.

For, indeed, to one is given by the Spirit the word of wisdom, as if the greater light, on account of those who are delighted with the light of manifest truth, as in the beginning of the day; but to another the word of knowledge by the same Spirit, as if the lesser light; to another faith; to another the gift of healing; to another the working of miracles; to another prophecy; to another the discerning of spirits; to another divers kinds of tongues. And all these as stars. For all these worketh the one and self-same Spirit, dividing to every man his own as He willeth; and making stars appear manifestly, to profit withal. But the word of knowledge, wherein are contained all sacraments, which are varied in their periods like the moon, and the other conceptions of gifts, which are successively reckoned up as stars, inasmuch as they come short of that splendour of wisdom in which the fore-mentioned day rejoices, are only for the beginning of the night. For they are necessary to such as he Thy most prudent servant could not speak unto as unto spiritual, but as unto carnal—even he who speaketh wisdom among those that are perfect. But the natural man, as a babe in Christ,—and a drinker of milk,—until he be strengthened for solid meat, and his eye be enabled to look upon the Sun, let him not dwell in his own deserted night, but let him be contented with the light of the moon and the stars.[58] Thou reasonest these things with us, our All-wise God, in Thy Book, Thy firmament, that we may discern all things in an admirable contemplation, although as yet in signs, and in times, and in days, and in years.

But first, 'Wash you, make you clean;'[59] put away iniquity from your souls, and from before mine eyes, that the dry land may appear. 'Learn to do well; judge the fatherless; plead for the widow,' that the earth may bring forth the green herb for meat, and the tree bearing fruit; and come let us reason together, saith the Lord, that there may be lights in the firmament of heaven, and that they may shine upon the earth. That rich man asked of the good Master what he should do to attain eternal life. Let the good Master, whom he thought a man, and nothing more, tell him (but He is 'good' because He is God)—let Him tell him, that if he would 'enter into life' he must 'keep the commandments;' let him banish from himself the bitterness of malice and wickedness; let him not kill, nor commit adultery, nor steal, nor bear false witness; that the dry land may appear, and bud forth the honouring of father and mother, and the love of our neighbour. All these, saith he, have I kept. Whence, then, are there so many thorns, if the earth be fruitful? Go, root up the woody thicket of avarice; sell that thou hast, and be filled with fruit by giving to the poor, and thou shalt have treasure in heaven; and follow the Lord 'if thou wilt be perfect,' coupled with those amongst whom He speaketh wisdom, Who knoweth what to distribute to the day and to the night, that thou also mayest know it, that for thee also there may be lights in the firmament of heaven, which will not be unless thy heart be there; which likewise also will not be unless thy treasure be there, as thou hast heard from the good Master. But the barren earth was grieved, and the thorns choked the word.

But you, 'chosen generation, you weak things of the world,' who have forsaken all things that you might 'follow the Lord,' go after Him, and 'confound the things which are mighty;' go after Him, ye beautiful feet, and shine in the firmament, that the heavens may declare His glory, dividing between the light of the perfect, though not as of the angels, and the darkness of the little, though not despised ones. Shine over all the earth, and let the day, lightened by the sun, utter unto day the word of wisdom; and let night, shining by the moon, announce unto night the word of knowledge. The moon and the stars shine for the night, but the night obscureth them not, since they illumine it in its degree. For behold God (as it were) saying, 'Let there be lights in the firmament of the heaven.' There came suddenly a sound from heaven, as it had been the rushing of a mighty wind, and there appeared cloven tongues like as of fire, and it sat upon each of them. And there were made lights in the firmament of heaven, having the word of life. Run ye to and fro everywhere, ye holy fires, ye beautiful fires; for ye are the light of the world, nor are ye put under a bushel. He to whom ye cleave is exalted, and hath exalted you. Run ye to and fro, and be known unto all nations.

Let the sea also conceive and bring forth your works, and let the waters bring forth the moving creatures that have life. For ye, who 'take forth the precious from the vile,' have been made the mouth of God, through which He saith, 'Let the waters bring forth,' not the living creature which the earth bringeth forth, but the moving creature having life, and the fowls that fly above the earth. For Thy sacraments, O God, by the ministry of Thy holy ones, have made their way amid the billows of the temptations of the world, to instruct the Gentiles in Thy Name, in Thy Baptism. And amongst these things, many great works of wonder have been wrought, likeas great whales; and the voices of Thy messengers flying above the earth, near to the firmament of Thy Book; that being set over them as an authority, under which they were to fly whithersoever they were to go. For 'there is no speech, nor language, where their voice is not heard;' seeing their sound 'hath gone through all the earth, and their words to the end of the world,' because Thou, O Lord, hast multiplied these things by blessing.

Whether do I lie, or do I mingle and confound, and not distinguish between the clear knowledge of these things that are in the firmament of heaven, and the corporeal works in the undulating sea and under the firmament of heaven? For of those things whereof the knowledge is solid and defined, without increase by generation, as it were lights of wisdom and knowledge, yet of these self-same things the material operations are many and varied; and one thing in growing from another is multiplied by Thy blessing, O God, who hast refreshed the fastidiousness of mortal senses; so that in the knowledge of our mind, one thing may, through the motions of the body, be in many ways set out and expressed. These sacraments have the waters brought forth; but in Thy Word. The wants of the people estranged from the eternity of Thy truth have produced them, but in Thy Gospel; because the waters themselves have cast them forth, the bitter weakness of which was the cause of these things being sent forth in Thy Word.

Now all things are fair that Thou hast made, but behold, Thou art inexpressibly fairer who hast made all things; from whom had not Adam fallen, the saltness of the sea would never have flowed from him,—the human race so profoundly curious, and boisterously swelling, and restlessly moving; and thus there would be no need that Thy dispensers should work in many waters, in a corporeal and sensible manner, mysterious doings and sayings. For so these creeping and flying creatures now present themselves to my mind, whereby men, instructed, initiated, and subjected by corporeal sacraments, should not further profit, unless their soul had a higher spiritual life, and unless, after the word of admission, it looked forwards to perfection.[60]

And hereby, in Thy Word, not the depth of the sea, but the earth parted from the bitterness of the waters, bringeth forth not the creeping and flying creature that hath life, but the living soul itself. For now hath it no longer need of baptism, as the heathen have, and as itself had when it was covered with the waters,—for no other entrance is there into the kingdom of heaven, since Thou hast appointed that this should be the entrance,—nor does it seek great works of miracles by which to cause faith; for it is not such that, unless it shall have seen signs and wonders, it will not believe, when now the faithful earth is separated from the waters of the sea, rendered bitter by infidelity; and 'tongues are for a sign, not to those that believe, but to those that believe not.' Nor then doth the earth, which Thou hast founded above the waters,[61] stand in need of that flying kind which at Thy word the waters brought forth. Send Thy word forth into it by Thy messengers. For we relate their works, but it is Thou who workest in them, that in it they may work out a living soul. The earth bringeth it forth, because the earth is the cause that they work these things in the soul; as the sea has been the cause that they wrought upon the moving creatures that have life, and the fowls that fly under the firmament of heaven, of which the earth hath now no need; although it feeds on the fish which was taken out of the deep, upon that table which Thou hast prepared in the presence of those that believe. For therefore He was raised from the deep, that He might feed the dry land; and the fowl, though bred in the sea, is yet multiplied upon the earth. For of the first preachings of the Evangelists, the infidelity of men was the prominent cause; but the faithful also are exhorted, and are manifoldly blessed by them day by day. But the living soul takes its origin from the earth, for it is not profitable, unless to those already among the faithful, to restrain themselves from the love of this world, that so their soul may live unto Thee, which was dead while living in pleasures,—in death-bearing pleasures, O Lord, for Thou art the vital delight of the pure heart.

Now, therefore, let Thy ministers work upon the earth,—not as in the waters of infidelity, by announcing and speaking by miracles, and sacraments, and mystic words; in which ignorance, the mother of admiration, may be intent upon them, in fear of those hidden signs. For such is the entrance unto the faith for the sons of Adam forgetful of Thee, while they hide themselves from Thy face, and become a darksome deep. But let Thy ministers work even as on the dry land, separated from the whirlpools of the great deep; let them be an example unto the faithful, by living before them, and by stimulating them to imitation. For thus do men hear not with an intent to hear merely, but to act also. Seek the Lord, and your soul shall live, that the earth may bring forth the living soul. 'Be not conformed to this world.' Restrain yourselves from it; the soul lives by avoiding those things which it dies by affecting. Restrain yourselves from the unbridled wildness of pride, from the indolent voluptuousness of luxury, and from the false name of knowledge; so that wild beasts may be tamed, the cattle subdued, and serpents harmless. For these are the motions of the mind in allegory; that is to say, the haughtiness of pride, the delight of lust, and the poison of curiosity are the motions of the dead soul; for the soul dies not so as to lose all motion, because it dies by forsaking the fountain of life, and so is received by this transitory world, and is conformed unto it.

But Thy Word, O God, is the fountain of eternal life, and passeth not away; therefore this departure is kept in check by Thy word when it is said unto us, 'Be not conformed unto this world,' so that the earth may bring forth a living soul in the fountain of life,—a soul restrained in Thy Word, by Thy Evangelists, by imitating the followers of Thy Christ. For this is after his kind; because a man is stimulated to emulation by his friend. 'Be ye,' saith he, 'as I am, for I am as you are.' Thus in the living soul shall there be good beasts, in gentleness of action. For Thou hast commanded, saying, Go on with thy business in meekness, and thou shalt be beloved by all men; and good cattle, which neither if they eat, shall they over-abound, nor if they do not eat, have they any want; and good serpents, not destructive to do hurt, but 'wise' to take heed; and exploring only so much of this temporal nature as is sufficient that eternity may be 'clearly seen, being understood by the things that are.' For these animals are subservient to reason, when, being kept in check from a deadly advance, they live, and are good.

For behold, O Lord our God, our Creator, when our affections have been restrained from the love of the world, by which we died by living ill, and began to be a 'living soul' by living well; and Thy word which Thou spakest by Thy apostle is made good in us, 'Be not conformed to this world;' next also follows that which Thou presently subjoinedst, saying, 'But be ye transformed by the renewing of your mind,'—not now after your kind, as if following your neighbour who went before you, nor as if living after the example of a better man (for Thou hast not said, 'Let man be made after his kind,' but, 'Let us make man in our image, after our likeness'), that we may prove what Thy will is. For to this purpose said that dispenser of Thine,—begetting children by the gospel,—that he might not always have them 'babes,' whom he would feed on milk, and cherish as a nurse; 'be ye transformed,' saith He, 'by the renewing of your mind, that ye may prove what is that good, and acceptable, and perfect will of God.' Therefore Thou sayest not, 'Let man be made,' but, 'Let us make man.' Nor sayest Thou, 'after his kind,' but, after 'our image' and 'likeness.' Because, being renewed in his mind, and beholding and apprehending Thy truth, man needeth not man as his director that he may imitate his kind; but by Thy direction proveth what is that good, and acceptable, and perfect will of Thine. And Thou teachest him, now made capable, to perceive the Trinity of the Unity, and the Unity of the Trinity. And therefore this being said in the plural, 'Let us make man,' it is yet subjoined in the singular, 'and God made man;' and this being said in the plural, 'after our likeness,' is subjoined in the singular, 'after the image of God.' Thus is man renewed in the knowledge of God, after the image of Him that created him; and being made spiritual, he judgeth all things,—all things that are to be judged,— 'yet he himself is judged of no man.'

But that he judgeth all things answers to his having dominion over the fish of the sea, and over the fowls of the air, and over all cattle and wild beasts, and over all the earth, and over every creeping thing that creepeth upon the earth. For this he doth by the discernment of his mind, whereby he perceiveth the things 'of the Spirit of God;' whereas, otherwise, man being placed in honour, had no understanding, and is compared unto the brute beasts, and is become like unto them. In Thy Church, therefore, O our God, according to Thy grace which Thou hast accorded unto it, since we are Thy workmanship created in good works, there are not only those who are spiritually set over, but those also who are spiritually subjected to those placed over them; for in this manner hast Thou made man, male and female, in Thy grace spiritual, where, according to the sex of body, there is not male and female, because neither Jew nor Greek, nor bond nor free. Spiritual persons, therefore, whether those that are set over, or those who obey, judge spiritually; not of that spiritual knowledge which shines in the firmament, for they ought not to judge as to an authority so sublime, nor doth it behove them to judge of Thy Book itself, although there be something that is not clear therein; because we submit our understanding unto it, and esteem as certain that even that which is shut up from our sight is rightly and truly spoken. For thus man, although now spiritual and renewed in the knowledge of God after His image that created him, ought yet to be the 'doer of the law, not the judge.' Neither doth he judge of that distinction of spiritual and carnal men, who are known to Thine eyes, O our God, and have not as yet made themselves manifest unto us by works, that by their fruits we may know them; but Thou, O Lord, dost already know them, and Thou hast divided and hast called them in secret, before the firmament was made. Nor doth that man, though spiritual, judge the restless people of this world; for what hath he to do to judge them that are without, knowing not which of them may afterwards come into the sweetness of Thy grace, and which continue in the perpetual bitterness of impiety?

Man, therefore, whom Thou hast made after Thine own image, received not dominion over the lights of heaven, nor over the hidden heaven itself, nor over the day and the night, which Thou didst call before the foundation of the heaven, nor over the gathering together of the waters, which is the sea; but he received dominion over the fishes of the sea, and the fowls of the air, and over all cattle, and over all the earth, and over all creeping things which creep upon the earth. For He judgeth and approveth what He findeth right, but disapproveth what He findeth amiss, whether in the celebration of those sacraments by which are initiated those whom Thy mercy searches out in many waters; or in that in which the Fish Itself is exhibited, which, being raised from the deep, the devout earth feedeth upon; or in the signs and expressions of words, subject to the authority of Thy Book,—such signs as burst forth and sound from the mouth, as it were flying under the firmament, by interpreting, expounding, discoursing, disputing, blessing, calling upon Thee, so that the people may answer, *Amen*. The vocal pronunciation of all which words is caused by the deep of this world, and the blindness of the flesh, by which thoughts cannot be seen, so that it is necessary to speak aloud in the ears; thus, although flying fowls be multiplied upon the earth, yet they derive their beginning from the waters. The spiritual man judgeth also by approving what is right and reproving what he finds amiss in the works and morals of the faithful, in their alms, as if in 'the earth bringing forth fruit;' and he judgeth of the 'living soul,' rendered living by softened affections, in chastity, in fastings, in pious thoughts; and of those things which are perceived through the senses of the body. For it is now said, that he should judge concerning those things in which he has also the power of correction.

But what is this, and what kind of mystery is it? Behold, Thou blessest men, O Lord, that they may 'be fruitful and multiply, and replenish the earth;' in this dost Thou not make a sign unto us that we may understand something? Why hast Thou not also blessed the light, which Thou calledst day, nor the firmament of heaven, nor the lights, nor the stars, nor the earth, nor the sea? I might say, O our God, that Thou, who hast created us after Thine Image,—I might say, that Thou hast willed to bestow this gift of blessing especially upon man, hadst Thou not in like manner blessed the fishes and the whales, that they should be fruitful and multiply, and replenish the waters of the sea, and that the fowls should be multiplied upon the earth. Likewise might I say, that this blessing belonged properly unto such creatures as are propagated from their own kind, if I had found it in the shrubs, and the fruit trees, and beasts of the earth. But now is it not said either unto the herbs, or trees, or beasts, or serpents, 'Be fruitful and multiply;' since all these also, as well as fishes, and fowls, and men, do by propagation increase and preserve their kind.

What, then, shall I say, O Thou Truth, my Light,—'that it was idly and vainly said'? Not so, O Father of piety; far be it from a minister of Thy word to say this. But if I understand not what Thou meanest by that phrase, let my betters—that is, those more intelligent than I—use it better, in proportion as Thou, O my God, hast given to each to understand. But let my confession be also pleasing before Thine eyes, in which I confess to Thee that I believe, O Lord, that Thou hast not thus spoken in vain; nor will I be silent as to what this lesson suggests to me. For it is true, nor do I see what should prevent me from thus understanding the figurative sayings of Thy books. For I know a thing may be manifoldly signified by bodily expression which is understood in one manner by the mind; and that that may be manifoldly understood in the mind which is in one manner signified by bodily expression. Behold, the single love of God and of our neighbour, by what manifold sacraments and innumerable languages, and in each several language in how innumerable modes of speaking, it is bodily expressed. Thus do the young of the waters increase and multiply. Observe again, whosoever thou art who readest; behold what Scripture delivers, and the voice pronounces in one only way, 'In the beginning God created heaven and earth;' is it not manifoldly understood, not by any deceit of error, but by divers kinds of true senses? Thus are the offspring of men 'fruitful' and do 'multiply.'

If, therefore, we conceive of the natures of things, not allegorically, but properly, then does the phrase, 'be fruitful and multiply,' correspond to all things which are begotten of seed. But if we treat those words as taken figuratively (the which I rather suppose the Scripture intended, which doth not, verily, superfluously attribute this benediction to the offspring of marine animals and man only), then do we find that 'multitude' belongs also to creatures both spiritual and corporeal, as in heaven and in earth; and to souls both righteous and unrighteous, as in light and darkness; and to holy authors, through whom the law has been furnished unto us, as in the firmament which has been firmly placed betwixt waters and waters; and to the society of people yet endued with bitterness, as in the sea; and to the desire of holy souls, as in the dry land; and to works of mercy pertaining to this present life, as in the seed-bearing herbs and fruit-bearing trees; and to spiritual gifts shining forth for edification, as in the lights of heaven; and to affections formed unto temperance, as in the living soul. In all these cases we meet with multitudes, abundance, and increase; but what shall thus 'be fruitful and multiply,' that one thing may be expressed in many ways, and one expression understood in many ways, we discover not, unless in signs corporeally expressed, and in things mentally conceived. We understand the signs corporeally pronounced as the generations of the waters, necessarily occasioned by carnal depth; but things mentally conceived we understand as human generations, on account of the fruitfulness of reason. And therefore do we believe that to each kind of these it has been said by Thee, O Lord, 'Be fruitful and multiply.' For in this blessing I acknowledge that a power and faculty has been granted unto us, by Thee, both to express in many ways what we understand but in one, and to understand in many ways what we read as obscurely delivered but in one. Thus are the waters of the sea replenished, which are not moved but by various significations; thus even with the human offspring is the earth also replenished, the dryness whereof appeareth in its desire, and reason ruleth over it.

I would also say, O Lord my God, what the following Scripture reminds me of; yea, I will say it without fear. For I will speak the truth, Thou inspiring me as to what Thou willest that I should say out of these words. For by none other than Thy inspiration do I believe that I can speak the truth, since Thou art the Truth, but every man a liar. And therefore he that 'speaketh a lie, he speaketh of his own;' therefore that I may speak the truth, I will speak of Thine. Behold, Thou hast given unto us for food 'every herb bearing seed,' which is upon the face of all the earth, 'and every tree in the which is the fruit of a tree yielding seed.' Nor to us only, but to all the fowls of the air, and to the beasts of the earth, and to all creeping things; but unto the fishes, and great whales, Thou hast not given these things. Now we were saying, that by these fruits of the earth works of mercy were signified and figured in an allegory, the which are provided for the necessities of this life out of the fruitful earth. Such an earth was the godly Onesiphorus, unto whose house Thou didst give mercy, because he frequently refreshed Thy Paul, and was not ashamed of his chain. This did also the brethren, and such fruit did they bear, who out of Macedonia supplied what was wanting unto him. But how doth he grieve for certain trees, which did not afford him the fruit due unto him, when he saith, 'At my first answer no man stood with me, but all men forsook me: I pray God that it may not be laid to their charge.' For these fruits are due to those who minister spiritual doctrine, through their understanding of the divine mysteries; and they are due to them as men. They are due to them, too, as to the living soul, supplying itself as an example in all continency; and due unto them likewise as flying creatures, for their blessings which are multiplied upon the earth, since their sound went out into all lands.

But they who are delighted with them are fed by those fruits; nor are they delighted with them 'whose god is their belly.' For neither in those that yield them are the things given the fruit, but in what spirit they give them. Therefore he who serves God and not his own belly, I plainly see why he may rejoice; I see it, and I rejoice with him exceedingly. For he hath received from the Philippians those things which they had sent from Epaphroditus; but yet I see why he rejoiced. For whereat he rejoices, upon that he feeds; for speaking in truth, 'I rejoiced,' saith he, 'in the Lord greatly, that now at the last your care of me hath flourished again, wherein ye were also careful,' but it had become wearisome unto you. These Philippians, then, by protracted wearisomeness, had become enfeebled, and as it were dried up, as to bringing forth this fruit of a good work; and he rejoiceth for them, because they flourished again, not for himself, because they ministered to his wants. Therefore, adds he, 'not that I speak in respect of want, for I have learned in whatsoever state I am therewith to be content. I know both how to be abased, and I know how to abound; everywhere and in all things I am instructed both to be full and to be hungry, both to abound and to suffer need. I can do all things through Christ which strengtheneth me.'

Whereat, then, dost thou rejoice in all things, O great Paul? Whereat dost thou rejoice? Whereon dost thou feed, O man, renewed in the knowledge of God, after the image of Him that created thee, thou living soul of so great continency, and thou tongue like flying fowls, speaking mysteries, —for to such creatures is this food due,—what is that which feeds thee? Joy. Let us hear what follows. 'Notwithstanding,' saith he, 'ye have well done that ye did communicate with my affliction.' Hereat doth he rejoice, hereon doth he feed; because they have well done, not because his strait was relieved, who saith unto thee, 'Thou hast enlarged me when I was in distress;' because he knew both 'to abound and to suffer need,' in Thee Who strengthenest him. For, saith he, 'ye Philippians know also that in the beginning of the gospel, when I departed from Macedonia, no Church communicated with me as concerning giving and receiving, but ye only. For even in Thessalonica ye sent once and again unto my necessity.' Unto these good works he now rejoiceth that they have returned; and is made glad that they flourished again, as when a fruitful field recovers its greenness.

Was it on account of his own necessities that he said 'Ye have sent unto my necessity'? Rejoiceth he for that? Verily not for that. But whence know we this? Because he himself continues, 'Not because I desire a gift, but I desire fruit.' From Thee, O my God, have I learned to distinguish between a 'gift' and 'fruit.' A gift is the thing itself which he gives who bestows these necessaries, as money, food, drink, clothing, shelter, aid; but the fruit is the good and right will of the giver. For the good Master saith not only, 'He that receiveth a prophet,' but addeth, 'in the name of a prophet.' Nor saith He only, 'He that receiveth a righteous man,' but addeth, 'in the name of a righteous man.' So, verily, the former shall receive the reward of a prophet, the latter that of a righteous man. Nor saith He only, 'Whosoever shall give to drink unto one of these little ones a cup of cold water,' but addeth, 'in the name of a disciple;' and so concludeth, 'Verily I say unto you, he shall in no wise lose his reward.' The gift is to receive a prophet, to receive a righteous man, to hand a cup of cold water to a disciple; but the fruit is to do this in the name of a prophet, in the name of a righteous man, in the name of a disciple. With fruit was Elijah fed by the widow, who knew that she fed a man of God, and on this account fed him; but by the raven was he fed with a gift. Nor was the inner man of Elijah fed, but the outer only, which might also from want of such food have perished.

Therefore will I speak before Thee, O Lord, what is true, when ignorant men and infidels (for the initiating and gaining of whom the sacraments of initiation and great works of miracles are necessary, which we believe to be signified under the name of 'fishes' and 'whales') undertake that Thy servants should be bodily refreshed, or should be otherwise succoured for this present life, although they may be ignorant wherefore this is to be done, and to what end; neither do the former feed the latter, nor the latter the former; for neither do the one perform these things through a holy and right intent, nor do the other rejoice in the gifts of those who behold not as yet the fruit. For on that is the mind fed wherein it is gladdened. And, therefore, fishes and whales are not fed on such food as the earth bringeth not forth until it had been separated and divided from the bitterness of the waters of the sea.

And Thou, O God, sawest everything that Thou hadst made, and behold it was very good. So we also see the same, and behold all are very good. In each particular kind of Thy works, when Thou hadst said, 'Let them be made,' and they were made, Thou sawest that it was good. Seven times have I counted it written that Thou sawest that that which Thou madest was 'good;' and this is the eighth, that Thou sawest all things that Thou hadst made, and behold they are not only good, but also 'very good,' as being now taken together. For individually they were only good, but all taken together they were both good and very good. All beautiful bodies also express this; for a body which consists of members, all of which are beautiful, is by far more beautiful than the several members individually are by whose well-ordered union the whole is completed, though these members also be severally beautiful.

And I looked attentively to find whether seven or eight times Thou sawest that Thy works were good, when they were pleasing unto Thee; but in Thy seeing I found no times, by which I might understand that Thou sawest so often what Thou madest. And I said, 'O Lord, is not this Thy Scripture true, since Thou art true, and being Truth hast set it forth? Why, then, dost Thou say unto me that in Thy seeing there are no times, while this Thy Scripture telleth me that what Thou madest each day, Thou sawest to be good; and when I counted them I found how often?' Unto these things Thou repliest unto me, for Thou art my God, and with strong voice tellest unto Thy servant in his inner ear, bursting through my deafness, and crying, 'O man, that which My Scripture saith, I say; and yet doth that speak in time; but time has no reference to My Word, because My Word existeth in equal eternity with Myself. Thus those things which ye see through My Spirit, I see, just as those things which ye speak through My Spirit, I speak. And so when ye see those things in time, I see them not in time; as when ye speak them in time, I speak them not in time.'

And I heard, O Lord my God, and drank up a drop of sweetness from Thy truth, and understood that there are certain men to whom Thy works are displeasing, who say that many of them Thou madest being compelled by necessity;—such as the fabric of the heavens and the courses of the stars, and that Thou madest them not of what was Thine, but, that they were elsewhere and from other sources created; that Thou mightest bring together and compact and interweave, when from Thy conquered enemies Thou raisedst up the walls of the universe, that they, bound down by this structure, might not be able a second time to rebel against Thee. But, as to other things, they say Thou neither madest them nor compactedst them,—such as all flesh and all very minute creatures, and whatsoever holdeth the earth by its roots; but that a mind hostile unto Thee, and another nature not created by Thee, and in everywise contrary unto Thee, did, in these lower places of the world, beget and frame these things. Infatuated are they who speak thus since they see not Thy works through Thy Spirit, nor recognize Thee in them.

But as for those who through Thy Spirit see these things, Thou seest in them. When, therefore, they see that these things are good, Thou seest that they are good; and whatsoever things for Thy sake are pleasing, Thou art pleased in them; and those things which through Thy Spirit are pleasing unto us, are pleasing unto Thee in us. 'For what man knoweth the things of a man, save the spirit of a man which is in him? Even so the things of God knoweth no man, but the Spirit of God. Now we,' saith he, 'have received not the spirit of the world, but the Spirit which is of God, that we might know the things that are freely given to us of God.' And I am reminded to say, 'Truly, "the things of God knoweth no man, but the Spirit of God;" how, then, do we also know "what things are given us by God?" ' It is answered unto me, 'Because the things which we know by His Spirit, even these "knoweth no man, but the Spirit of God." For, as it is rightly said unto those who were to speak by the Spirit of God, "It is not ye that speak," so is it rightly said to them who know by the Spirit of God, "It is not ye that know." None the less, then, is it rightly said to those that see by the Spirit of God, "It is not ye that see;" so whatever they see by the Spirit of God that it is good, it is not they, but God who "sees that it is good." ' It is one thing, then, for a man to suppose that to be bad which is good, as the forenamed do; another, that what is good a man should see to be good (as Thy creatures are pleasing unto many, because they are good, whom, however, Thou pleasest not in them when they wish to enjoy them rather than enjoy Thee); and another, that when a man sees a thing to be good, God should in him see that it is good,—that in truth He may be loved in that which He made, who cannot be loved unless by the Holy Ghost, which He hath given. 'Because the love of God is shed abroad in our hearts by the Holy Ghost which is given unto us;' by whom we see that whatsoever in any degree is, is good. Because it is from Him who Is not in any degree, but He Is that He Is.

Thanks to Thee, O Lord. We behold the heaven and the earth, whether the corporeal part, superior and inferior, or the spiritual and corporeal creature; and in the embellishment of these parts, whereof the universal mass of the world or the universal creation consisteth, we see light made, and divided from the darkness. We see the firmament of heaven, whether the primary body of the world between the spiritual upper waters and the corporeal lower waters, or—because this also is called heaven—this expanse of air, through which wander the fowls of heaven, between the waters which are in vapours borne above them, and which in clear nights drop down in dew, and those which being heavy flow along the earth. We behold the waters gathered together through the plains of the sea; and the dry land both void and formed, so as to be visible and compact, and the matter of herbs and trees. We behold the lights shining from above,—the sun to serve the day, the moon and the stars to cheer the night; and that by all these, times should be marked and noted. We behold on every side a humid element, fruitful with fishes, beasts, and birds; because the density of the air, which bears up the flights of birds, is increased by the exhalation of the waters. We behold the face of the earth furnished with terrestrial creatures, and man, created after Thy image and likeness, in that very image and likeness of Thee (that is, the power of reason and understanding) on account of which he was set over all irrational creatures. And as in his soul there is one power which rules by directing, another made subject that it might obey, so also for the man was corporeally made a woman, who, in the mind of her rational understanding should also have a like nature, in the sex, however, of her body should be in like manner subject to the sex of her husband, as the appetite of action is subjected by reason of the mind, to conceive the skill of acting rightly. These things we behold, and they are severally good, and all very good.

Let Thy works praise Thee, that we may love Thee; and let us love Thee, that Thy works may praise Thee, the which have beginning and end from time,—rising and setting, growth and decay, form and privation. They have therefore their successions of morning and evening, partly hidden, partly apparent; for they were made from nothing by Thee, not of Thee, nor of any matter not Thine, or which was created before, but of con-created matter (that is, matter at the same time created by Thee), because without any interval of time Thou didst form its formlessness. For since the matter of heaven and earth is one thing, and the form of heaven and earth another, Thou hast made the matter indeed of almost nothing, but the form of the world Thou hast formed of formless matter; both, however, at the same time, so that the form should follow the matter with no interval of delay.

We have also examined what Thou willedst to be shadowed forth, whether by the creation, or the description of things in such an order. And we have seen that things severally are good, and all things very good, in Thy Word, in Thine Only-Begotten, both heaven and earth, the Head and the body of the Church, in Thy predestination before all times, without morning and evening. But when Thou didst begin to execute in time the things predestinated, that Thou mightest make manifest things hidden, and adjust our disorders (for our sins were over us, and we had sunk into profound darkness away from Thee, and Thy good Spirit was borne over us to help us in due season), Thou didst both justify the ungodly, and didst divide them from the wicked; and madest firm the authority of Thy Book between those above, who would be docile unto Thee, and those under, who would be subject unto them; and Thou didst collect the society of unbelievers into one conspiracy, in order that the zeal of the faithful might appear, and that they might bring forth works of mercy unto Thee, even distributing unto the poor earthly riches, to obtain heavenly. And after this didst Thou kindle certain lights in the firmament, Thy holy ones, having the word of life, and shining with an eminent authority preferred by spiritual gifts; and then again, for the instruction of the unbelieving Gentiles, didst Thou out of corporeal matter produce the sacraments and visible miracles, and sounds of words according to the firmament of Thy Book, by which the faithful should be blessed. Next didst Thou form the living soul of the faithful, through affections ordered by the vigour of continency; and afterwards, the mind subjected to Thee alone, and needing to imitate no human authority, Thou didst renew after Thine image and likeness; and didst subject its rational action to the excellency of the understanding, as the woman to the man; and to all Thy ministries, necessary for the perfecting of the faithful in this life, Thou didst will that, for their temporal uses, good things, fruitful in the future time, should be given by the same faithful.

We behold all these things, and they are very good, because Thou dost see them in us,—Thou who hast given unto us Thy Spirit, whereby we might see them, and in them love Thee.

O Lord God, grant Thy peace unto us,—for Thou hast supplied us with all things,—the peace of rest, the peace of the Sabbath, which hath no evening. For all this most beautiful order of things, 'very good' (all their courses being finished), is to pass away, for in them there was morning and evening.

But the seventh day is without any evening, nor hath it any setting, because Thou hast sanctified it to an everlasting continuance; that that which Thou didst after Thy works, which were very good, resting on the seventh day, although in unbroken rest Thou madest them, that the voice of Thy Book may speak beforehand unto us, that we also after our works (therefore very good, because Thou hast given them unto us) may repose in Thee also in the Sabbath of eternal life.

For even then shalt Thou so rest in us, as now Thou dost work in us; and thus shall that be Thy rest through us, as these are Thy works through us. But Thou, O Lord, ever workest, and art ever at rest. Nor seest Thou in time, nor movest Thou in time, nor restest Thou in time; and yet Thou makest the scenes of time, and the times themselves, and the rest which results from time.

We therefore see those things which Thou madest, because they are; but they are because Thou seest them. And we see without that they are, and within that they are good, but Thou didst see them there, when made, where Thou didst see them to be made. And we were at another time moved to do well, after our hearts had conceived of Thy Spirit; but in the former time, forsaking Thee, we were moved to do evil; but Thou, the One, the Good God, hast never ceased to do good. And we also have certain good works, of Thy gift, but not eternal; after these we hope to rest in Thy great hallowing. But Thou, being the Good, needing no good, art ever at rest, because Thou Thyself art Thy rest. And what man will teach man to understand this? Or what angel, an angel? Or what angel, a man? Let it be asked of Thee, sought in Thee, knocked for at Thee; so, even so shall it be received, so shall it be found, so shall it be opened. *Amen.*

# NOTES

Notes followed by the initials *JGP* are drawn from those supplied by J. G. Pilkington, translator of the present version of the *Confessions*, which was first published in 1876. The remaining notes have been selected and adapted from those supplied by the Rev. Edward B. Pusey for the translation which he published in 1838, and which was largely a revision of the William Watts version of 1631.

1. *page 1*   *St. Ambrose, from whom were the beginnings of his conversion and by whom he was baptized.*

2. *page 6*   *Ex. xvi. 15. This is one of the alternative translations put against 'it is manna' in the margin of the authorized version. It is the literal significance of the Hebrew, and is so translated in most of the old English versions. Augustine indicates thereby the attitude of faith. Many things we are called on to believe (to use the illustration of Locke) which are above reason, but none that are contrary to reason. We are but as children in relation to God, and may therefore only expect to know 'parts of His ways.' Even in the difficulties of Scripture he sees the goodness of God. 'God,' he says, 'has in Scripture clothed His mysteries with clouds, that man's love of truth might be inflamed by the difficulty of finding them out. For if they were only such as were readily understood, truth would not be eagerly sought, nor would it give pleasure when found.'— De Ver. Relig.   JGP*

3. *page 10*   *A rite in the Western Churches, on admission as a catechumen, previous to baptism, denoting the purity and uncorruptedness and discretion required of Christians.*

4. *page 11*   *Baptism was in those days frequently (and for similar reasons to the thought in Note 2) postponed till the hour of death approached. The doctors of the Church endeavoured to discourage this, and persons baptized on a sick-bed ('clinically') were, if they recovered, looked on with suspicion. The Emperor Constantine was not baptized till the close of his life, and he is censured by Dr. Newman for presuming to speak of questions which divided the Arians and the Orthodox as 'unimportant,' while he himself was both unbaptized and uninstructed. JGP*

5.   page 13    The 'vail' was an emblem of honour, used in places of worship, and subsequently in courts of law, Emperors' palaces, and even private houses. That between the vestibule and the school itself, besides being a mark of dignity, may, as St. Augustine perhaps implies, have been intended to denote the hidden mysteries taught therein, and that the mass of mankind were not fit hearers of truth.

6.   page 22    Also called Madauros. Formerly an episcopal city; now a small village. At this time the inhabitants were heathen. St. Augustine calls them 'his fathers,' in a letter persuading them to embrace the Gospel.

7.   page 27    Souls in their very sins seek but a sort of likeness of God, in a proud and perverted and, so to say, slavish freedom.

8.   page 31    He alludes to the sea of Sodom, which is said to bubble out a pitchy slime, into which other rivers running, are there lost in it and, like the lake itself, remain immovable, wherefore it is called the Dead Sea.

9.   page 33    Eversores. This appears to have been a name which a pestilent and savage set of persons gave themselves, licentious alike in speech and action. They seem to have consisted mainly of Carthaginian students, whose savage life is mentioned again.

10.  page 35    There was something peculiarly enthralling to an ardent mind like Augustine's in the Manichæan system. That system was kindred in many ways to modern Rationalism. Reason was exalted at the expense of faith. Nothing was received on mere authority, and the disciple's inner consciousness was the touchstone of truth. The result of this is well pointed out by Augustine (Con. Faust.): 'Your design, clearly, is to deprive Scripture of all authority, and to make every man's mind the judge of what passage of Scripture he is to approve of, and what to disapprove of. This is not to be subject to Scripture in matters of faith, but to make Scripture subject to you. Instead of making the high authority of Scripture the reason of approval, every man makes his approval the reason for thinking a passage correct.' JGP

11.  page 37    The strange mixture of the pensive philosophy of Persia with Gnosticism and Christianity, propounded by Manichæus, attempted to solve this question, which was 'the great object of heretical inquiry' (Mansel's 'Gnostics'). It was Augustine's desire for knowledge concerning it that united him to this sect, and which also led him to forsake it when he found therein nothing but empty fables (De Lib. Arb.). Manichæus taught that evil and good were primeval, and had independent

existences. *Augustine, on the other hand, maintains that it was not possible for evil so to exist (De Civ. Dei), but, as he here states, evil is 'a privation of good.' The evil will has a 'causa deficiens,' but not a 'causa efficiens,' as is exemplified in the fall of the angels.* JGP

12. page 39     *Here, as three paragraphs later, he alludes to the typical and allegorical charac-ter of Old Testament histories. Though he does not with Origen go so far as to disparage the letter of Scripture, but upholds it, he constantly employs the alle-gorical principle. He (alluding to the patriarchs) goes so far, indeed, as to say (Con. Faust.) that 'not only the speech but the life of these men was prophetic; and the whole kingdom of the Hebrews was like a great prophet'; and again: 'We may discover a prophecy of the coming of Christ and of the Church both in what they said and what they did.' This method of interpretation he first learned from Ambrose.* JGP

13. page 41     *The Patriarchs.*

14. page 41     *According to this extraordinary system, it was the privilege of the 'elect' to set free in eating such parts of the divine substance as were imprisoned in the vegetable creation (Con. Faust.). They did not marry or work in the fields, and led an ascetic life, the 'hearers' or catechumens being privileged to provide them with food. The 'elect' passed immediately on dying into the realm of light, while, as a reward for their service, the souls of the 'hearers' after death transmigrated into plants (from which they might be most readily freed), or into the 'elect,' so as, in their turn, to pass away into the realm of light.* JGP

15. page 42     *He alludes here to that devout manner of the Eastern ancients, who used to lie flat on their faces in prayer.*

16. page 46     *Vindicianus. St. Augustine calls him 'the great physician of our times.'*

17. page 48     *The Manichæans, of whom St. Augustine was then one, could not but reject baptism, or any rite employing a material substance. They purified matter, not matter them.*

18. page 57     *Augustine tells us (De Civ. Dei) that Varro, in his lost book 'De Philosophia,' gives two hundred and eighty-eight different opinions as regards the chief good, and shows us how readily they may be reduced in number.* JGP

19. page 58     *It may assist those unacquainted with Augustine's writings to understand the last three paragraphs, if we set before them a brief view of the Manichæan specu-lations as to the good and evil principles, and the nature of the human soul:*

*(1) The Manichæans believed that there were two principles or substances, one good and the other evil, and that both were eternal and opposed one to the other. The good principle they called God, and the evil, matter or Hyle (Con. Faust.). Faustus, in his argument with Augustine, admits that they sometimes called the evil nature 'God,' but simply as a conventional usage. Augustine says thereon: 'Faustus glibly defends himself by saying, "We speak not of two gods, but of God and Hyle"; but when you ask for the meaning of Hyle, you find that it is in fact another god. If the Manichæans gave the name of Hyle, as the ancients did, to the unformed matter which is susceptible of bodily forms, we should not accuse them of making two gods. But it is pure folly and madness to give to matter the power of forming bodies, or to deny that what has this power is God.' Augustine alludes in the above passage to the Platonic theory of matter, which resulted after his time in pantheism, and which was entirely opposed to the dualism of Manichæus. It is to this 'power of forming bodies' claimed for matter, then, that Augustine alludes in our text as 'not only a substance but real life also.' (2) The human soul the Manichæans declared to be of the same nature as God, though not created by Him—it having originated in the intermingling of part of His being with the evil principle, in the conflict between the kingdoms of light and darkness (in Ps.). Augustine says to Faustus: 'You generally call your soul not a temple, but a part or member of God' (Con. Faust.); and thus, 'identifying themselves with the nature and substance of God,' they did not refer their sin to themselves, but to the race of darkness, and so did not 'prevail over their sin.' That is, they denied original sin, and asserted that it necessarily resulted from the soul's contact with the body. To this Augustine steadily replied that as the soul was not of the nature of God, but created by Him and endowed with free will, man was responsible for his transgressions. Again, referring to the Confessions, we find Augustine speaking consistently with his then belief when he says that he had not then learned that the soul was not a 'chief and unchangeable good,' or that 'it was not that nature of truth'; and that when he transgressed 'he accused flesh' rather than himself; and, as a result of his Manichæan errors, 'contended that God's immutable substance erred of constraint, rather than admit that his mutable substance had gone astray of free will, and erred as a punishment.' JGP*

20. page 59    'The categories enumerated by Aristotle are rendered—as adequately as perhaps they can be in our language—substance, quantity, quality, relation, place,

time, situation, possession, action, suffering. The catalogue (which certainly is but a very crude one) has been by some writers enlarged, as it is evident may easily be done by subdividing some of the heads; and by others curtailed, as it is no less evident that all may ultimately be referred to the two heads of "substance" and "attribute," or, in the language of some logicians, "accident" ' (Whately's 'Logic'). JGP

21. page 62   Augustine frequently recurs to the idea that in God's overruling Providence, the foulness and sin of man do not disturb the order and fairness of the universe. He illustrates the idea by reference to music, painting, and oratory. 'For as the beauty of a picture is increased by well-managed shadows, so, to the eye that has skill to discern it, the universe is beautified even by sinners, though, considered by themselves, their deformity is a sad blemish' (De Civ. Dei). JGP

22. page 71   The waters of baptism.

23. page 74   The ordinary opinion as to the Academics was that they were universal sceptics; St. Augustine states his conviction that they held, concealed, positive truth, but publicly contented themselves with refuting the opposed errors.

24. page 78   This was the main weapon of the Manichees.

25. page 81   Baptism.

26. page 82   The swine is in the law classed as unclean, as not ruminating, not as being its fault but its nature. But there are men signified by this animal—unclean by their fault, not by nature—who, hearing the words of wisdom gladly, reflect not thereon.

27. page 84   2 Cor. iii. 6. The spiritual or allegorical meaning here referred to is one that Augustine constantly sought, as did many of the early Fathers, both Greek and Latin. He only employs this method of interpretation, however, in a qualified way—never going to the length of Origen or Clement of Alexandria. He does not depreciate the letter of Scripture, though, as we have shown previously (Note 12), he went as far as he well could in interpreting the history spiritually. He does not seem, however, quite consistent in his statements as to the relative prominence to be given to the literal and spiritual meanings, as may be seen by a comparison of portions of book xvii. of the 'City of God.' His general idea may be gathered from the following passage in book xiii.:

'Some allegorize all that concerns paradise itself, where the first men, the parents of the human race, are, according to the truth of Holy Scripture, recorded to have been; and they understand all its trees and fruit-bearing plants as virtues and habits of life, as if they had no existence in the external world, but were only so spoken of or related for the sake of spiritual meanings. As if there could not be a real terrestrial paradise! As if there never existed these two women, Sarah and Hagar, nor the two sons who were born to Abraham, the one of the bond-woman, the other of the free, because the apostle says that in them the two covenants were prefigured! or as if water never flowed from the rock when Moses struck it, because therein Christ can be seen in a figure, as the same apostle says: "Now that rock was Christ" (1 Cor. x. 4). . . . These and similar allegorical interpretations may be suitably put upon paradise without giving offence to any one, while yet we believe the strict truth of the history, confirmed by its circumstantial narrative of facts.' JGP

28. *page 87* Perhaps Valentinian the Younger, whose court was at Milan when Augustine was Professor of Rhetoric there.

29. *page 90* The games in the provinces of the empire were on the same model as those held in the Circus Maximus at Rome, though not so imposing. This circus was one of those vast works executed by Tarquinius Priscus. Hardly a vestige of it at the present time remains, though the Cloaca Maxima, another of his stupendous works, has not, after more than 2,500 years, a stone displaced, and still performs its appointed service of draining the city of Rome into the Tiber. In the circus were exhibited chariot and foot races, fights on horseback, representations of battles (on which occasion camps were pitched in the circus), and the Grecian athletic sports introduced after the conquest of that country. JGP

30. *page 90* Augustine, in book v. above, refers to the reputed sanctity of Manichæus, and it may well be questioned whether the sect deserved that unmitigated reprobation he pours out upon them in his 'De Moribus,' and in parts of his controversy with Faustus. Certain it is that Faustus laid claim, on behalf of his sect, to a very different moral character to that Augustine would impute to them. It is difficult to understand that Manichæanism can have spread as largely as it did at that time, if the asceticism of many amongst them had not been real. JGP

31. *page 96* 'I was entangled in the life of this world, clinging to dull hopes of a beauteous wife, the pomp of riches, the emptiness of honours, and the other hurtful and destructive pleasures' (Aug. De Util. Credendi). 'After I had shaken off the Manichæans and escaped, especially when I had crossed the sea, the Academics

long detained me tossing in the waves, winds from all quarters beating against
my helm. And so I came to this shore, and there found a pole-star to whom to
entrust myself. For I often observed in the discourses of our priest [Ambrose],
and sometimes in yours [Theodorus], that you had no corporeal notions when you
thought of God, or even of the soul, which of all things is next to God. But I
was withheld, I own, from casting myself speedily into the bosom of true wisdom
by the alluring hopes of marriage and honours; meaning, when I had obtained
these, to press (as few singularly happy had before me) with oar and sail into
that haven, and there rest' (Aug. De Vita Beata). JGP

32. page 103   St. Augustine frequently uses this argument against the Manichees; and when,
in the conference with Fortunatus, the latter had nothing to answer to it, St.
Augustine subjoins, 'I knew that you had nothing to say, and when I was a
"hearer" among you, I could never discover what to say; and this was to me a
warning from God to leave that error, and turn, or rather return, to the Catholic
faith, through His mercy, who allowed me not to be held fast for ever in these
deceits.'

33. page 111   'This,' says Watts, 'was likely to be the book of Amelius the Platonist, who
hath indeed this beginning of St. John's Gospel, calling the apostle a barbarian.' This Amelius was a disciple of Plotinus, who was the first to develop
and formulate the Neo-Platonic doctrines, and of whom it is said that he would
not have his likeness taken, nor be reminded of his birthday, because it would
recall the existence of the body he so much despised.

The Neo-Platonic ideas as to the 'Word' or Logos which Augustine contrasts
during the remainder of this book with the doctrine of the Gospel, had its germ
in the writings of Plato. The Greek term expresses both reason and the expression
of reason in speech; and the Fathers frequently illustrate, by reference to this
connection between ideas and uttered words, the fact that the 'Word' that was
with God had an incarnate existence in the world as the 'Word' made flesh. By
the Logos of the Alexandrian school something very different was meant from the
Christian doctrine as to the incarnation, of which the above can only be taken
as a dim illustration. JGP

34. page 113   We find the lentil to be an Egyptian food, for in Egypt it abounds; whence the
Alexandrian lentil is highly prized, and is brought even to our country, as if the
lentil did not grow here. Esau, then, by desiring the Egyptian food, lost his
birthright. So also the people of the Jews, of whom it is said, 'In their heart they

turned back into Egypt,' after a sort longed for the lentils, and so lost their birthright.

35. page 118    A 'skin' denotes mortality.

36. page 119    'The Photinians ascribe to the Son of God a beginning from the virgin's womb, and will not believe that He was before.'

37. page 121    St. Paul (1 Cor. xv. 9). JGP

38. page 122    Simplicianus became a successor of the most blessed Ambrose, Bishop of the Church of Milan. To him St. Augustine wrote two books and calls him 'father,' speaks of his 'fatherly affection from his most benevolent heart not recent or sudden, but tried and known,' requests his 'remarks and corrections of any books of his, which might chance to fall into his holy hands.'

39. page 125    That is, he became a 'catechumen.' JGP

40. page 125    The Apostles' Creed, which was delivered orally to the catechumens to commit to memory, and by them 'delivered back,' publicly repeated before they were baptized.

41. page 131    He was born A.D. 251. St. Augustine speaks of him as 'a holy and perfect man, who is extolled as having, without any knowledge of letters, by hearing learnt the Divine Scriptures, and by thoughtful reflection understood them.'

42. page 132    Their employments were, to gather in the Emperor's tributes, to fetch in offenders, provide corn, ride of errands like messengers of the chamber, lie abroad as spies and intelligencers; they were often preferred to places of magistracy in the province.

43. page 136    For this is the punishment requited to the disobedient in himself, that he in turn should not be obeyed even by himself.

44. page 147    The former are the three disputations against the Academics, the substance of the viva voce discussion of a few days, shortly after he had gone into the country: 'De Vita Beata,' begun on his birthday, November 15, and the two books, 'De Ordine.' The latter are his 'Soliloquies,' two books in which, 'being alone, he held a dialogue with himself, he and his reason, as though they were two.'

45. page 149    Their life is nothing else than to gaze, to strive, to eat, to drink, to sleep, and in their thoughts but to embrace phantastic images, which they derive from that life.

46. *page 151*   They were baptized at Easter, and gave up their names before the second Sunday in Lent, the rest of which they were to spend in fasting, humility, prayer, and being examined in the scrutinies. Therefore they went to Milan, that the bishop might see their preparation. Augustine was baptized by St. Ambrose himself.

47. *page 170*   Anaximenes of Miletus was born about 520 B.C. According to his philosophy the air was animate, and from it, as from a first principle, all things in heaven, earth, and sea sprung, first by condensation and after that by a process of rarefaction. JGP

48. *page 192*   Against the Manichees, who forbade the eating of flesh. According to them, the most impure food of all was insects.

49. *page 195*   The beginning of a hymn of St. Ambrose, which they were wont to sing at the commencement of night.

50. *page 207*   The hour-glasses of his time went by water.

51. *page 228*   'In God, all things are ordered and fixed; nor doth He any thing, as by a sudden counsel, which He did not from eternity foreknow that He should do.'

52. *page 230*   Tacitly opposed to the Manichees, with whom darkness was a self-existent substance.

53. *page 232*   Because at the first creation, it had no form nor thing in it.

54. *page 237*   The Manichees, who rejected the Old Testament, wherefore he wishes that they should be smitten, to their healing, with the 'two-edged sword' of the Old and New Testaments.

55. *page 261*   'Each Person in the Blessed Trinity having the attributes of the Others, so that the distinction of Persons whereby They be, in some incomprehensible way, distinguished from Each Other, coalesces in the Unity of the Godhead.'

56. *page 262*   'This is said on account of Christ Himself, Who in Scripture is continually called a mountain.' His reason for putting repentance and light together is that baptism was anciently called illumination.

57. *page 264*   'The sayings of dead men, because they were not theirs, but through them were His, who "stretched out the heavens as a skin," remain to our posterity. For after death the Prophets and Apostles were more widely known; for they were not so known, when they lived; Judea alone possessed the Prophets when living; dead, all nations. For while they lived, the "skin" was not yet stretched out, not as yet were the heavens stretched out to cover the whole world.'

58. *page 268*  *He alludes to the primitive practice which admitted not their catechumens or unbaptized to hear the higher points of religion handled till they were enlightened, that is, baptized; yet these he advised to rest contented with their catechetical knowledge.*

59. *page 268*  *He alludes to the sacrament of baptism.*

60. *page 270*  *He means that baptism, which is the sacrament of initiation, was not so profitable without the Lord's Supper, which ancients called the sacrament of perfection, or consummation.*

61. *page 271*  *'And because they abide with unshaken belief in the baptism which they have received, therefore it is said, "He hath established the earth upon the waters." '*